SPEECH COMMUNICATION

SPEECH COMMUNICATION: A RATIONAL APPROACH

JOHN C. ZACHARIS
COLEMAN C. BENDER
Emerson College
Boston, Massachusetts

John Wiley & Sons, Inc.   New York   London   Sydney   Toronto

Copyright © 1976 by John Wiley & Sons, Inc.

Library of Congress Cataloging in Publication Data:

Zacharis, John C
  Speech communication.

  Includes index.
    1. Oral communication. I. Bender, Coleman C.,
1921– joint author. II. Title.

PN4121.Z3   808.5   75-45057
ISBN 0-471-98054-4

Printed in the United States of America

10 9 8 7 6 5 4 3 2 1

To our many friends and professional colleagues
and to, especially, Evelyn and Marillyn who encouraged
the completion of the manuscript.

PREFACE

Speech Communication: A Rational Approach is a message-oriented text that stresses your many options within the communicative act. Options begin right from the moment you choose to speak or remain silent. From there, you begin to select the most appropriate and effective options for communication. You, the student, begin to understand your choices by, first, looking at communication systems, second, understanding yourself, third, understanding the nature of your listeners, and fourth, knowing about your message choices.

The process of selecting your options is rational. It requires that you look at your many choices only after you understand how each works.

We favor the type of communication that is reasoned, rational, and well researched. Effective message design is not found in the cookbook approach, so we do not provide systems as easy recipes for successful communication. Therefore, when you do look at the many ways of structuring your message that we provide throughout the text, do so with the understanding that they can and should be molded to your specific needs and interests.

From here, you should begin to develop conceptual ways of looking at the complex nature of communication. You will find in the opening parts of the book that communication can be a maze. Mind managers and manipulators attempt to control your ways of thinking and speaking. As a rational communicator, you can begin to resist patterns of communication in which you are controlled.

Your life is a series of choices. And whatever options you select will determine the direction of your everyday existence. Interacting with other human beings is a major part of your development as an individual. Rational judgment and effective participation are the twin goals of this text. The application of effective communication techniques will work toward the betterment of your personal, academic, and professional life.

John C. Zacharis
Coleman C. Bender

Boston, Massachusetts
December 1975

vii

CONTENTS

SPEECH COMMUNICATION

CHAPTER 1   A RATIONAL APPROACH TO THE COMMUNICATION GENERATION

CHAPTER 1 A RATIONAL APPROACH TO THE COMMUNICATION GENERATION

THE DIMENSIONS OF COMMUNICATION

The Scene

The alarm awakens you. The radio with its programing geared to keep pace with your early morning activity gets you in step with a thing called *contemporary life*. You hear the latest music, the latest news, and about the latest products. You are alive, or so it seems.

The newspaper is at the front door. Its convenient early arrival, which you take casually, was made possible by an enormously complex industry. You glance at big headlines with half-hearted interest. Time allows you to read some articles, forces you to skip others. A few minutes must be spared for breakfast. You notice that your bread or cereal is, according to its package, filling your vitamin and protein deficiencies. "Energy building" the package says. The words somehow juice you up but by 11:00 A.M. you feel as if you have had no breakfast at all.

On the way to class you read billboards and posters and hear more news. Everyone seems anxious to feed you more information. "Buy this!" "Believe that!" The world's events are crammed into four minutes, preceded by and ended with an orchestrated fanfare. You are told that a president has resigned, a war has ended, terrorists are holding a diplomat hostage. Interwoven are split-second quotations by politicians with ideas on everything: housing, a local school bill, desegregation, and taxes. Everything is deplorable, they claim, but it is correctable if they are elected. Such confusion. Whom do you believe?

You arrive at school. Out of friends flow more talk and opinions. There are whispers that several black athletes have resigned in protest over their coach. The college is changing its requirements. "What do you think?" "Will you graduate?" "Have you heard about the big drug arrest?" "What will Prof. Kay ask today?"

In class, you are prodded to defend your views on history, philosophy, and economics. "Give me an example; please clarify yourself; what do you mean?" are only a few of the many questions. You want to say, "Give me a break," but you don't. Out of despera-

2

tion, you begin sputtering the familiar, commonplace ideas. They are the comfortable ones you hear every day.

If you manage to escape the ordeal of school, something else awaits you. A husband or wife or friend wants to know what you think. It seems you are always defending yourself—at home or at school.

With all the conveniences and progress that modern communication has produced, it has somehow victimized you. You are tense and don't know why. We've always taken communication to be a good thing. Free speech and the expression of ideas are one's rights. But the constant flow of communication can be, as described above, tyrannical if left unchallenged. It can be manipulative, unnoticed, and as debilitating as polluted air.

Is there a way out, a defense, a way of taking control, and a way of influencing without always being influenced? We think there is. And that is the reason for the structure, chapters, and advice of this text. You begin plotting the overthrow of the negative effects of communication by (1) recognizing their existence and dimensions, (2) understanding how their processes work, and (3) knowing what it takes to function as an effective communicator. The following pages will, we hope, help you make progress in these directions.

Evolution of Communication: An Overview

What advance of civilization has brought you to the point where your time, ideas, choices, and activities all seem to be influenced by the ever-present effects of communication? The implications of communication have become awesome. Man has moved from a prehistoric time when gestures and sound were sufficient to relay a message to an era when electronics makes possible sending millions of bits of information within seconds. Telegraph, telephone, radio, television, film, newspapers, advertisements, magazines—everything—fill our time. We are living in a generation which seems dominated by the forces of communications.

But first, to what extent has this affected the individual communicator—the person whose goal it is to interact more effectively with others in person-to-person or large-group situations? At the most basic level, It is essential to comprehend the complexity of communication before you can attempt to use it. The hypothetical morning scene described above illustrates how you can be totally caught up in the information and effects of communication without a sense of its environmental potency.

Bettmann

"The Gutenberg communicator—for the past 500 years patiently transmitting experience line by line, usually left to right, down the printed page—is no longer relevant. TV man has become conditioned to a total communication environment, to constant stimuli which he shares with everyone else in society."

Tony Schwartz

But you could ask, "Must I beware of everything *as communication?*" "Can I not think of my relationships with others naturally, or about shopping for groceries, or about history, without always thinking about communication?" Of course you can. We discuss and analyze communication only to understand its special effects that influence our thinking and our lives. At certain points it is necessary to know that you are not reacting naturally to the events around you but that your behavior is being determined by an overload of artificial or irrelevant ideas. Briefly, what are some of these "special effects" about which we speak?

For one thing, the evolution of communication technology has created a problem of time. The rapid flow of events relayed to you in a matter of seconds forces instant digestion, instant judgments, and instant decisions. Moreover, vital information may bypass you altogether. Without time to think, your decisions become uncertain, your ideas become fuzzy.

Second, the problem of quantity presents a similar difficulty. No one can hear, see, and read everything. You can never be totally informed. Thus, there is a constant need for selectivity. Ineffective and random selectivity can ruin your ability as a communicator.

Third, there is the phenomenon of diverse sources of information. The more information there is to understand, the more difficult it is to identify your own beliefs and of those of others. With new fads, people take on new personalities. Their identities are not solely determined by their immediate environment but by new information and new images.

The Evolution of Communication: Background and Scope

We have been brought to this point by some extraordinary advances in communication. Marshall McLuhan, the internationally known communication theorist whose works include *The Medium is The Massage, The Gutenberg Galaxy,* and *Understanding Media: The Extensions of Man* has described the history and phases of communication in several stages.

McLuhan discusses how human beings in their oral communication stage of development used sounds to establish a complex language system that was coded with many meanings and variations. History and culture were passed from generation to generation by means of stories and songs. In the next stage of communication development, man began to record his ideas in writing. Ideas could be saved by the scribe, the individual who copied thoughts and ideas onto paper. An ability to read became more important as man began to rely less on oral communication to transmit history.

In the printing stage, the next phase of development, ideas were made permanently available to large masses of people. More information became more available to more people, but concurrently, print became a substitute for experience. People began to rely heavily upon print as the source of truth.

Finally, in the electronics stage, people began using highly complex systems, such as the telegraph, telephone, radio, television, and computer, to pass on information. Speed became the key. In addition, television incorporated both the visual and audio aspects the earlier development stages of communication. Through television communication again became experiential.[1]

The history of speech and communication in America is rich with the heritage of the town meeting, the protest rhetoric and literature that led to the Revolutionary War, and the oratory of great religious leaders such as Jonathan Edwards and Henry Ward Beecher. Abolitionists and feminist orators held forth in the nineteenth century, preserving the platform as a political force in American government.

In the twentieth century, Franklin Delano Roosevelt became the first president to make major use of radio with his "Fireside Chats" in which he discussed the problems and legislation of the 1930s. With the coming of World War II, electronic media systems began to be used all over the globe. The emergence of television and the computer following World War II has accelerated what has often been called the "communications explosion."

Radio and Television
The growth in the communications industry over the past thirty years since World War II is exemplified by the growth of radio and television. Today, over 97 percent of households in the United States have radio receivers. In addition, over 50 million radios are in automobiles. Television households increased from 13 percent in 1950 to 68 percent in 1955 and to 90 percent in 1962. By "1961, television viewing per home, per day, went up to six hours and four minutes in the average television home."[2] A.C. Nielsen estimated in 1974 that the United States was moving toward two *or more* television sets per household and that at least 28 million households were in that particular category. The availability of multiple channels through cable television, which is now in over 7 million households, has further broadened the impact of television in America.[3]

Advertising has given an incredible boost to the development of radio and television. In 1972, over $23 billion was being spent in advertising.[4] By 1980, Cox Broadcasting estimates that the expenditure could run as high as $60 billion! To comprehend fully the impact of advertising, consider the money spent in the various communication outlets in 1973:[5]

COMMUNICATION-OUTLET	DOLLARS (IN MILLIONS)
Newspapers	7,595
Magazines	1,448
Form publications	65
Television	4,493
Radio	1,690
Direct mail	3,698
Business papers	865
Outdoor	308
Miscellaneous	4,958
Total	25,120

Similarly, the government has spent large amounts of money on communications and public relations. J. William Fulbright in *The Pentagon Propaganda Machine* has stated that the Department of Defense has the largest advertising agency in the world.[6]

Film

The growth of film reflects a similar pattern both at home and abroad. The United States film industry dominates the world film market. "It is estimated that 67 percent of the screening time in the United Kingdom, 65 percent in Brazil, 55 percent in Italy, and 29 percent in West Germany, 28.5 percent in France and 21 percent in Japan is given to American films, while certain other countries play United States films up to 90 percent of the total time."[7]

In addition to commercial "movies," noncommercial and government documentary films are expanding enormously into specialized markets such as industrial, medical, religious, and educational groups.

The World Reaches of Communication

The dramatic spread of low-cost transistors has revolutionized world-wide communication. Radio has grown rapidly: Africa, in ten years, went from 140 radio transmitters to 370. In the same period, those of Europe rose from 566 to 2700, South America doubled, Asia tripled, and the USSR quadrupled.[8] The world total of television sets rose from 11 million in 1950 to 130 million in 1963. Television linkage such as Eurovision, by means of which eighteen Western European countries exchange programs, has greatly enhanced world communication.[9]

These developments have not spread communication equally around the world, however. The United Nations Educational, Scientific, and Cultural Organization (UNESCO) has stated: "Today, some 2,000 million persons, living in 100 countries and representing 70 percent of the world population, still lack adequate communication facilities."[10]

The United States, by comparison, may be suffering from over-communication.

Communication in Space

A most important phenomenon in the development of communication has been the innovation of the communication satellite. Following the establishment of the Communication Satellite Act in 1962 by Congress, space satellites have made possible direct dial international phone calls, the transmission of electroencephalograms from England to the Mayo Clinic, and the international transmission of weather photographs.[11]

On July 22, 1974, Western Union bought two full pages in the *Wall Street Journal* to announce the second transmission of the message, "What hath God wrought?" (the first was sent on May 22, 1844, by Samuel Morse). The message was sent from New York to Los Angeles via Western Union's Westar satellite. On August 8, 1974, page nine of the *Wall Street Journal* announced: "This full page is printed from a satellite signal." The entire page had actually been printed from the image received. The advertisement claimed that the American Satellite Corporation could produce the same results for all forms of private line communications. They stated: "Our system has the full capabilities to transmit voices, high or low speed data, and facsimile signals—to and from business and government centers across the country, and with significant cost savings as compared with conventional communication methods."[12]

Communication in the Future

With extraordinary expansion, communication will bring with it changes and problems. Forrest Warthman has succinctly summarized some of the changes:

☐ Replacement of some print by facsimile print or television
☐ More information from nationally centered data banks
☐ More private closed circuit telecommunication networks
☐ More homes linked by cable
☐ Magnetic tape, cassette libraries, and interactive access to central libraries
☐ Two-way television systems to businesses and homes
☐ Monitoring of the physical movements of people
☐ More electronic security systems

Warthman further makes a point that is especially pertinent to some of the problems described earlier: "Life in the future city will be carried on at a faster pace of communicating, learning, producing, consuming, and moving on to different experiences." He later comments: "To the extent that these devices and networks improve the inconvenience and comforts of urban life, leaving more time for social interaction, they will be beneficial. But to the extent that they isolate us socially, they will impair our well-being."[13]

A denser social structure, a greater input of communication, and the possibility of more conflict and choices brought on by more dimensions in the communication process can make you noncommunicative and passive observers. Once you have given up your right to free speech because of your inability to cope with free speech, you will become consumers and not users of communication.

José Luis L. Aranguren offers this recommendation:

> . . . it is necessary to learn the skills of listening, watching, separating the relevant from the irrelevant and ranking the different pieces of news according to their source, consistency or inconsistency, reliability and credibility. This means that we must overcome the precedent alternatives and not content ourselves with being either simple consumers of informative raw material or simple acceptors of already digested, interpreted information; we ourselves, ought to be the organizers, evaluators and critics of the received information. Of course, this is not an easy task.[14]

Gaining Access

One major difficulty with modern communication systems is that they tend to be one-way. They send you the message, but you have little opportunity to respond. With one-way systems, "it becomes easier for government and corporate entities to reach us when they wish," states Benjamin Singer, "while at the same time it becomes more difficult for us to make contact with them. This communication imbalance became the cause of a profound disengagement from the belief of the legitimacy of the social institutions that play paramount roles in maintaining our society."[15]

The focus of this text is largely on how you communicate publicly within groups, both large and small, and not necessarily on how you communicate with the media. You will, however, have the opportunity to interact with media systems as they begin to open feedback systems from the public. Some evidence is beginning to demonstrate that this is taking place and that there will be greater opportunities in the future. Letter writing to newspapers, phone-in talk shows, open-line radio shows created by politicians and political groups, citizens' television panels on both commercial and noncommercial stations, and town-meeting–type programs are but a few of the ways in which people are gaining access to the media. In addition, cities are beginning to establish more information centers that allow for two-way contact between the government and the public. In Boston, the establishment of the Little City Halls has brought government dialogue and decision making to neighborhoods.

RATIONALITY, CONTROVERSY, AND THE FUNCTIONS OF SPEECH COMMUNICATION

Our major concern is how you as part of your communication environment can, as Aranguren has implied, sort out information and communicate in rational ways. There always will be controversy and many sides to many questions. And you will always be forced to select your direction. Your opinions and actions will subsequently help to determine the growth and quality of your life.

Rational communication is one of the methods by which you seek to accomplish this end. It is one of the means by which you weigh your choices and options.

Communication and Societal Balance

Democratic institutions are designed to encourage diversity while resolving conflict. Our government has functioned for 200 years because through free expression and voting rights a citizen can advocate his own views. When and if injustice occurs, each person has the platform, the press, the courts, or the street corner from which to protest. Although controversy has helped to destroy many political systems, it has somehow evolved as a strength in our system. The result of man against society, pressure group against majority groups, and political groups against each other is a more just social system. Where the system disintegrates is where groups forgo the wisdom to test out and weigh the opinions of others.

In the absence of reasoned discourse, democratic societies begin to flounder. They drift into postures where emotional arguments and quick solutions seem legitimate. Such solutions are usually temporary, however, and it is not long before conflict erupts into violence and subsequently upsets the balance of democracy. Citizens must, therefore, possess clear goals and views built on unbiased information.

The factors that form public opinion are infinitely complex. Information, attitudes, and positions are offered by all political sides and sources: conservatives and liberals, scholars and journalists, Republicans and Democrats, socialists and capitalists, labor and management, theologians and atheists, and the new generation and the old. The media sort out and report their own interpretation of all views.

The result is that a bias factor is always afloat, "polluting" the truth. And yet, to sift out all the accurate information on a given issue is a task of near impossibility. A system of discrimination is needed—one that weighs ideas, examines their sources, tests their validity, poses contradictory viewpoints, and ultimately weighs their worth.

Rational communication provides society with such a system. For a society constantly in flux it is a means of balancing all considerations with reason. It is a way of promoting the truth or exposing fraudulent ideas. It is the ultimate defense against manipulation and irrational decision making. In effect, rational communication produces the judge—not one dressed in courtroom regalia—but one able to examine society, laws, and ideas where they are ideologically in conflict. It is therefore integral to the entire educational process.

Speech Communication as a Function of Liberal Education

The purposes of a liberal education are multifold, involving the development of the individual. The educated person must:
- [ ] Eliminate prejudices.
- [ ] Develop insights.
- [ ] Tolerate and examine opposing views.
- [ ] Express views.
- [ ] Learn the principles of investigation.
- [ ] Weigh and analyze facts.
- [ ] Apply the values of education to life.

It is sometimes easy to forgo these goals by becoming a receiver of information only. By listening, taking notes, and memorizing, students assume they are learning. However, knowledge is less meaningful and "less easily remembered" if it is not expressed, challenged, and reconsidered.

The process of speech communication places you at the crossroads of a liberal education. You listen; you read; you analyze;

and you communicate. Knowledge becomes integrated with your behavior as a thinking and working adult.

Prejudices are Minimized

If you can see the distinction between the irrational and the rational, valid and invalid premises, and biased and unbiased information, you may be able to minimize your prejudices. During a political debate between two presidential candiates, you should see things beyond the interpretation of your own party. The charisma of the candidate should be forgotten for the moment so that his ideas have meaning on their own. Generalized and glossy opinions should be set aside; objectivity should be stressed.

Insights are Increased

Hostility is sometimes difficult to hold back, but it is true that a less emotional response to a viewpoint may produce additional insights. By considering new information gotten from differing viewpoints, you can synthesize thoughts into fresher and more insightful concepts.

Opposing Views are Tolerated and Examined

The conflict of ideas and positions forces you as a rational communicator to probe issues far beyond the conventional stereotypes of the mass media. Given a situation in which arguments are to be examined with logical scrutiny, irrational outbursts of opinion are decreased.

Views are Expressed

Although the democratic process requires the expression of views, we often rely on our elected representatives to speak on issues. Pressure groups fill the void when rational citizens fail to speak. More participation in the dialogue on a given issue, will add depth.

The Principles of Investigation are Practiced

Opinions easily obtained from popular sources may be useful for the purpose of generating ideas. Reporters, however, are forced by deadlines to report things quickly, succinctly, and with emphasis on whatever is attention-getting. Little time or space is allowed for the distillation and documentation of opinions. You, as a rational communicator, should look deeply into all issues related to a topic. Statistics, objective opinions, and other forms of evidence become the basis for clear thinking and perceptive communication.

Facts are Weighed and Analyzed

Investigation is only the first step of what must be an on-going process of examining information for consistency, biases, and distortions. The process takes time. You may spend hours researching an idea for a speech and then discover the idea to be bogus. But you have profited from the learning experience.

The Values of Education are Applied to Life

Through communication, you learn that expression, logic, and the tools of criticism are also useful for looking at yourself. Common sense, judgment, and expression aid in developing clearly articulated goals and life directions.

The Vocational Values of Speech Communication

When you leave the university, you must face a world that is somewhat different. Whereas contemplation is the function of education, making a living will probably be your first priority on graduation.

The values of an education, however, have universal applicability to whatever occupation you may pursue. In particular, the elements of speech communication are listed by the U.S Department of Labor's *Occupational Outlook Handbook* as essential to many professions. Speaking, listening, writing, interacting with others, a knowledge of groups and people, organizational abilities, analysis, research skills— all those factors with which we will be concerned—are daily listed in classified advertisements as necessary tools for employment. We are not talking about only speech and communication-related occupations but *all* occupations. Individuals who speak and present themselves well are often the first to be hired. The interview itself is the most fundamental and basic test of speech communication skills. Without an effective interview, you may never have the chance to prove yourself in other areas. Therefore, good speech skills becomes critical to employment and advancement.

Careers in the following areas are *directly related* to an in-depth concentration in speech and communication studies:

Business and sales
Sales training and development
Organizational communication
Public relations
Advertising
Personnel

Education
Educational media
Marketing
Radio
Television
Theatre
Speech pathology
Writing occupations
Politics and government
Law
Social Services
International communication and diplomacy

Those interested in other careers may be surprised by the frequency with which communication is used as an important if not essential aspect of those professions. Consider how important communication skills are to the following occupations:

Occupation	Communication Skills That Are Useful
All jobs in labor	Labor-management negotiation and communication
All jobs in management	Communicating through the organization
Agriculture	Writing for agricultural publications, sales, advertising
Air Force, air transportation	Leadership, interacting with people
Airline stewardess	Poise, confidence, dealing with people
Banking	Report writing, public relations, dealing with customers
Book publishing	Editing, management, sales
Civil engineering	Presenting ideas, demonstrating concepts, training others to perform tasks
Food retailing	Concepts of persuasion, packaging
Foreign service	Language, diplomacy, nonverbal communication
Government	All aspects of communication

Hotel management	Customer relations, public relations, organizational skills
Health services	Public relations, training, interpersonal communication
Industrial engineering	Analyzing human behavior patterns, visual presentations, teaching
Interior design	Dealing with people, presenting ideas, selling, understanding behavior
Insurance	Persuasion, direct selling, poise, confidence
Law	Reasoning, organization, outlining, public speaking
Law enforcement	Interacting with the public, police training, persuasion, reasoning, organization
Nursing	Interpersonal relations, audio visual training, teaching and demonstrating
Own business	All phases of communication: from letter writing to selling
Pharmacy	Dealing with public
Real estate	Selling, developing advertisements
Restaurant work	Public relations

Exercise: Match your own career objectives with the skills mentioned throughout this text.

AN AGENDA FOR YOUR DEVELOPMENT AS A SPEECH COMMUNICATOR

Managing Your Communication System

You are about to set out on the task of improving on, or making modifications in, yourself as a speech communicator. *Management of self* is an important place to start because it implies that you are in control of what you do. The mere fact that you examine yourself, the communication situation, the messages you send, and the impact you have suggests that you are aware of your choices and options.

As a manager of your communication system, you will have many tasks. And for an overview of the tasks you face, we turn to one of the nation's leading authorities on management, Peter Drucker. In his book, *The Effective Executive,* he suggests that the effective executive has five basic patterns of activity.[16] Consider how they apply to you as you begin to acquire the tools of the rational communicator. Drucker suggests that one must know:

1. Where time goes and how it is spent
2. How to focus on outward contributions
3. How to build on strengths
4. How to concentrate on a few major areas where superior performance will produce outstanding results
5. How to make effective decisions

Where Time Goes and How it is Spent

Just as the effective executive must know where his or her time goes, you too must be aware of how to allocate your time when developing a speech. How much time should you spend on research and planning? To what extent should you use time in building up certain sections of your message? How much does your audience want to hear on certain sections of your speech? Is it too much? Too little? These are but a few of the questions that will have great bearing on your effectiveness as a communicator.

How to Focus on Outward Contributions

The effective communicator is alert to what contributions he or she brings to the speech situation. If there are special attributes in your background as they relate to the topic, then you should draw on them. The level of importance that you place on ideas will determine the outward contributions that you make.

How to Build on Strengths

It is important to evaluate your strengths and weaknesses with an eye to how you can build on strengths. Survey the various sections of this book. Find what it is that you do particularly well. Then proceed to amplify and develop that ability. You will find that exceptional strength in certain areas will greatly enhance your effectiveness even though other aspects still require work.

How to Concentrate on a Few Major Areas Where Superior Performance will Produce Outstanding Results

To be sure, consideration of a few major areas where superior performance will produce outstanding results is not unlike understanding your strengths and weaknesses. But here you will be more concerned with what it is that you are selecting and saying in a speech. Which points deserve prominence? Which issues require more research? How much humor should be used? These questions should cause you to think about how to focus on the task of getting superior results.

How to Make Effective Decisions

Rational decision making is a theme that is woven throughout this entire text. Each speech, each situation, each problem, and each audience will require that you personally make rational choices and decisions concerning the direction your message takes. A constant awareness of decision making is essential to rational communication. It is the factor that encourages you to develop a well-balanced and effective message.

Rational Options and Growth

Now that you know something about the various aspects of communication and rational approaches to it, it is important to begin the task of building on your abilities as a speech communicator. This text is divided into chapters that are sequenced to provide you with an essential perspective of the important areas of communication. You may, however, wish to pursue this task in a different order. Those with a fear of speaking before groups may, for example, wish to read Chapter 13 first. In that chapter you will learn how to improve the physical delivery of a speech through the elimination of stage fright.

The agenda for your development will emerge as follows:

In Chapter 2 we examine communication as a dynamic process—how it functions to weld groups together or, conversely, tear them apart. The process of communication will be examined from the point of view of models with a suggested operational model that allows for options.

In Chapter 3 we discuss the various communication settings with emphasis on the self as it relates to situations and audiences.

In Chapter 4 we focus on the formulation of an idea as it evolves pertinent to a situation. Methods of research are outlined.

In Chapter 5 we analyze the process of selecting information to evidence ideas. The element of establishing probability is explored as well as how evidence is tested for validity.

In Chapter 6 we look at the means of structuring the informative message. Patterns for the informative approach are presented, we well as advice on using visual support.

In Chapter 7 we discuss the approaches to the persuasive option offering a optional sequencing system for developing the persuasive message.

In Chapter 8 we examine the uses of the logical option as it is useful for the development, amplification, and clarification of ideas.

In Chapter 9 we present the various components of the psychological option, including approaches to understanding attitudes, needs, and appeals. Strategies for the psychological option are also discussed.

In Chapter 10 we explore the role of the rational evaluator: one who listens to, analyzes, and responds to concepts.

In Chapter 11 we move into the realm of rational decision making, with particular emphasis on the reflective thinking pattern as a device for problem solving. The elements of group leadership and group participation are also discussed.

In Chapter 12 we look at language and tell how through symbols, clarity, appropriateness, and color you can further enhance your message.

In Chapter 13 we examine the various styles of presentation, with particular emphasis on communicative behavior as it is manifested in vocal and nonverbal means of presentation.

Consider, above all, that it is you who should be making rational choices that enhance your individuality as a speech communicator.

SUMMARY

You are surrounded by demands for your attention. Communication is an ever-present part of our environment. Advances in communication have moved at a startling pace in quantity, speed, and variety. The selling of products and politicians has become a major industry.

Rational communication is the means by which you can weigh your choices and options. The survival of democracy depends on rational analysis and reasoned discourse. Ideas must be expressed, challenged, and reconsidered.

Your skills in rational speech communication will also be directly applicable to your vocational aims. Many careers are specifically related to speech and communication studies.

Finally, you need to consider yourself as a self-manager in the communication process. You need to focus on outward contributions, build on strengths, concentrate on selected areas of improvement, and make effective decisions. The selecting of appropriate communication options is the recurring theme of the text.

Review and Exercises

1. Do a frequency study of the number of times you get information from the telephone, television, radio, newspapers, magazines, and other sources. In an average week, what is your major source of information? What ranks second, third, and fourth?
2. How do you see the future development of communication? What new modes can be expected? Will society be controlled? Is Orwell's *1984* a possibility?
3. What institutions and groups would be most disrupted by the lack of communication? Justify your choices.
4. Do a survey of yourself as a communicator, listing all strengths and weaknesses. Project into the future a goal for development. What will be necessary to achieve that end?
5. Select one or two career objectives. List the communication skills necessary for those careers. Where do you need development?
6. What changes in behavior and communication would occur if all telephones were changed to "video phones"?
7. Do a survey of your class members for a summary of their attitudes toward various communication media.

Additional Readings

Bagdikian, Ben H., *The Information Machines: Their Impact on Men and the Media,* Harper and Row, New York, 1971.

Berelson, Bernard, and Janowitz, Morris, eds., *Reader in Public Opinion and Communication,* 2nd ed., The Free Press, Glencoe, Illinois, 1966.

Bowers, John W. and Ochs, Donovan J., *The Rhetoric of Agitation and and Control,* Addison-Wesley, Reading, Mass., 1971.

Dunlap, Orrine E., Jr., *Communications in Space,* Harper and Row, New York, 1970.

Emery, Edwin, Ault, Philip H., and Agee, Warren K., *Introduction to Mass Communication,* 3rd ed., Dodd, Mead, New York, 1970.

Goffman, Erving, *Relations in Public: Microstudies of the Public Order,* Basic Books, New York, 1971.

Lomas, Charles W., *The Agitator in American Society,* Prentice-Hall, Englewood Cliffs, N.J., 1968.

Matson, Floyd W., and Montague, Ashley, eds., *The Human Dialogue: Perspectives on Communication,* Free Press, New York, 1967.

McLuhan, Marshall, *Understanding Media: The Extensions of Man,* McGraw-Hill, New York, 1964.

Schramm, Wilbur, et al., eds., *The Handbook of Communication,* Rand McNally, Chicago, 1971.

Shostrom, Everett L., *Man, The Manipulator,* Abingdon Press, New York, 1967.Toffler, Alvin, *Future Shock,* Random House, New York, 1970.

Footnotes

[1] See Marshall McLuhan, *The Medium is the Massage* (New York: Bantom Books, 1967) Copyright © 1967 by Bantam Books, Inc. By permission of the publisher, and *Understanding Media* (New York: McGraw-Hill, 1964).

[2] From *World Communications. Press Radio Television film.* (New York: UNESCO Publishing Center, 1964), p. 172. Reproduced by permission of UNESCO, copyright © UNESCO 1964.

[3] *The World Almanac and Book of Facts* (1975), p. 445. Copyright © 1975 by The World Almanac; Newspaper Enterprise Association, Inc., New York, 1974.

[4] Robert Coen, *Advertising Age,* February 19, 1973, p. 64. Copyright © 1973 by Advertising Age. Reprinted by permission of the publisher.

[5] *The World Almanac and Book of Facts* (1975), p. 446.

[6] J. William Fulbright, *The Pentagon Propaganda Machine* (New York: Liveright, 1970).

[7] *World Communications,* pp. 172–173.

[8] *World Communications,* p. 27.

[9] *World Communications,* pp. 34–40.

[10] *World Communications,* p. 5.

[11] Leonard Jaffe, *Communication in Space* (New York: Holt, Rinehart and Winston, 1966).

[12] *Wall Street Journal,* August 8, 1974, p. 9.

[13] Forrest Wartham, "Telecommunication and the City," *Annals of the American Academy of Political and Social Science,* **412** (March 1974), pp. 127–39.

[14] José Luis L. Aranguren, "Freedom, Symbols and Communication," *Annals of the American Academy of Political and Social Science,* **412** (March 1974), pp. 11–20.

[15] Benjamin Singer, *Feedback and Society* (Lexington, Mass.: D.C. Heath, 1973), pp. 1–2.

[16] Peter F. Drucker, *The Effective Executive* (New York: Harper and Row, 1967). Copyright © 1967 by Harper and Row. Reprinted with permission of the publisher.

CHAPTER 2 EXAMINING THE PROCESS OF COMMUNICATION

COMMUNICATION AS PROCESS
THE FUNCTIONS OF COMMUNICATION
    The Social Functions of Communication
    The Function of Role in Communication
    The Symbolic Functions of Communication
    The Organizational Functions of Communication
    The Cultural Function of Communication
    Message Functions: The Development of a Code
EXAMINING COMMUNICATION AS A SYSTEM
    The Cellular Message
    Personal Message Systems
EXAMINING COMMUNICATION: THE MODELS
APPROACH
    The S-R Model
    Rhetorical Model
    Schramm's Model
    Berlo's Model
    Wendell Johnson's Model
    Organizational Communication Model
    An Option Model

CHAPTER 2 EXAMINING THE PROCESS OF COMMUNICATION

COMMUNICATION AS PROCESS

The impact of communication is staggering. You could look from within a society intertwined with communication systems and ask, "Can it all be unraveled?" "Am I not hopelessly caught in a system that manipulates me?"

You can, to an extent, control communication by understanding the variables of its process. The word *process* is important. Communication is considered a process because it is on-going. It is dynamic. Nothing can catch it and wrap it in a bag. It moves and it is unstoppable. How you adjust to it will depend on how you adapt, dynamically, to its ever-changing phenomena. By knowing the variables and reasons why it does change, you can begin the constructive process of developing your own individualistic approach.

You first need an approach—a way of looking at communication and how it functions for your purposes. Many persepctives have been used and are the basis of investigative studies into the nature of communication. For example, communication has been looked at as a mathematical problem by Claude Shannon who, while working for the Bell Telephone Laboratory, produced a mathematical model of communication. The theory was amplified and developed in a publication written with Warren Weaver entitled, *The Mathematical Theory of Communication.*[1]

Wilbur Schramm approached the study of communication from the point of view of the mass media. His approach acknowledges the major impact of the media on our culture in the book, *The Process and Effect of Mass Communication.*[2] Another view of communication was taken by Wendell Johnson who, as a person with background in speech therapy and general semantics, focused on problems in *People in Quandaries*[3]—a book about the impact of language and meanings.

Jurgen Ruesch and Gregory Bateson have examined communication from a medical and psychiatric viewpoint in the book entitled *Communication: The Social Matrix of Psychiatry.*[4] In another approach, a group of researchers have examined communication from the point of view of persuasion and how it influences the psychological behavior of listeners. Their book, *Communication and*

Persuasion,[5] by Carl Hovland, Irving Janis, and Harold Kelly is but one of the many works in this area.

Many writers have applied communication concepts to very practical concerns. Willard V. Merrihue's book, *Managing by Communications,*[6] is useful for business and organization settings. For those interested in the problems of listening as they affect the communication act, there is Ralph G. Nichols' and Leonard Stevens' book, *Are You Listening?*[7] Nonverbal aspects of communication have been dealt with in many books including the Jurgen Ruesch and Weldon Kees book, *Nonverbal Communication,*[8] and another, *Kinesics and Context,* by Ray Birdwhistell.[9]

The list goes on, but it only further illustrates the broad range of viewpoints. This chapter attempts to isolate and consider some of these perspectives as they may be pertinent to building your own theory, as well as sensitizing you to the many variables and considerations that affect the communicative act.

THE FUNCTIONS OF COMMUNICATION

We have said that communication is dynamic and that it is an ongoing process. It serves several functions that are the focus of the following section.

The Social Functions of Communication

The family group is considered the most influential of social groups in the development of the individual. Here patterns of behavior, language, and attitudes are started. The child begins very early to discover connections. Cries function to bring food and attention. Within the family, the child begins to learn the systems of cooperation and competition. He learns the acceptable and unacceptable ways of communication.

From there, the child is introduced into other social groups including groups of relatives, play groups, religious groups, community groups, school groups, and work groups—each functioning to influence communicative behavior. An understanding of the group's values and structure can serve as an excellent indicator of a person's thinking pattern and behavior. If, for example, the individual was heavily into scouting for a long period of time, you can make certain assumptions about his attitudes. These influences on the child are important to the understanding of the communicative act; they explain certain types of reactions, the nature of special "in" language, and something about human motives.

The Function of Role in Communication

In the process of being socialized, persons learn to establish certain roles. The child early creates the role of an independent-dependent creature by his communication with those around him. He learns ways of manipulating his surroundings by cries, smiles, and sounds. He discovers that certain nuances in his sound patterns will bring food, comfort, and change.

As groups change, so do the roles of the individual. Leadership roles, student roles, and coordinator roles are tried. The individual learns the language, customs, and mannerisms of each role, including ways of sitting, walking, and standing.

And so it is throughout our lives. We try roles, succeed in some, and fail in others, but in each we try communicative skills and behavior. Some situations allow for many variations; others are quite rigid. In certain speech situations, customs might dictate that we can speak only after being acknowledged or raising a hand. In lecture situations, interruptions may not be permitted.

The Symbolic Functions of Communication

Later, in Chapter 12, we will talk about the function of symbols and language and how we can make improvements. However, in the initial process of understanding communication, you should be aware that certain symbols signal feelings and attitudes. You should consider that words can be loaded—positive, negative, neutral, literary, scientific, fun, or spiteful. Symbols serve as the basis for establishing the language patterns of groups—both small and large. Word symbols are the basis of highly persuasive advertisements; they are the matter from which slogans are built.

The Organizational Functions of Communication

The social, role, and symbolic functions of communication are all part of larger organization patterns that are established by the language we use to interact with one another.

Each of us, for example, takes on an assigned place in the strata of organizations. Teachers have one function within a university; administrators have another. It is necessary to understand the hierarchy in order to maintain verbal exchanges. The patterns are essential to understanding how we can be effective.

The ways of communicating within an organization are sometimes identified by organizational charts that define the lines of communication and describe how the business or organization is tied together. The special interests of the organization also indicate how their communication patterns operate. Consider how nonsmokers, Alcoholics Anonymous, and Weight Watcher groups develop their own organizational communication patterns.

The Cultural Function of Communication

Considered broadly, culture can be looked at as a network of man's values, beliefs, and behavior. Each of these is a learned system. Culture can also be seen as a combined result of music, dance, art, literature, clothes, customs, governmental systems, and so on. It sets codes of behavior (for example, "Big boys don't cry"); it sets norms ("We expect you to go to college"); and it sets social pressures ("Don't eat with your fingers").

Just as language patterns differ from group to group, so there are larger differences from culture to culture—the most obvious of which are the languages themselves. To an American, all turbans (the wrapped headdress of Asian cultures) tend to look alike, but to a person raised in a turban culture, the method of wrapping and the shape identify the status of the wearer. The information that is learned within a culture is subsequently the basis for communication patterns but is not transferred easily across cultures.

Edward T. Hall, social anthropologist and author of *The Silent Language*[10], has indicated that distance and time are cultural factors that create cross-cultural communication problems. Proper distance between persons in a communicative act in the same culture is different from culture-to-culture distance. Two people chatting might discover that each is either stepping backward or forward if they are from cultures where people stand far apart from one another. This process may result in their moving around a room in a circle without fully realizing what is happening. Attitudes toward time in different cultures also differ. In certain cultures, being late is acceptable, but in our culture if a business conference is scheduled for a certain time, being late is not likely to be welcomed. In Hawaii, for example, you can ask if an appointment is according to "Hawaiian Time," which can be later than mainland time.

All this serves to indicate that the understanding of communication between groups and cultures transcends the mere consideration of words. Willingness to learn the customs and codes is essential for putting into practice what will render our speech communication effective.

Message Functions: The Development of a Code

Communication can be examined from the point of view of message construction. This means that you can take all the information that needs to be presented in a given situation and, with respect to all the functions and variables of communication, structure a message in the form of, say, a fifteen-minute speech that will either impact knowledge or convince listeners to believe in a certain point of view. Written out, the message can become an entity in and of itself—separated in fact from the living communication situation. The message can be an extremely complex process, either artful or scientific in its design. Before we begin to examine its components in subsequent chapters, we ought to look at the message as a "code"—or as a communication system that goes through many levels of interaction, adapts to many variables, and subsequently elicits responses from participating units.

To do so, we can look at communication as moving from cellular messages to societal messages—from one singular unit to larger interrelated units. The transformations are fascinating and provide ways of isolating and understanding the points of development in the entire communication process system.

EXAMINING COMMUNICATION AS A SYSTEM

The Cellular Message

Gunther S. Stent has said, "The capacity to communicate is a fundamental feature of living cells. The genetic information of an organism is embodied in the precise sequence of the four kinds of nucleotide base—ademine, guanine, thymine and cytosine in the DNA molecules of the nuclei of its cellular constituency."[11] In other words, the cell has specific instructions that enable it to function as a manufacturing, functioning package that carries out "catalytically facilitated metabolic reactions." These metabolic communications can occur when released molecules influence other cells. Hormones are examples of this special communication. Cells also communicate with nervous information. They have extensions or axons that combine to form a network. Electrical signals may be sent in response to physical or chemical stimuli.

Briefly, cells may communicate with a genetic code so that they can reproduce themselves or combine with genetic material to form other cells. Groups of cells have combined to serve special functions in the higher animals. Nerve cells have combined to form special receptor functions to light stimulus or sound stimulus. Other cells have combined for the special functions of processing chemicals, such as cells in the stomach and lungs.

Complete packages of cells may communicate with other packages of cells. Your eyes (a package of nerve cells) communicate with your brain (another package), which may generate certain reactions in your stomach (a package of chemical processing cells).

Cells are complicated systems. They communicate internally but have to monitor their own internal activity. They can communicate externally, sending messages to other cells. Moreover, they can combine for special functions. They can become organs with specialized activities.

Cells serve many kinds of other activities. They can develop communication networks. They may receive, transmit, and actuate. They can also miscommunicate. A virus infection may cause a cell to change the manufacturing code. They may stop communicating, misinterpret information, or pass on inaccurate information.

This rather simplified version of cellular communication indicates what is at the base of our communication system. It is also an analogy of all the factors that take place when humans communicate with one another. After all, what are we but larger packages of cells?

Personal Message Systems

Our brief story about cells demonstrated some principles about the process of communication. Consider now how human beings establish their own personal message systems. The basic components of a communication system are:

The receiving unit
The processing unit
The transmitting unit

The *receiving unit* accepts data from the five senses: hearing, touching, smelling, tasting, seeing. Some are more sensitive than others. A friend may have, for example, an extremely sensitive nose. She can always tell when and where people have been smoking; she smells it on clothes, in rooms, and in automobiles.

Each human being is unique in this respect. Certain taste sensitivities are genetic; this is the case with touch systems that are sometimes quite delicate. Very slight pressures on skin surfaces will produce bruises. Some people have allergies; others wear glasses. All these factors determine what you pay attention to and subsequently have a strong impact on personal communication patterns.

The *processing unit* collects information from the *receiving unit* and proceeds to store and influence it. There is evidence that the processing storage action is an electrochemical procedure. Human beings also appear to have two memory systems: one short term and the other long term. There is considerable research currently underway to examine the complexities of the brain processing system.[12]

Although our knowledge is imprecise, we do know that the brain stores, processes, and recalls information. Computers work in a similar manner. They can function to produce certain mathematical computations much faster than human beings; however, the complexity of our own brain is demonstrated by the fact that it can accomplish far more sophisticated tasks than can computers. Your ability to associate certain phenomena into ideas and emotions suggests the complexity at which your brain operates. Something like thinking of your childhood at grandmother's house when you smell fresh baked bread, for example, tells something important about the communication process.

In the processor unit called the brain, you store a language system, cultural behavior patterns, an attitude system, and a system for selecting and filtering information. These systems allow you to use symbols to represent ideas. You can talk about things that are not in your immediate physical presence, or about things that have happened, or about events that may happen in the future. You can build a world of fantasy, and you can create purely symbolic worlds that do not have a resemblance to physical reality.

These abilities take part in modifying, strengthening, eliminating, and multiplying information. It is this system of processing that makes you unique as an individual, and it is the factor you have to consider when addressing messages to others. The differences between people may be extremely widespread, as in the case of the open-minded person who is willing to change versus the closed-minded person who rejects information that does not fit into his preconceived belief systems.[13]

The *transmitting unit* is the verbal and nonverbal means that you use to send messages: your voice, body, and gestures. The type of vocal behavior that you select will determine how you communicate a message. This factor will be further discussed in Chapter 13, but it is important to know at this point that a high or low, soft or slow voice can imply many different things. There is a way of saying "hi" that is quite friendly as opposed to a "hi" that suggests aggression.

Your body language, namely your movements and posture, will communicate some good and some curious things. How does a posture that is straight and at attention appear? What about somehow who leans on a wall or on a podium? These things can convey interest or disinterest in our listeners.

In talking about the cultural functions of communication, we mentioned distance as a nonverbal factor. Some persons will back off if you invade what is called their "personal zone."[14] Similarly, gestures can drive people apart or bring them together. The failure to use gestures may imply a lack of involvement. Excessive gestures may have negative overtones. The nature of the message determines what requires much animation and when the lack of movement is more appropriate.

The face, too, is a major communicator. Children use their faces expressively whereas adults tend to disguise their inner selves. Insincerity is an attitude that is difficult to hide. Some speakers say, "I'm happy to be here," while conveying, facially, the feeling that they are sorry to be there. A smile may say many things.[15] (See figures 1-5.)

In our society we resist touch as a form of communication unless, of course, it is with someone we know. Other societies find touch acceptable. It could serve some very positive functions. Ashley Montagu has suggested that we return to touching to improve our interaction with others.[16]

We have seen three key components of human communication system.

Receiving
Processing
Transmitting

At this point, we will begin to examine the lines of communication: the interaction between persons.

EXAMINING COMMUNICATION: THE MODELS APPROACH

Because communication is dynamic, it would seem difficult to diagram the process. However, constructing a model is useful in the identification of factors and how they relate to one another. Models are a way of visualizing the communication system.

Figure 1

What do the facial expressions of this woman mean?

Reprinted with permission of Saturday Review.

Figure 2

Figure 3

Figure 4

Figure 5

Models further force you to select those features that are relevant to the process under study. In building a model airplane, for example, you look at key features and eliminate others that seem irrelevant. Similarly, a model may be used to test a theory. Model airplanes have been used to test theories of aerodynamics in wind tunnel tests. The features of your own communication theories can be tried out in test and real-life situations.

As a simple frame of the process of communication, the model can serve as the basis for a more complex theory. New subtleties, components, and different lines of communication can be added to see the further dimensions of communication.

Finally, models are useful as a device of explanation. They clarify theories and point to ways in which concepts can be improved. Communication becomes, therefore, less of a hit-or-miss venture. You can try things, see if they work, and reject those elements that do not.

The following models are but a few common examples of how you can diagram the communication process. Think, as you go through each, how they can be used. Look at their components and their processes while considering how new and different models can be constructed to build more precise diagrams of the special kinds of communication situations you face.

The S-R Model

The stimulus–response (S–R) Model is a diagram of communication in its most basic form. It represents a stimulus–response relationship.

Stimulus ⟷ Response

To many theorists, this simplistic diagram demonstrates communication in a nutshell. If someone winks, and you respond, it is a S–R pattern of communication. The stimulus–response concept can be seen in an infinite number of situations. Certain words, gestures, pictures, actions will all stimulate others to respond in certain ways. Therefore, you could consider the process as an exchange or transfer of information of ideas. The process becomes reciprocal and has many effects, each of which can suggest a new dimension to the communication act.

Consider that if I smile at you, and you smile back, the process is a simple S–R.

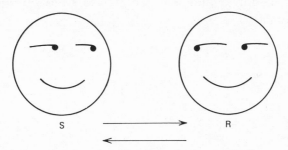

However, your response may make me continue to smile or "feel good" so that I smile at others, or it make you feel good that I smiled at you. The S–R process can, of course, work negatively. From this

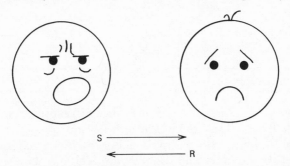

simple pattern, you can begin to build the complexity of communication. It is important to notice, however, that whatever you say is *al-*

ways going to elicit a response—the S–R Model is constantly at work. Many are totally unaware of the fact that what they say is registering an effect. An awareness of the basic fact of S–R is essential to the improvement of communication behavior.

The Rhetorical Model

In the Aristotelian sense, rhetoric is the study of all the available means of persuasion. This is a wide and inclusive definition, yet it is taken most frequently to mean *the way in which one person influences or stimulates meaning in the mind of another by the use of a message.* It is, therefore, message oriented—or concerned with the content, organization, style, and delivery of the message. Other elements such as the speaker's reputation, or *ethos,* are considered part of the message itself.

The features of the message itself that inform, persuade, and render a reaction or decision are the focus of the rhetorical approach to understanding the communication process. Consider the following rhetorical model:

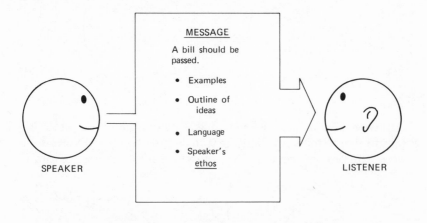

Schramm's Model

Another communication model is that of Wilbur Schramm, mentioned earlier as the author of *The Process and Effect of Mass Communication.* Central to the Schramm model is the consideration of the functions of the encoder and the decoder. The encoder is the source of the message; the decoder is the recipient or destination of the message. Both the source and the destination operate in their own fields of experience (that is, the world in which they live), and so the source can encode and the destination can decode only in terms of his or her own experience. If we do not know Greek, we can neither encode nor decode in that language. If a central New Guinea native has never seen or heard of an airplane, the plane may seem to him to be a bird.

The Schramm model appears as follows:

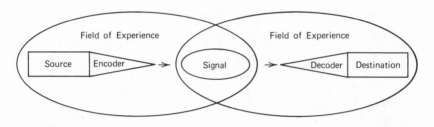

Berlo's Model

One of the most widely known models is that of David K. Berlo who, in the book *The Process of Communication,* divides the process into four major components: source, message, channel, and receiver (commonly known as SMCR).[18] The source is the place from which communication originates. The message is the content. The channel is man's senses. The receiver is the recipient of the message. The Berlo Model appears as follows:

S	**M**	**C**	**R**
SOURCE	**MESSAGE**	**CHANNEL**	**RECEIVER**
Communication skills	Content	Seeing	Communication skills
Attitudes	Treatment	Hearing	Attitudes
Knowledge	Code	Touching	Knowledge
Social system	Elements	Smelling	Social system
Culture	Structure	Tasting	Culture

Wendell Johnson's Model

Wendell Johnson, an international expert in communication, has listed a series of events that may occur in a single communication act.[19] The series of steps begins with an event or person that may serve as a stimulus to another person called Mr. *A.* As this event or person stimulates Mr. *A,* he then translates the stimulus into concepts or words. In making his verbal contact, Mr. *A* then selects and arranges words which he vocalizes such as, "Hi, there."

The resulting sound waves and light waves are transmitted to Ms. B who is stimulated by these impulses. She translates these impulses into concepts and words, selects an appropriate response, and sends a verbal message back to Mr. A, "Hi to you, too." The following diagram illustrates the steps.

1. An event: Ms. B stimulates Mr. A. Impulses travel to Mr. A's brain, producing feelings.

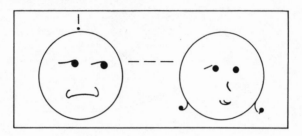

2. Mr. A selects and arranges a message that, by means of sound and light, is sent to Ms. B.

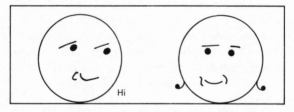

3. Ms. B is stimulated by impulses, and she too selects and arranges a message.

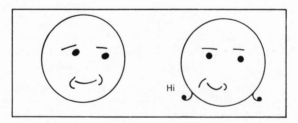

The Organizational Communication Model

A useful way of examining the communication process is by diagraming the communication pattern of a business or organization. You have probably already seen organizational charts that show the various departments, the lines of authority, and the levels of administration. The nature of communication will be determined by the particular functions of the larger group. Consider how the following model of an academic institution can suggest specialized patterns of interaction.

CHART OF COMMUNICATION CHANNELS

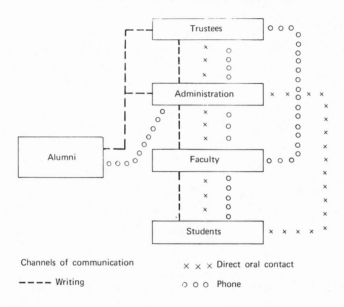

An Option Model

The option model has been developed by us. It is designed to suggest that you have many choices from which you can construct your own theories about communication. Moreover, it suggests that you can have many varied approaches to developing your own patterns of communication.

As we will see in later sections of this book, different considerations change the directions of communication that you take. For example, you have the option to communicate or not to communicate with anyone with whom you might come into contact. Consider that in a public situation someone may gesture a handwave in your direction. Whether you respond or not will suggest whether you wish to be friendly or not. If your choice is to respond, then you have the options of a wave, a verbal "hello" or "hi" (formal or informal), a handshake, a short conversation, a long conversation, a hug, a kiss, an invitation to dinner, or whatever. The options are many. What you select will be determined by cultural conditions, attitudes, intents, and by prejudgments of the responses you intend to receive.

The same principle applies to message construction. Each situation has unique conditions that dictate different options. If you use only one set style of communication, your entire approach to speaking to others will be severely limited.

We encourage, therefore, an attitude and approach that examines all considerations—one that forces you to make choices at all points in the communicative act. As you continue to function as a decision maker in every step, you will establish a rational approach to speech communication. Consider the following option model.

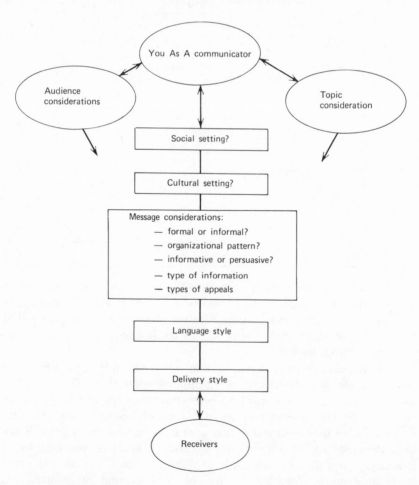

SUMMARY

Understanding communication models may help you to understand the communication system in which you must function. Families, organizations, groups, industries—all have communication systems. In your college or university you need to know the acceptable or nonacceptable communication systems. You soon learn that Professor Starr doesn't permit interruption in a lecture but that Professor Fletcher encourages and welcomes comments or questions. In more formal organizations you will find that the patterns of communication are usually well defined. In a military organization the communication options are definitely stated and usually rigidly followed. Failure to work within the communication system and to use the options allowed will usually be followed by specific penalties. In a formal presentation you need to consider a wide variety of options such as time option, opening options, speaker position options, environmental options, speaker style options, and so on. The designing and delivery of effective messages may improve if you understand your options and rationally select the most appropriate.

Review and Exercises

1. What are some special communication patterns that you can characterize as distinctly belonging to one group? Compare it with another.
2. Compare some of the communication patterns of another culture with that of the United States.
3. For sending messages to another person develop an elementary code system that does not use the ordinary structure of the English language.
4. Describe your own communication behavior in terms of the major roles you perform in your life. *How* does it differ from role to role? *Why* does it differ?
5. Compare animal and human communication patterns.
6. In what ways are your own communication patterns similar and different from others in your own age group?
7. Construct your own communication model. Compare it with one of the models in the text.

Additional Readings

Cherry, Colin, *On Human Communication,* M.I.T. Press, Cambridge, Mass., 1957.

Dance, Frank E. X., ed., *Human Communication Theory: Original Essays,* Holt, Rinehart and Winston, New York, 1967.

Hall, Edward T., *The Hidden Dimension,* Doubleday, Garden City, N.Y., 1969.

Lenneberg, E. H., *Biological Foundations of Language,* Wiley, New York, 1967.

Mead, Margaret, *Continuities in Cultural Evolution,* Yale University Press, New Haven, 1964.

Rogers, Everett M., and Shoemaker, F. Floyd, *Communication of Innovations: A Cross-Cultural Approach,* Free Press, New York, 1971.

Smith, Alfred G., ed., *Communication and Culture,* Holt, Rinehart and Winston, New York, 1966.

Footnotes

[1] Claude Shannon and Warren Weaver, *The Mathematical Theory of Communication* (Urbana, Ill.: University of Illinois Press, 1949).

[2] Wilbur Schramm, *The Process and Effect of Mass Communication* (Urbana, Ill.: University of Illinois Press, 1954).

[3] Wendell Johnson, *People in Quandaries* (New York: Harper and Brothers, 1946).

[4] Jurgen Ruesch and Gregory Bateson, *Communication: The Social Matrix of Psychiatry* (New York: W. W. Norton and Company, 1951).

[5] Carl Hovland, Irving Janis, and Harold Kelley, *Communication and Persuasion* (New Haven: Yale University Press, 1953).

[6] Willard V. Merrihue, *Managing by Communication* (New York: McGraw-Hill, 1960).

[7] Ralph G. Nichols and Leonard A. Stevens, *Are You Listening?* (New York: McGraw-Hill, 1957).

[8] Jurgen Ruesch and Weldon Kees, *Nonverbal Communication* (Berkeley: University of California Press, 1956).

[9] Ray L. Birdwhistell, *Kinesics and Context* (Philadelphia: University of Pennsylvania Press, 1970).

[10] Edward T. Hall, *The Silent Language* (New York: Doubleday, 1966).

[11] Gunther S. Stent, "Cellular Communication," *Scientific American* **227** (September 1972), pp. 43–51. Reprinted with permission of *Scientific American.*

[12] Steven Rose, *The Conscious Brain* (New York: Alfred A. Knopf, Inc., 1973).

[13] Milton Rokeach, *The Open and Closed Mind* (San Francisco: Jossey-Bass, 1968). Copyright © Jossey-Bass Publisher. Reprinted by permission of the publisher.

[14] Edward T. Hall, *The Silent Language.*

[15] Paul Ekman, Wallace V. Friesen, and Phoebe Ellsworth, *Emotion in the Human Face* (New York: Pergamon Press, 1972).

[16] Ashley Montagu, *Touching: The Human Significance of Skin* (New York: Columbia University Press, 1971).

[17] Wilbur Schramm, *The Process and Effects of Mass Communication,* Urbana, Ill.: University of Illinois Press, 1955, pp. 4–8. Copyright © 1954 by the Board of Trustees of the University of Illinois. Reprinted by permission of the University of Illinois Press.

[18] From David K. Berlo, *The Process of Communication: An Introduction to Theory and Practice,* (New York: Holt, Rinehart and Winston, 1960), p. 72. Copyright © 1960 by Holt, Rinehart and Winston, Publishers. Reprinted by permission of Holt, Rinehart and Winston, Publishers.

[19] Wendell Johnson, "The Communication Process and General Semantic Principles," in *Mass Communication,* edited by Wilbur Schramm (Urbana, Ill.: University of Illinois Press, 1960), pp. 307–15.

CHAPTER 3 APPRAISING THE COMMUNICATION SETTING

CHAPTER 3 APPRAISING THE COMMUNICATION SETTING

We have looked at the communication process in an effort to understand its functions and variables, and we have talked about how it influences our lives as a distinctive part of the environment in which we live.

Now the focus will change somewhat. We will begin to concentrate on how these elements affect your roles as a communicator. Each setting is unique, and therefore each requires some special insights as to how your role changes accordingly. It is important, however, to note that many of your communication patterns and insights are *applicable to all settings*. You cannot talk about human interaction as if there are different formulas for different situations. Rather, it is the awareness of the differences that ought to clarify the lines of communication you take.

In order to appraise the communication setting, it is important to know something about the uniqueness of yourself—how do you fit into the situation? Which aspects of your "self" are you presenting in special occasions? Next, we'll look at three basic types of communication situations: the dyad, the small group, and the audience. How each alters the construction of the message is the subject of the following chapters.

UNDERSTANDING YOURSELF

You can create many images of yourself—each of which may influence the approach to communication. Understanding these self-concepts and ways of looking at self should help you to understand your own communication system.

How important are self-images? Extremely important. Consider, for example, the view of Maxwell Maltz, a widely known plastic surgeon, who became interested in changes in self-concepts as related to changed appearances. He states: "The 'self-image' is the key to human personality and human behavior. Change the self-image and you change the personality and behavior."[1]

In other words, human beings develop self-concepts that influence the ways in which they communicate. Some research indicates that a low self-concept obstructs communication. If you have been told frequently that you are stupid, you may have developed a negative self-concept that is reflected in your entire communication behavior.[2] Such behavior may not, in fact, be appropriate.

To identify your self as it functions in different ways, consider some of the following perspectives. You are, for example, an organizing self. You have learned ways of assembling things. Given a picture that only partly shows an image, you will complete it by visualizing the missing parts. Your ability to organize also enables you to put things into categories: small, large, friendly, unfriendly, colorful, or drab. This ability, which is often referred to as "closure," may either help or mislead you. Inaccuracies in organizing can lead to many difficulties in how you perceive reality.

Earlier we spoke about the function of role on communication. Consider how it relates to yourself. You do, after all, play many roles; some are comfortable, others are not. Individuals learn appropriate male and female role behavior when they are young. Later they may confuse the two roles or, perhaps, determine that the distinction is unimportant. The role of public speaker is one that is uncomfortable to many. Gaining skill is essential to establishing the confident role.

You are also a linguistic self with special and unique language patterns and vocabulary. You know when to use formal language and when informal patterns are more appropriate. Your special vocabularies include words unique to mathematics, music, science, and sports. Your grammatical pattern may reflect something about the neighborhood or geographical area in which you were raised. There are certain words that you use with your peers, the argot that shows you are included in a group.

Similarly, you have an attitudinal self that determines your thoughts and actions. You know that you like or dislike sports, movies, the theatre, chemistry, statistics, reading the newspaper, or whatever. If your public speaking experiences have not been good ones, you will probably have a negative attitude about that.

Attitudes determine biases, and to a certain extent we can also say that you have a biased self. Even though we do not wish to admit it, we are all biased in some directions. Biases function somewhat differently from attitudes because they are a form of "insisting" or "protecting" your thoughts and interests. They do not allow for variations that may alter the basic character of your attitudes.

You also have a social self. As a member of small or large, local or cultural, artistic or religious groups, you will acquire certain habits and behavior patterns. Rural Kansas as opposed to urban Chicago will present different group structures, each of which requires adjustments in communication.

The ritualistic self is the part of you that determines your manners, how you enter a room, the ways in which you behave on hearing religious or rock music, and so on. Ritual is a significant part of communication because certain behavior patterns may adversely affect anything you say. A podium at a head table, for example, indicates that there is an expectation for you to speak from it. Try moving the podium to the middle of the room and see how it affects communication.

You could identify the various forms of self in countless ways: athletic self, outdoors self, sexual self, aesthetic self, financial self, vocational self, and so on. Such designations are important, however, only as they describe your communication patterns and how you will operate in your interaction with others. Where are you placing your values? What self are you using? How does it match up with the selves of others?

One perspective that is useful for further analyzing yourself and determining where alterations can be made in your communication patterns is the script. Eric Berne, the psychiatrist, has said that each human as a child writes scripts under the influence of parents. These scripts determine the part you play; they determine your behavior. These scripts may be quite negative—they may follow a pattern that presents you constantly in an inferior role. For those who wish to break out of bad script patterns, he offers advice in his book, *What Do You Say After You Say Hello?*[3] He indicates that you have "tape recordings" in your head of conversations. These conversations, or scripts, may be things that you heard your parents, friends, or relatives say. Under many circumstances, you will play back these "tapes." Your personality follows, therefore, a predictable script.

There are ways to change this. You can determine your own script: the direction you take in your relationship with others. If you are being interviewed for a job, you may select a specific script that suggests that you are submissive and not a troublemaker. The old "tapes" of your parents saying, "Wash your hands, don't speak until spoken to, and don't talk too much," will come in handy.

On the other hand, you may decide that the position calls for aggression. You will need, then, to recall the scripts that say, "Speak up, assert yourself, if you don't take care of yourself no one else will," and so on. Playing out these scripts, you may find yourself being quite dynamic and strong as a personality.

The Emergence of Ethos

An understanding of self will determine how you influence others. Your character, or as it was called by the ancient Greeks, *ethos,* has a strong effect on your ability as a persuader. Ethos includes such factors as confidence, reputation, mannerisms, rituals, the feelings that you show for others, morals and ethics, and concerns. You are, after all, a source of information and the extent to which others believe you will be determined by how they see your role.

UNDERSTANDING COMMUNICATION SITUATIONS

Three basic communication situations are the dyad, the small group, and the audience. Each has characteristics that surface somewhat differently, and you should look for the special conditions, problems, and options they pose.

The Dyad Situation

The dyad situation involves person-to-person, or one-to-one, communication. The special concern of the dyad situation is the closeness or intimacy necessary for communication. And yet, the telling and sharing of feelings and ideas is a task often filled with many obstructions and many inhibitions. How people attempt to share their inner thoughts with others has been the concern of philosophers, poets, artists, filmmakers, dancers, and actors.

What are some of your options in person-to-person communication? You have, of course, the option to talk or remain silent. Silence can imply many things: a desire to listen attentively or a desire not to be disturbed. It can reflect the wish not to be manipulated or downgraded. Its effects are many and profound.

However, if the choice is to make contact, it can be done by a selection process. You make a careful choice as to whom you want to contact, and then through nonverbal signals such as a smile or the closing of physical distance you begin the act of communication. You might want to compare your own nonverbal behavior in opening contact situations with two widely known books: *How to Read A Person Like a Book*[4] by Gerald Nierenberg and Henry H. Calero and *Body Language*[5] by Julius Fast. The self roles about which we spoke earlier will play a significant part in the initial contact stage because you will be condensing a few aspects of your personality into a relatively short time span.

A key factor, however, in the dyadic communication situation is the concept of trust. It is this concept on which one-to-one relationships are built. Past experiences may make us distrust others, and so it is important to realize that making contact will always involve some risk. The failure to obtain trust, through taking risks, will inhibit communication. The principle of self-disclosure can be used to analyze the extent to which you are willing to let things be known about you. According to the concept of the "Johari Window,"[6] you can analyze your levels of self-disclosure:

	Information Known to Self	Information Not Known to Self
Information known to others	Open area	Blind area
Information not known to others	Hidden area	Unknown area

Joseph Luft and Harrington Ingham created the "Johari Window" to explain areas of awareness. In this visual, Luft and Ingham graphically illustrate that each human being's self-awareness and communication patterns create a unique relationship between individuals. Each of the areas in the Johari Window will vary in size depending on the individual's awareness and his openness to others. If the individual is open, the "open area" in the window will be larger than the other areas. If the individual is unaware and noncommunicative, the "unknown area" will be much larger than the other three areas. The "blind area" is large when the individual does not have information about self that other persons have. The "hidden area" is larger if the individual has high self-awareness but does not allow others to gain access to this information.

Through self-disclosure, you allow more information about yourself to be known to others. You subsequently open more channels through which trust can develop.

Another way of analyzing the dyadic situation is to conceive of it as a form of transaction. Usually we think of transaction as a form of exchange: we exchange money for goods or services, for example. Communication takes place in a similar way. In the book, *Games People Play,* Eric Berne looks at communication as a form of a transactional game.[7]

In *I'm O.K., You're O.K.,* Thomas A. Harris sees communication as dialogue patterns that reflect general life positions.[8] He states basically that people carry on transactions with one another in four basic ways. In the first way, you can take the position that "I'm not O.K., and you're not O.K.," or the both-of-us-are-wrong attitude. In another way, you can take the position that "I'm O.K., you're not O.K." This reflects a positive attitude about self but a negative attitude about the other person. In a third way, you can say or imply, "I'm not O.K., you're O.K." This point of view sustains negative feelings about self and allows the other to maintain a superior posture. Finally, there is the ideal way, which is "I'm O.K., you're O.K.," suggesting an equal and positive relationship between individuals.

There are many more complexities than the ones we have mentioned in our short discussion of the dyad, but it is important to notice that the dyad represents communication at a very personal level and must, therefore, be thought of from the perspective of close contact. (See figures 1-5.)

Figure 1

The Small Group Situation

Later, in Chapter 11, we will discuss in more detail the operation of the group discussion process. At this point, we are primarily interested in the special characteristics of the small group situation.

Small groups generally range anywhere from three to fifteen persons. The nature of the communication may, to a large extent, be determined by the purposes of the group's meeting. We suggest there are three basic purposes. First, there is an interactional purpose—people get together to socialize or learn more about one another. Second, there is a topical purpose—people get together to explore a

Figure 2

subject. And, third, there is a decisional purpose—people get together to make a decision about a problem area.

In small group communication, several characteristics are important. First is that of involvement. Each group requires that each person have, to some extent, a concern for its members. Whether this concern takes place at a very personal level involving feelings of love, friendship, or belonging, or whether concern takes place at a more abstract level of group goals will determine the levels of involvement of each individual. Without a commitment to some group ideal or goal, persons are unlikely to obtain a high level of interaction and communication.

The second characteristic is that of individual identity. Self roles have already been discussed, but consider that those roles must acquire a new dimension. They must, in some way, be in concert with the roles of the other individuals in the group. When all assume aggressor roles, for example, breakdown in interaction is predictable. There will be some group pressures for individuals to be agreeable and sometimes submissive, and you should not lose sight of your own identity. Some analysis of how your role will emerge and of how much latitude you are going to allow in meeting others half-way, is critical.

The third characteristic is that of leadership. The election of a leader is, seemingly, the easiest way to solve the issue of leadership. But even when leaders are elected or assigned, the impulse to lead in a group is hard to contain. If you do emerge as a leader, will you be willing to exercise your authority judiciously? Will you be objective? Will your leadership role be used to show off your personality? All these factors must be dealt with either in yourself or in the behavior of others.

The fourth characteristic is that of group standards. Each group develops rituals, structures, behavior patterns, and sometimes rules by which it operates. Each of these group standards determines the parameters that define the purpose of the group and also give it its identity. Wide deviation from the standards generally results in breakdowns in communication. Some variation is usually permitted in more creative and productive groups.

The Audience Situation

Any format that separates the role of the speaker from that of the listener can be designated as an audience situation. Such settings include public symposiums, panels, and debate presentations. The most familiar is the public-speaking situation: one speaker addressing a larger group.

In the dyad or small group situation, there is a constant exchange of ideas. In the audience situation, exchange generally takes place either at designated *times* (at the end of the speech) or by designated

Figure 3

means (a raise of the hand to be acknowledged by the speaker or chairperson).

Time allocations are usually set up for the speaker, and those who fail to follow expected time limits usually incur the irritation of the audience. Similarly, a special area is indicated for the speaker, and to some extent the physical place suggests the level of control and authority of the speaker over his or her audience.

There is always a degree of formality associated with the audience situation. Ideas are prepared, comments are less spontaneous, the audience sits and the speaker stands, and the boundaries of behavior follow expected norms. Even where there are heckling and interruptions, the roles are clear and apparent. Everyone has a place.

A symposium is a discussion in which the topic is divided into subareas on which each member of the symposium speaks. It is not customary for symposium members to speak directly to one another but rather to address ideas toward the audience. This format is somewhat different from the panel discussion in which the participants speak to one another, allowing for the audience to observe and ask questions.

A debate, on the other hand, identifies two opposing sides to a topic. Speakers address themselves to a particular side, usually under time rules and other formalized procedures. The public interview is another special form of the audience situation. Television talk shows of a light or serious nature are typical of the public interview.

Figure 4

Figure 5

All audience situations have one thing in common. The speaker–listener relationship places the speaker in a position of being, to some extent, an authority on the subject being discussed. Some feature about his background or his research has given him the authority to address others on the subject. To that extent, the speaker is usually expected to maintain a higher level of responsibility for what is being said. Because he is influencing others, or presenting information to them, he may be expected to defend his concepts.

UNDERSTANDING YOUR AUDIENCE

If your setting involves a speaker–audience relationship, you will need to know some things about its social composition. Your methods and opportunities for gathering information will vary greatly. At times you will be able to do an in-depth survey of your audience; at other times you will need to make assumptions with a minimum of information.

What kinds of data are useful to a communicator? First, you might ask what your audience's attitudes are toward you. If that is difficult information to come by, you might ask, if you are a student, what their attitudes toward college students are in general.

Further questions are involved. For example, what are their attitudes toward your topic? If you are speaking on relaxing environmental controls to a strong group of conservationists, you will have special problems of adaptation. Thus, you need to attempt some classifications. Is your audience favorable, neutral, or unfavorable toward your topic? Some measurement of the strength or weakness of their attitudes would help; the lighter the attitude, the more easy it is to persuade. Consider using a chart in which you divide up their feelings.

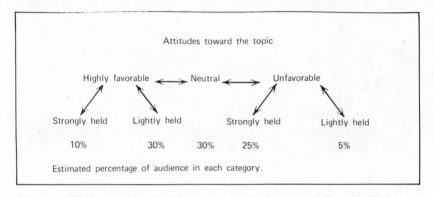

Attitudes are one thing, but interest level is another. Even when attitudes are strong, the interest may not be present. Many persons have strong attitudes in favor of safe driving, but their interest in such a topic may be low. This may be particularly true if you are speaking to a group of individuals under the driving age or to persons whose driving record is excellent.

You must also ask how much your listener knows about the topic. Knowledge levels are critical to planning a speech. Some speeches will insult your listeners. Others will be beyond their comprehension. The intelligence line is sometimes difficult to estimate. You may attempt some sort of estimate in the following way:

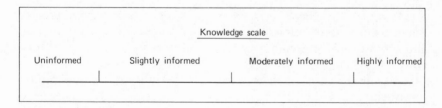

Age range is often an easy factor to estimate and it will be helpful in selecting information and examples appropriate to the interests and life-styles of your audience. Centuries ago, Aristotle suggested that youth lack self-control, are spirited, and have strong desires. Older people are more confident and cautious. Older people may be cynical.[9] Things do not appear to have changed, do they? As a youth-oriented culture, we tend to value highly those things that are symbolic of a younger age.

The person born into a middle-class suburb will have a different life orientation from those whose lives have been spent in the inner-city. There are those who have rejected materialism in favor of communes and natural existence. Their respect for the value of life will be, predictably, strong.

You might also probe into the major events that have made an impact on the audience. The Kennedy assassination? The Vietnam War? Unemployment? The resignation of Nixon? Such events may provide you with the basis for certain ideas. The special experiences of the audience may similarly be useful. College students have stood in registration lines, been concerned about tests and grades, and have had to make curriculum choices. These are all common ground areas that provide you with the opportunity to identify with audience interests and experiences.

The social and economic background of the audience is also vital information. Those who lived through the bread-line economy of the 1930s depression may have strong opinions about unemployment.[10] People who have lived in affluence may be either casual or concerned about a declining economy.

The audience's sex may affect their attitudes toward you, and it may affect their views about your examples and ideas. Who would be more effective, for example, in recruiting women for a police force, a male or female speaker?

You need also to ask what are the audience's reading and viewing patterns. We are intellectually shaped by the kinds of information and entertainment we consume. Knowledge of these factors will sharpen your perspective.

Finally, to what special groups or organizations does the audience belong? These are important clues. Organizations tell much about the people who belong to them. The group's values help to pinpoint the individual's values. You can assume, for example, that members of the American Legion will have strong feelings about patriotism. Members of art and music societies will have strong attitudes about art and music, and so forth.

To summarize your investigation about audience attitudes, consider the list:

Age
Sex

Economic class
Attitudes on topic
Interest level
Knowledge of topic
Class background
Educational status
Ethnic background
Reading habits
Group memberships

Changing Attitudes and Values

Are attitudes and values changing? Yes and no. There appear to be certain values that permanently become part of a culture when it is stable. Of course, there are always those individuals who are the exceptions.

The study of social attitudes and values has caught the attention of sociologists, communication experts, business groups, and research teams. Interviewers are measuring attitudes about political candidates, energy, television programing, and the marketability of products. At the University of Michigan, for example, the Survey Research Center has studied consumer attitudes since 1946. Every three months a research team with a budget of $250,000 surveys 1500 representative consumers.[11]

In 1951 Robin M. Williams reported a sociological approach to value measurement in *American Society: A Sociological Interpretation.*[12] He indicated that American society does not have a completely consistent value structure, yet he also pointed to some values that have broad acceptance. Achievement and success are two particular values important to our culture. We are interested in the "winner," and in most success stories. Activity and work are also two important values; even the extremely affluent usually attempt to find some useful activity. Other values that were widely accepted, according to Williams, were "moral orientation, humanitarian mores, efficiency and practicality, progress, material comfort, freedom, external conformity, science and secular rationality, nationalism and patriotism, democracy, and individual personality."

Have these values changed since 1951? Have Watergate, Vietnam, and the energy crisis modified our views? A sample of attitude change measurement was commissioned by the Virginia Slim Company. They wanted to determine the changes in the attitudes of American women toward marriage and the family. Marriage still rated high with 96 percent of the women polled feeling that it was "the most satisfying and interesting way of life." Another interesting attitude concerned the education of children. Ninety percent felt that cooking classes for boys was a good idea, but only 76 percent felt that boys should enroll in sewing classes. About 52 percent felt that girls should take woodworking classes.[13]

The Stanford Research Institute has been engaged in the study of values and attitudes as they relate to life styles. In a recent report, they examined some of the variations in our culture and suggested that people fall into the following six categories: Makers, Preservers, Takers, Changers, Seekers, and Escapers. Each category has its own life goals and values (see the table on page 60–61).

The same report indicates that there is still strong support for traditional points of view. Over 93 percent support the statement, "The Golden Rule is very important." Ninety percent agreed with the statement, "Nothing is more important than family, love, and respect." The major concerns and worries were with violence, inflation, crime, and drugs.[15]

As a rational communicator, you will need to understand the values and attitudes of the general culture. Where do values change? Within what groups? How can this information be put to use in the construction of the message?

SUMMARY

Understanding yourself is an important step in functioning within the communication setting. You have many concepts of self including your organizing self, your linguistic self, your attitudinal self, your social self, and your ritualistic self. To understand yourself, you may attempt to understand the scripts that determine your personality and how these scripts may be rewritten.

In the dyad situation, you are involved in a one-to-one setting that you can analyze from the point of view of intimacy or distance, contact or noncontact, and trust or nontrust. The dyad can be looked at as a form of transaction that involves general life positions that reflect attitudes about self and others.

The small group situation involves considerations of involvement, group roles, leadership, and group standards. The audience situation determines the roles of the speaker and listeners, and there is generally a larger degree of formality than in the dyad or small group situation.

Surmised Demographics of the Life Ways

	Makers	Preservers	Takers	Changers	Seekers	Escapers
Typical Occupations	Business executives Career women Political leaders Efficient housewives Successful white collar Administrators	Retired Successful white and blue collar Conservative executives Strict parents	Unsuccessful white and blue collar Tenured workers Political hangers-on Indifferent parents	Liberal students Radicals Social critics Professional and amateur advocators and libbers	No typical groups	No typical groups
Typical Educational Level	Medium to high	Medium	Medium to low	High	High	Low and high
Typical Class	Middle and upper	Middle and lower	Middle and lower	Upper and middle	None	Middle and lower
Typical Political Inclination	Middle of road	Very conservative Populist	Conservative	Liberal or radical Independent	Liberal	Apolitical
Typical Age Pattern	Mid to older	Older	All age groups	Younger	All	Younger
Typical Place of Residence	Suburbs Large cities	Rural areas Small towns Suburbs, tracts	Large cities Middle size cities Inner cities, tracts	Large cities College towns	None	Center cities Communes
Typical Income Level	High	Medium	Low	Medium	High or low	Low
Mobility	High	Low	Low	High	Medium	Low or drifting

Source: Stanford Research Institute, Menlo Park, California. Copyright © 1973 by Stanford Research Institute.

Contrasts in Typical Life Way Profiles

	Maker	Preserver	Taker	Changer	Seeker	Escaper
Life Goal	accomplishment	maintain traditions	family security	changed social systems	inner harmony	happiness
Sources of Meaning	work	family	appearances	societal involvement	esthetics	religion
Sources of Truth	empiricism	authority	rationalism	rationalism	intuition	revelation
Psychological Need	achievement	security	to be accepted	mastery	unfolding	self-fulfillment
Belief System	behaviorism	fundamentalism	neo-Freudianism	existentialism	transcendentalism	immanentism
Morality Pattern	duty	eye-for-an-eye	approval-seeking	social contract	universalistic	deference to authority
Time Orientation	future-present	past	present	future	present-future	blurred

Source: Stanford Research Institute, Menlo Park, California. Copyright © 1973 by Stanford Research Institute.

Your understanding of your audience is essential for selecting the most appropriate communication options. You need to know their attitudes and values, their interest level, their knowledge level, their special affiliations, their social and economic background, and their age and sex. Life style patterns is another way of looking at audience classifications.

Review and Exercises

1. What are the major factors that have helped you shape your own self-concept?
2. Are there other aspects to yourself that this chapter has not discussed?
3. How do you rate your own communicative effectiveness in person-to-person relationships as opposed to small group or audience situations? What about with members of the opposite sex? What about with persons over seventy?
4. What communication roles do you find easiest to assume?
5. What ritualistic forms of communication can you identify in your daily patterns?
6. Interview a classmate and have him or her interview you. What differences were there? Have the class rate your effectiveness in an interview situation.
7. Do an audience survey of your class to assess their general attitudes.
8. How do these attitudes relate to a specific topic?
9. How do you identify your own life style? Maker? Preserver? Taker? Changer? Seeker? Escaper? Of what pertinence are these categories to communication?

Additional Readings

Bois, J. Samuel, *The Art of Awareness*, 2nd ed., William C. Brown, Dubuque, Iowa, 1973.

Buber, Martin, *Between Man and Man*, trans. by Ronald G. Smith, Macmillan, New York, 1968.

Clevenger, Theodore, Jr., *Audience Analysis*, Bobbs-Merrill, Indianapolis, 1971.

Homans, George C., *The Human Group,* Harcourt, Brace and World, New York, 1950.

Johnson, David W., *Reaching Out: Interpersonal Effectiveness and Self-Actualization,* Prentice-Hall, Englewood Cliffs, N.J., 1972.

Kahn, Robert L., and Cannell, Charles, F., *The Dynamics of Interviewing,* Wiley, New York, 1957.

McCall, George J., and Simmons, J. L., *Identities and Interactions,* Free Press, New York, 1966.

Rogers, Carl, *On Becoming a Person,* Houghton Mifflin, Boston, 1961.

Wenburg, John R., and Wilmot, William M., *The Personal Communication Process,* Wiley, New York, 1973.

Footnotes

[1] Maxwell Maltz, *Psycho-Cybernetics* (New York: Prentice-Hall, 1969), p. ix. Copyright © 1960 by Prentice-Hall, Inc. Reprinted by permission of the publisher.

[2] George H. Mead, *Mind, Self, and Society* (Chicago: University of Chicago Press, 1934).

[3] Eric Berne, *What Do You Say After You Say Hello?* (New York: Grove Press, 1972).

[4] Gerald L. Nierenberg and Henry H. Calero, *How to Read a Person Like a Book* (New York: Pocket Books, 1973).

[5] Julius Fast, *Body Language* (New York: M. Evans and Company, 1970).

[6] Joseph Luft, *Of Human Interaction* (Palo Alto, Calif.: National Press, 1963).

[7] Eric Berne, *Games People Play* (New York: Grove Press, 1964).

[8] Thomas A. Harris, *I'm O.K. You're O.K.* (New York: Harper and Row, 1967).

[9] Aristotle, *Rhetoric.*

[10] Jack Daniels, "The Poor: Aliens in a Affluent Society: Cross-Cultural Communication," *Today's Speech,* **18,** No. 1 (1970), pp. 15–21.

[11] *Wall Street Journal,* December 12, 1974.

[12] Robin M. Williams, *American Society: A Sociological Interpretation* (New York: Alfred A. Knopf, Inc., 1951).

[13] *Family Guide,* **86** (January 1975), p. 22.

[14] *Life Ways and Life Styles,* A Research Report by the Long Range Planning Service (Stanford Research Institute, 1973). Palo Alto, Calif.

[15] *Ibid.*

CHAPTER 4 FORMULATING AN IDEA

CHAPTER 4 FORMULATING AN IDEA

You surely know what ideas are. They are as natural to your system as breathing—sometimes as frequent. You know which ones are unpopular and which ones are not. But if you have never "gone public" with your ideas—that is to say, if you rarely present them in settings beyond your circle of acquaintances and relatives—you might be treading with some insecurity. To some, the thought of stating ideas before a group is frightening.

The ideas about which we speak are neither those that float in and out of our minds nor those that meet the standards of the *Great Books*. They are, rather, thoughts that have had the benefit of some nurturing through reading and reflection. Or they are the product of our experiences—experiences that we seek to share with others. Formulating and verbalizing an idea, sometimes referred to as "encoding," "is the process of translating a preconceived idea into a message for transmission to a receiver."[1]

This entire text deals with how all the factors concerning the subject, situation, yourself, and the audience influence communication, but here we will be concerned simply with some basics of topic selection.

CRYSTALLIZING A TOPIC

Ideas usually come to us in rough form. They need polishing and refinement. Assigned to deliver a speech, you might say, "I think I'll talk about the energy crisis." But the subject is too broad. You need to ask questions of yourself and the subject that will focus on a point of view. Are you, for example, simply going to tell us there is a problem with energy? Or are you going to present some solutions? Or both? Are you going to advocate that the government do something? Or are you going to tell us about the technology of off-shore drilling? To make your message manageable—for yourself, for the time allotted, and for the audience—you will need to infuse your subject with an apparent purpose.

That purpose might be achieved by simply whittling your subject down to size. By taking a broad subject and reducing it, you will achieve a clearer purpose. An area of focus will be apparent to yourself and the audience. Consider for example:

General Subject Area:	Energy
General Category:	Oil
Specific Category:	Middle Eastern oil
Specific Topic:	The economic impact of Middle Eastern oil prices.

Another example of the process of focus is as follows:

General Subject Area:	Communication
General Category:	Persuasion and Propaganda
Specific Category:	Nazi Propaganda
Specific Topic:	The uses and purposes of Nazi propaganda in the 1930s.

In short, you make your ideas more manageable by limiting them.

YOUR TOPIC IN THE RHETORICAL SITUATION

As we have stated, knowledge of the subject, situation, yourself, and the audience is essential to shaping the topic, but the variables, or factors, that affect each and every act of communication present some mind-boggling problems. Some situations are very tense. Others are passive and receptive. The physical setting might be cold, wet, hot, dry, noisy, or whatever. And there are all types, shapes, and ages of audiences.

Here we will consider some basic, yet intriguing, rudiments of topic selection. The first involves the selection of a broad subject area. This must relate to your interests, your background, and the research sources available to you. Moreover, you will need to decide whether it is your intent to inform, persuade, or solve a problem. The selection of a broad subject area should be relatively simple, but if you need some hints, turn to the list of ideas at the end of the chapter.

The second step is to *find your place* in the territory of the subject. In other words, you may have selected a broad subject such as energy but you may feel at ease in talking only about your use of gasoline. This consideration is not meant to discourage you from exploring new areas but rather to make you aware of the fact that you are likely to be most effective as a communicator when you restrict yourself to what you know and what you have experienced. Some other questions that may aid you in determining *your place* in the subject are:

1. At what point do you begin to experience difficulties with the complexity of the subject? Can you talk with ease about nuclear energy?
2. To what extent do you want to be committed, or uncommitted, to the actions implied by what you say? If you are an advocate of public nudity, will you follow through?
3. Is your background best suited for dealing with the subject broadly, or narrowly?
4. How has the subject affected you personally in the past?

The third step is to analyze how your listeners should, or should not, influence the formulation of your idea-subject-topic. We know that communication is a reciprocal event: Audience feedback will affect both the manner and content of your speech. Some anticipation of audience attitudes should help you to define your direction. Audience attitudes will be the subject of a more detailed analysis in Chapter 9, but here you should ask some basic questions concerning this important factor. For example,

1. What can you expect an audience to accept from a person with your background? Although you should not be intimidated by an audience, neither should you attempt to speak over your head.
2. What can you estimate is the commitment of your audience to a side, or position, on the topic? Should your topic be worded accordingly?
3. What is the background of your audience on the topic?
4. Is there a point at which you can predict they will cease listening to what you say?

TEN RHETORICAL SCENARIOS

The questions asked above pose some difficult, sometimes unanswerable, problems. Moreover, it is difficult to see how they work in the abstract. For this reason, we have constructed ten rhetorical scenarios that could be typical of the type of situation you might face.

What is a scenario? A scenario is a make-believe situation (similar to reality) in which you can decide on a possible course of action depending on what contingencies the situation presents. In other words, it is a game of deciding what you would say if the situation were such-

and-such. A scenario is useful because you can apply principles to a situation that is similar to reality.

The following scenarios are presented as case studies from which you can determine which direction your subject should take. They are also useful for mapping out communication strategies that we will discuss in later chapters. Here we are interested in how they might affect the limitations and boundaries of your topic.

In the first scenario, which involves you as a speaker on drugs, we have presented three different situations as they affect the single topic: drugs. Notice how your topic can take on different shadings and dimensions according to the setting.

Scenario I

Let us assume you are a student in college and, although you are not a user of drugs, you have an interest in the subject and have done research in the area. You consider your attitude to be moderate. Although you have seen abuses and feel compelled to warn people about them, you do not wish to appear as if you are meddling with their personal habits. You have stronger feelings against the use of hard drugs than against the use of marijuana.

Situation A

In the first situation you have been given a "persuasive" speech assignment. The classroom audience is not really concerned about the harms of drugs. Like cigarettes, drugs seem undesirable and desirable at the same time. Your audience has heard several speeches on the same topic.

If you expect to have any impact at all, your topic will have to be phrased in rather jolting language. It could be something like, "The Lethal Side-Effects of Last Night's High." The topic may very well draw on your listeners' immediate experiences; if so, it will have some personal meaning.

Situation B

In the second situation you have been asked to talk about the drug problem in college to a group of high school students who are members of a social service organization (such as the YMCA) in your hometown. You know (1) that most have either had some contact with, or have smoked, marijuana, and (2) that they are fully aware of the harmful effects of hard drugs.

Any speech on the harmful effects of drugs will, in all likelihood, overwork a topic that by now has become uninteresting to your audience. On the other hand, a speech with the subject "The Symptoms of the Drug Culture in College and How to Escape It" might create a picture of a social setting that your audience has not yet faced. You could talk about the stress, the depression, the sexual prolems, and the tensions of studying that accompany the aftermath of drug use. You could also suggest that your audience will be involved in the drug culture whether they smoke or not. Think of another approach that might be interesting.

Situation C

In the third situation, you are attending a dormitory meeting following the attempted suicide of a well-known student. The mood is solemn. Administrators, faculty, and students are present. All accept the fact that their casual attitudes may have contributed to this situation.

In this situation, it would be unnecessary to address yourself to the problem of drugs. It is obvious. A topic describing a course of action, on the other hand, might be welcomed. You might state, "The establishment of a drug clinic has been talked about long enough. Now is the time to get it off the ground."

Scenario II

In a lighter vein, this scenario involves you, a student, working as a summer tour guide at the house of a famous historical personality. You are asked to prepare a five-minute talk to supplement the standard guide speech about "in this room General Greeley was born." Most of the tourists know a few basic facts about the house. Greeley was a well-known figure. The situation calls for something interesting.

A standard, but reliable, approach in this setting is the spicy story formula. As you approach his wine cellar, you might talk about "Greeley's Weaker Moments." Similarly, a topic about "Some Mysterious Facts about the Greeley Homestead" would be equally successful.

Scenario III

While attending college, you have served as a magazine salesperson. After three years, you have established a good reputation for your sales ability and integrity. Your company is constantly recruiting new sales personnel—many in your own age bracket. The company's training program teaches its personnel what to say and how to say it, but they have asked you to talk about your ingredients for success. How do you phrase your topic?

A "go get 'em" hyped-up sales approach is probably not appropriate. The new personnel have probably not yet developed any loyalty to the company. Their interest is earning money for school. They are probably approaching their first assignment with some reservations. The situation probably calls for a blunt treatment of reality such as, "How to Cope With Your First Failures."

Scenario IV

You are a first-year law student. Your hometown is small, rural, and has one major industry. The industry is causing a water pollution problem. You decide to attend a town meeting at which the subject is to be debated. Previous discussions have indicated that the problem can be solved without major expense. The townspeople are uncertain as to how to approach the subject. They are unaware of their legal rights; they do not wish to offend their major source of income.

A militant statement calling for immediate legislation could upset a delicate relationship between the town and the industry. The situation calls for clarity and mediation. The best type of speech would involve some information on how to frame legislation, how to implement it, and how to avoid litigation over water rights. An informative speech about how another town faced a similar problem and solved it to the satisfaction of both parties would be excellent.

Scenario V

You are, say, twenty-eight years old. You are moderately successful in a small business in a suburban town. As an active member of a church, you have been asked to speak to a group of businessmen about contributing to the church. Most are conservative and most have already donated something to the church.

Your audience has shown that they are willing to give by the evidence of their past contributions. The problem in persuasion involves getting more of the same. Perhaps one approach is to demonstrate that the past fund-raising campaign still left the church with some debts. Another approach might involve "New Tax Advantages for Donations." Think of other topics.

Scenario VI

You are an advocate of greater equality and opportunity for women. As a successful woman who works for a company with an outstanding record in equal job opportunities, you have been asked to speak before an organization whose sole interest is the advancement of women.

Too often, in social movements, advocates find themselves telling others things they already believe. Persuasion is not always necessary in situations of this sort. What is needed, usually, is information. You could probably provide an insider's view of the more subtle "Techniques of Discrimination" that they should be aware of in industry.

Scenario VII

You are a first-year medical student who, as an undergraduate, was very interested in social causes. As a young activist, you got involved in the problems of the aged. You have been asked to speak before a group of retired men and women at a community for the elderly.

The situation hardly calls for a gloomy speech about the neglect of the aged. The concentration level of your audience is not high, and therefore a detailed address about health is also not likely to be fully appreciated. An enjoyable speech about "Avoiding Boredom" or "Some Light Activity for Light Moments" might be well appreciated. "Sexual Potency After 100" ought to generate some fun.

Scenario VIII

You are the parent of a black child who is creative and intelligent. Your child is attending a school known for its liberal policies and advanced outlook in education. Nevertheless, you have reason to believe that the school system is somehow discriminating against your child, and her growth has been inhibited. From conversations with a small group of other black parents, you sense that they share your experience. A group of these parents have gotten together at your home to discuss the matter. They have asked you to lead the discussion. How should the problem be stated?

Because the school is advanced, it is possible that as many, or more, black parents will disagree with you as will agree with you. The administration of the school feels comfortable with its policies but is open-minded and willing to listen to whatever you say. A very specific listing of discriminatory circumstances, corroborated by the experiences of others, is essential. "The Nature of Discrimination in Testing Procedures" might be a topic that would give focus to your complaints.

Scenario IX

You are a college freshman. In high school you were popular: a class officer, an athlete, and a good student. You have been invited back to your high school to deliver a talk that will open, or keynote, a career day. Many of the students remember you as an organizer, perhaps somewhat of a manipulator. What sort of topic do you choose?

You have not yet embarked on a career, so it might be presumptuous of you to talk about opportunities in the real world. You are, nevertheless, considered an authority of sorts on getting ahead. A topic, such as a humorous slant on "How to Succeed in College" might provide some enjoyment.

Scenario X

As a last scenario, let us create a near impossible task. You believe in U.F.O.'s (Unidentified Flying Objects). Your belief is that they are from other planets where life is of a higher order than that on earth. You claim to have seen U.F.O.'s, and the "people" who pilot them. You have been asked to speak before a group of skeptics. They not only disclaim the legitimacy of your position but consider it as some form of subversion. A large percentage of the group is made up of war veterans.

A description of what you have seen might whet their curiosity and provide some food for laughter, but you are not likely to be taken seriously. If, however, you draw on their presumed respect for the military by talking about "The U.S. Air Force's Records Concerning U.F.O.'s," you might make some headway. Although the goal of convincing them of your position is an impossibility, you may mitigate some biases.

Review and Perspective

We have talked about focusing and limiting a topic. We have discussed the variables that may influence the wording of your topic. And we have presented several scenarios in which you can put some topics to the test of situational considerations. We are now concerned with providing some guidance in the development and understanding of your topic.

INVESTIGATING AN IDEA

No communicator can be expected to enter into a rhetorical situation in total command of the subject. Investigating information that is beyond the limits of your past experiences will more than likely be necessary. If for no other reason than to stimulate some new ideas, you will want to seek out pertinent facts.

The process of research can have many roadblocks and pitfalls—any of which can divert you into the area of biased opinions, distortions, and uncorroborated facts. How to discriminate between useful and poor information will be the focus of the next chapter. Here we are concerned with providing some direction for obtaining information and data from which you can develop and distill your ideas.

Without some procedures, the task of research can seem tedious and overwhelming. So consider that your task should follow five basic steps.

First, you should survey your own personal knowledge of the topic, jotting down whatever main categories, ideas, or related areas come to mind. If you wish to talk about Japan, list the things you know: gardens, Tokyo, Toyotas, Hiroshima. You may then ask how each area can fit into your topic—keeping in mind avenues for research.

Second, you should begin reading—anything and everything that is pertinent. A broad perspective is necessary before you can begin to select that which is *most* pertinent and *most* interesting.

Third, you should begin to set some specific objectives concerning the type of information you are seeking.

Fourth, you should develop a system for recording and organizing the information as it relates to the specific subheadings of your topic.

Fifth, you should begin recording all ideas and information from nonprinted sources such as conversations, your own observations, televisions programs, radio news broadcasts, and motion pictures.

The Library: Your Primary Source

Fundamental to researching a topic is the library—an efficiently designed data-storage system. An understanding of its system will make available to you much valuable information. The means of retrieving information depends, simply, on an awareness of how the library can direct you to specific works. Once those works are discovered, you will find other sources listed within that source or on neighboring shelves.

The Card Catalogue

The alphabetical card catalogue provides a key system for efficiently locating books in a library. Familiarity with the system will reduce the amount of time it takes to discover a basic source and will subsequently increase the speed of message construction. The title of each work is printed on a card and filed either according to author's last name, the title heading, or the subject heading. In the majority of libraries, you can locate the work under all three categories. For example, a book entitled *Aggressiveness Among Welfare Recipients* by Karen Z. Fletcher might be found under three separate divisions.

1. Author's name—Fletcher, Karen Z.
2. Title—*Aggressiveness Among Welfare Recipients*
3. Subject—Social Psychology

Once the source card is located, you should immediately record the author, title, and the *reference number.* The number is used for one of two purposes: locating the book on a shelf or acquiring the book from the librarian. Larger libraries, in lieu of open stacks, employ staff members to deliver the book.

Periodicals

Both popular magazines and scholarly periodicals are useful to the communicator. By the very nature of their purpose magazines are generally concerned with those topics most frequently discussed in public—subjects that are contemporary, informative, and often controversial. Scholarly periodicals, for example *Foreign Affairs* or *Northwestern Law Review,* can be expected to be more analytical and more factual than the ordinary magazine, hence offering you additional insights and facts.

Periodicals are usually found in separate sections of the library, and their location is discovered by a quick glance in the card catalogue. Special resource guides are available in the reference section of the library, which lists countless articles on current topics.

Reference sources include the *Reader's Guide to Periodical Literature*—an excellent and available source for finding specific topics in magazines. The *Reader's Guide,* although published each month, is available in large yearly volumes that contain a cumulative index of articles for over a hundred different magazines over the past half-century. An article can be found merely by selecting the volume, according to the appropriate date, and then turning to the proper subject heading.

Other periodical and special indexes are also available, such as *International Index to Periodicals,* which has been renamed the *Index to the Humanities and Social Sciences.* It catalogues scholarly articles from the most well-known learned journals. *Poole's Index to Periodical Literature* covers the period from 1802 to 1906. Other sources include *The Business Index, Education Index, Agricultural Index, Art Index, Music Index, Industrial Arts Index, Bulletin of the Public Affairs Information Service, Newsweek Index,* and *Time Index.*

Newspapers

As a record of daily factual material, the newspaper services are an invaluable tool to the communicator. Although journalists are not always free of bias, you can expect to find the most factual information available on a given subject in newspapers. Back issues, however, are not always available. With the exception of the *New York Times,* most local libraries save little else other than the town newspaper. University libraries generally offer more newspapers to the researcher, but the most complete collection is to be found at the Library of Congress.

The *New York Times Index* is the most helpful guide available for newspaper research. Because the *Times* itself is thorough, the *Index* carries reference to all events of international and domestic significance. Moreover, indexed items appear with titles and brief summaries; this saves you valuable time.

The *Times Index* can also indirectly lead you to similar items in other newspapers. By locating the date of a particular event through the *Times Index,* you can assume that a similar article may have appeared in, say, the *Boston Globe* on the same day. If the desired newspaper is not available in the local library, you might seek a photostatic copy from either (1) the publisher, (2) the Library of Congress, or (3) the local library in the place of publication.

Other newspaper indexes include *The London Times Index, Palmer's Index,* which catalogues items from 1790, and the *Official Index,* which has a comprehensive listing since 1906.

Government Sources

The United States government each year produces massive quantities of information pertaining to nearly all current subjects of executive, legislative, and judicial concern.

Often a short cut to obtain a government publication is to locate the author of a legislative bill through the newspaper and to request specific materials through his office. If this is not possible, special indexes and bibliographies are available.

The *Monthly Catalogue: United States Government Publications* lists numerous governmental pamphlets. The *Statistical Abstract of the United States* and the *United States Census Reports* index statistics on the country. Particularly useful is Boyd's *United States Government*

Publications: Sources of Information for Libraries, which contains those bibliographies distributed by the government.

The Reference Room

Library reference rooms will provide numerous other sources helpful for specific purposes, such as *Dictionary of American Biography, Dictionary of National Biography, The Encyclopedia Britannica, Encyclopedia Americana, Who's Who, Who's Who in America, American Men of Science, Directory of American Scholars,* and *Webster's Biographical Dictionary.*

The Communicator as a Source

We mentioned previously that man is obliged to expand beyond himself for information and analysis. Skills of observation and recording can be developed so as to enhance the communicator as a source himself. If, for example, you are more alert to the environment around you, you may be able to perceive ideas that exceed printed ideas. Interesting observations may come to mind.

A speech on poverty can, for example, become more vivid and convincing if you take time to visit and observe the agony of the ghetto. Your view becomes more human, hence less statistical and less impersonal. Your receivers will subsequently listen with more sympathy.

Conversation with others, listening, debating, and all other forms of communication—be they visual, olfactory, or whatever—can be the source of countless insights. Poets, for example, purposefully place themselves in new situations to acquire new, fresh insights. After all, man is a being who responds and creates according to his sense impressions. You should therefore allow your senses to record your environment keenly.

Television and radio can be good sources. By selecting good programs and being attentive to their verbal and nonverbal content, you will obtain additional insights.

RECORDING IDEAS AND MATERIALS

Personal observations and sense impressions may be recorded at anytime on anything, but for printed, factual, and researched materials, the communicator needs to create a viable system. Sheets of paper and notebooks can be cumbersome and awkward. Too many bits of information may clutter one piece of paper and clutter your mind as well.

The best storage and retrieval system designed for the individual speaker is the 4 × 6 or 3 × 5 notecard system. Single bits of information—a fact, an opinion, an example, a source, or whatever—can be recorded on a single card and later reshuffled for organization and coherence. Moreover, the same cards can be used for reference during the communicative act.

The notecard can be designed for optimum efficiency by keeping in mind three principles:

1. The *subject* should be indicated in the appropriate place.
2. The *information* should be precise and accurate.
3. The *source* should be recorded.

SHOE INDUSTRY DECLINE IN NEW ENGLAND
   "Foreign imports are responsible for the disastrous decline of shoe production in Massachusetts. Over the last three years, 52 factories have closed."
Virginia and Helen Costarides, *The Declining Shoe Industry,* (Boston: Chadwick Press, 1975), p. 44.

A LIST OF IDEAS

Included below is a list of subjects designed to stimulate some of your own thinking about topics. Some may provide you with an instant topic. Others will present starting points from which you may explore numerous areas.

Your selection of topics will depend, of course, on the options that you have chosen. It will be necessary to narrow your topic down to meet the considerations of time and situation. The amount of information and commitment to the position that you bring to the subject will be equally important considerations.

Each subject contains in it the options of the informative, persuasive, or problem-solving approach.

Consider the example of *energy:*

Informative topic:	Recent advances in the use of solar *energy.*
Persuasive topic:	Rocktown should develop a solar *energy* plant.

Problem-solving topic: What can be done to solve
the *energy* crisis?

National and International Policy
  HEALTH
    New Vaccines
    Pediatrics
    Geriatrics
  POPULATION CONTROL
    Diets
    Contraception
    Abortion
  TRADE POLICY
    Wheat
    Arms
    Automobiles
  EDUCATION
    Progressive versus Traditional
    I.Q. and Testing
    Busing
  AGRICULTURE
    Farm Subsidies
    Futures
    Inflation Control
  HOUSING
    Low-cost
    Mobile Homes
    Condominiums
  ECOLOGY
    Recycling
    Water Pollution
    Pesticides
  TRANSPORTATION
    Train
    Airplane
    Automobile
  TECHNOLOGY AND MODERNIZATION
    Retooling of Industry
    Refuse as Energy
    The Modern City

Exotic Places
  EASTER ISLAND
  KATMANDU
  OLDUVAI GORGE

MT. KILIMANJARO
INCA RUINS
MT. EVEREST
THE NILE
KYOTO
NEW ZEALAND
TRANSYLVANIA

Economics

INFLATIONS, RECESSIONS, DEPRESSIONS
COST OF ENERGY
OIL COSTS
PSYCHOLOGY OF THE STOCK MARKET
THE GOLD STANDARD
UNEMPLOYMENT
PUBLIC WORK
GUARANTEED NATIONAL INCOME
WORLD MONETARY SYSTEM
FREE TRADE

Myths versus Fact

WITCHCRAFT IN SALEM
VISITORS FROM OUTER SPACE
THE LOCH NESS MONSTER
THE HISTORY OF DRACULA
GHOSTS IN ENGLAND
DAVY CROCKETT
INDIAN WARS AND BATTLES
VOODOOISM
HOUDINI
THE DISCOVERY OF AMERICA

Notorious Criminals

HITLER
EICHMANN
JOHN WILKES BOOTH
LEE HARVEY OSWALD
CHARLES MANSON
JOHN DILLINGER
BONNY AND CLYDE
JACK THE RIPPER
AL CAPONE
NERO

Futurism
> CLONING
> SPACE TRAVEL
> RADIATIONAL MUTATIONS
> ARTIFICIAL ORGANS
> FUTURISTIC ART
> LASERS
> 2000 A.D.
> ATOMIC ENERGY
> UNDERWATER HABITATION
> EARTHQUAKES AND HOLOCAUSTS

Sports
> THE SPAWNING OF PROFESSIONAL TEAMS
> THE NATIONALIZATION OF THE OLYMPICS
> COLLEGE RECRUITMENT
> FAMOUS MOMENTS IN SPORTS
> FAMOUS COACHES AND PLAYERS
> THE HISTORY OF SAILING
> SPORTS SCANDALS
> BROKEN BONES AND ARTIFICIAL TURF
> WOMEN VERSUS MEN, BOYS VERSUS GIRLS
> THE ABOLITION OF VIOLENT SPORTS
> THE DANGERS OF SKYDIVING

Morality and Ethics
> CENSORSHIP AND THE LAW
> MORAL VERSUS NATIONAL INTERESTS IN THE MAKING
>   OF FOREIGN POLICY
> PROSTITUTION
> THE FUTURE OF ORGANIZED RELIGIONS
> ZEN BUDDHISM
> KARMA
> EUTHANASIA
> CAPITAL PUNISHMENT
> WHITE COLLAR CRIME
> VIVISECTION

Military History
> GETTYSBURG
> BATTLE OF THE BULGE
> D-DAY, THE SIXTH OF JUNE
> THE BOMBING OF HIROSHIMA
> STALINGRAD

PEARL HARBOR
IWO JIMA
THE ALAMO
THE SIX-DAY WAR
THE BOSTON MASSACRE

SUMMARY

We are usually prone to think first of a general topic. Reducing this broad concept to a more specific area calls for consideration of self-interest, special purpose, and audience background and interests. Your development of an idea can be more productive if you follow a systematic research procedure: Survey your own knowledge, begin pertinent reading, narrow your objectives, use a standard head or subhead identification system for notes, and record print and nonprint information. Improve your library research techniques because it is your fundamental source of information.

Review and Exercises

1. Select a general subject area and break it down into a general category, a specific category, and a specific topic.
2. Make a list of specific topics that interest you as a speaker. Submit the same list to your class and have them rank the topics according to their interests.
3. Construct a hypothetical scenario using the ones listed in the text as a guide. Develop a topic that would be appropriate for this scenario.
4. How could the same topic be adapted to a different scenario?
5. Using the library, locate an article on each of the following topics:

      A. Animal communication
      B. The government's position on U.F.O's.
      C. The American Medical Association's position
          on the dangers of smoking.

6. Using the *New York Times Index,* locate five major speeches by John F. Kennedy and Richard Nixon in 1960.

7. Develop a bibliography for one of the topics listed under the heading of "Morality and Ethics."

Additional Readings

Aldrich, Ella Virginia, *Using Books and Libraries,* Prentice-Hall, Engle-wood Cliffs, N.J., 1960.

Berelson, Bernard, *Content Analysis in Communication Research,* The Free Press, New York, 1952.

Oliver, Robert T., Arnold, Carroll C., and White, Eugene E., eds., *Speech Preparation Sourcebook,* Allyn and Bacon, Boston, 1966.

Winchell, Constance M., *Guide to Reference Books,* American Library Association, Chicago, 1967.

Footnotes

[1] James C. McCroskey, *An Introduction to Rhetorical Communication,* 2nd edition (Englewood Cliffs, N.J.: Prentice-Hall, Inc., 1972), p. 140. Copyright © 1972 by Prentice-Hall, Inc. Reprinted by permission of the publisher.

CHAPTER 5 SELECTING INFORMATION: THE USES OF EVIDENCE

CHAPTER 5 SELECTING INFORMATION: THE USES OF EVIDENCE

RATIONAL PURPOSES

Either you speak from experience or from information obtained from other sources.

In either case you are selecting, condensing, and interpreting information. Moreover, you are converting it into your own language—with all its ambiguities and idiosyncrasies. If you expect that those with whom you communicate will choose to listen to and believe what you say, then some kind of sorting-out process is necessary. The information you use must show your listeners what it has shown to you.

Evidence is the term we have chosen to use for information. It is the kind of information that you select to make the truth of your message *evident*. Because of the limitations of time, your language, the situation, and even your own memories, you cannot present all the information available. Words are, after all, only a *representation* of reality. So you must select the best and most representative information to make the truth outwardly apparent. You could say that the process of selection itself converts information into evidence. In a courtroom, for example, lawyers and prosecutors use bits of information to construct the reality of what happened. This is evidence.

The use of evidence as it is discussed on the following pages is directed primarily toward you, the rational sender of messages, but its criteria should also be applied by you as the receiver–listener. Because communication is a two-way process, you will participate at both ends. Consider evidence in that light.

The purposes of evidence are to clarify, amplify, and prove ideas. Each piece of evidence should meet all three criteria—not only one or the other. The objectives are interrelated. What proves a point should also clarify it. What amplifies should also prove.

Purposes of Evidence
   C larify
   A mplify
   P rove

Evidence *clarifies* by making ideas *understandable*. A speech about how a copier machine works might compare the process to a

86

magnet: The chemically treated paper magnetizes particles to reproduce the printed matter on a page. This comparison, or analogy, clarifies the copying process by comparing the audience's known information about magnets to their unknown information about copiers. Evidence has made the concept clearer.

Evidence *amplifies* by illustrating and expanding an idea. A speech that is intended to impress on an audience the need for automobile safety may include several descriptions, or examples, of accidents. Each description amplifies and magnifies the need for safety by illustrating the results of unsafe driving.

Evidence *proves* by drawing together information so that conclusions are apparent. It makes an idea valid and apparent by presenting information that supports that idea. It may do so by synthesizing facts. You might say, "Ten of the twenty-two people who did not stop their cars at the corner of Chadwick and South Elm Streets were in accidents. Therefore, people ought to stop at that corner." By either its quantity or quality, the evidence provides the audience with a rationale for believing the truth of what is being said.

Many variables influence the use of evidence, and you cannot assume that its use will automatically and instantaneously convince others of what you say. For one thing, what you know and believe to be true may not be apparent to others. A listener's previous knowledge of the subject may bias his or her interpretation of what you say. How the listener views you, the speaker, will determine your believability as well.

How evidence affects communication has, therefore, been the subject of considerable research.

In analyzing what is necessary for evidence to be effective, William Dresser states that "at least three conditions will have to be met for evidence to have an impact. The assertion to be supported must be one that the listener would doubt if evidence were not offered. The evidence must *not* be doubted by the listener. And the relationship existing between the evidence and the assertion must seem both clear and valid to the listener once it is pointed out."[1]

It is apparent that evidence will, to one degree or another, influence the communicative act. In reporting several studies on evidence, James McCroskey concludes: "These nine studies provide substantial justification for the generalization that initial credibility and evidence usage interact to produce attitude change and perceived credibility."[2] Of another study, he indicates that "evidence must be new to the audience before it can have an impact on their immediate attitude change or their perception of the message source."[3]

It is our point of view that you heighten the effectiveness of evidence by understanding some important considerations of what to look for—how to discriminate between useful and poor evidence. A first question involves the nature of facts.

A Fact is a Fact, Or is It?

The first criterion in the selection and use of evidence is to know what a fact is. On the surface, the answer seems obvious, but consider for a moment the following statements. Do they sound like facts?

1. It rained in Boston on July 11, 1974.
2. A chair has four legs.
3. Mike is ugly.

Let us examine how you could approach determining the validity, or *factual* nature, of each statement. The first, "It rained in Boston on July 11, 1974," could be verified as a fact by several means. Expert testimony by a meteorologist might be enough. Official records of the United States Weather Bureau would be very convincing. However, a statement by a Bostonian that, "I think it rained on that day," would make the "fact" seem a dubious one.

The second statement, "A chair has four legs," poses several questions for analysis. Each is a question of definition.

1. Is a chair, by definition, a piece of furniture with four legs?
2. Does a chair always have four legs?
3. If you removed one leg from a chair, is it still a chair?
4. If you sit on a four-legged table, does it become a chair?

You could approach answering these questions by first establishing a definition that is acceptable and then proceeding to ask whether or not the object under consideration meets the criteria of the definition. If a definition is not established, then your fact might be suspect. The fact of "rain in Boston" could be questionable if you had defined "rain" as a few drops for two seconds after midnight.

The question of definition might, in and of itself, require additional evidence. You might consult several experts in home furnishing and ask, "In your judgment does a chair always have four legs?" Your statement might subsequently maintain that "According to four out of five experts questioned, a chair must have four legs to be classified as a chair."

The statement, "Mike is ugly," is the most difficult to verify as a fact. The question of "ugliness" is a value judgment and subject to a wide range of opinion. The distinction must subsequently be made between fact and opinion with the full realization that opinions, based purely on value judgments, can rarely be considered facts.

However, you could try—again, by using definition. You might state that "ugliness" is something that is "displeasing to the eye," but then you still have the problem of telling your audience whose eye was used for the test. Another approach might be to ask several people who know Mike. If you are able to say that "most of his friends and acquaintances consider him ugly," you may not have established his ugliness as an indisputable fact but you might have established probability.

Often it is necessary to qualify such "facts" with phrases such as:

According to experts . . .
In the opinion of Dr. Smith . . .
The records show . . .
Five witnesses agree that . . .
It is probable that . . .

In summary, then, you can see that facts are subject to questions. Those that are generally accepted are usually not discussed, but those that are used to establish probability must meet certain criteria and tests including those of source reliability, definition, and other forms of corroboration.

THE ETHICS OF EVIDENCE

The manner in which facts are selected and used can pose some interesting questions involving ethics. It would be comforting to believe that information speaks for itself, but unfortunately this is not the case. You are speaking for it. It is being filtered through your own attitudes and experiences after, perhaps, it has been worked over by someone else. How you frame a fact, dress it up, insult it, or whatever, will greatly affect its appearance. The right fact in the wrong context can shed an entirely different light on a subject.

However, so long as you assume that your *goals* of communication are ethical, you will probably ask, "Need every piece of evidence be scrutinized for its ethical implications?" Not necessarily. Nor can ethics be avoided. We tend to think of ethics as associated with the larger issues in life: life, death, love, and war. The truth of the matter is that there may be ethical considerations in anything you say—especially if is influencing someone else's behavior or well-being.

So we frequently tend to dismiss the impact of what we say. Because we are concerned with our own lives, and perhaps also because of tinges of insecurity, we do not realize our influence on our own environment. Even a seemingly harmless discussion with your neighbor as to how he can paint his house might carry with it some serious ramifications: namely, safety and cost. In relating the evidence of your own experience, you may casually say: "You can paint one side of your house in a couple of hours." But to you, "a couple of hours" actually means "a few hours." And what you can do in a few hours may take others a day and a half. The evidence of your experience could cause your neighbor to be hasty. You may have set the scene for an accident.

If you further doubt the necessity of applying ethics, think of the frustrations that you have suffered because of poor advice or incomplete directions. How you go about considering ethics and their bearing on communication is the subject of the following brief but critical discussion.

Acquiring an Ethical Eye

The ability to determine what is ethical, given the considerations of the situation, topic, and audience, is a continuous task. The term *situation ethics* is the title of a contemporary philosophy that holds that there are no absolute laws by which we may determine the good and the bad. Rather, each situation contains its own conditions that determine its own set of ethics. The example of the advice that one never shouts fire in a crowded theatre, even if there is a fire, demonstrates that the consideration of panic should make you think twice about shouting the truth.

Because there is no standard applicable to all situations, this type of philosophy may seem to lead you nowhere with regard to the selection of evidence and what you say. Just the opposite is true. Each situation contains *some* ethical considerations. You are, therefore, required to add the dimension of ethics to the rational choices that you make.

An easier task is the cultivation of an eye for what is falsified, exaggerated, or distorted evidence. We will talk later in the chapter about how you can make such distinctions. Often your own common sense will tell you much. If, for example, a subject has been open to dispute for many years, you should know enough to exclude evidence that states something like: "It's a known fact that there is life on Mars."

Another ethical consideration involves resisting the temptation to select and use only that evidence that lends support to your point of view. It is only natural to see things according to our biases. We all tend to categorize things on the side most favorable to us. The goal of one-sidedness works in strange ways. First, our message is likely to be less developed if we have not sought answers for what appear to be contradictory viewpoints. Second, some audiences can easily spot the individual whose mind is closed to opposing views.

Eliminating Some Common Habits

Some of the above discussion involves making intentional ethical choices. However, there are some common habits of selection and usage that can unwittingly lead to unethical viewpoints and conclusions.

The Sin of Incomplete Research

The task of obtaining all information on a subject is almost impossible. Although this is true, it is not an excuse for laziness. Ignorance of the law is no justification for violation of the law. In other words, if you are missing vital information pertinent to your persuasive or informative speech, you are responsible.

The Sin of Omission

Even though you have researched your subject fully and extensively, you may leave out relevant data in the organizational process. A speech that projects the success of the World Football League could draw on statistics of attendance of some franchises while leaving out the poor attendance of others. There is a very strong impulse to make things fit. Avoid it. You can still establish a good case by including seemingly contradictory information.

The Sin of Irrelevance

Piling on pointless and irrelevant information can lead audiences into concluding, falsely, that a contention has been proven when it has not. If you are advocating the need to limit the arms race, statistics about our stockpiling of arms can be irrelevant unless you indicate that the stockpile is not necessary. Similarly, evidence about the number of hospitals or doctors in the country may be irrelevant to the contention that compulsory health insurance is needed.

A Situational Test of Ethics

The following is a presentation of evidence in support of a contention. On the surface it appears to suggest the need for a solution:

Ten out of twenty-two people who did not stop their cars at the corner of Chadwick and South Elm Street were in accidents. Therefore, a street light should be installed.

Could the use of the above evidence be considered ethical if the following information was provided?

1. The information was collected over a five-year period.
2. The ten persons have poor eyesight, were under the influence of alcohol, or failed to observe the stop sign.
3. The corner was icy at the time of the accidents.

Closing the Credibility Gap

The political orator or medicine salesman who stumped the backwoods of early America had an unfair advantage. The audience had little access to information that might prove the speaker wrong.

Today, exactly the opposite is true. Almost everyone has an opinion, and most sides are reported in the papers. In the aftermath of Watergate the public is skeptical. And although the term "credibility gap" is likely to remain with us for a while, some political advocates continue to speak as if it did not exist. White House correspondent Hugh Sidney has said: "We need a public rhetoric that matches in level the intelligence and awareness of the American people."[4]

To close the credibility gap between you and your listeners, consider the following.

Draw Information from Various Sources

Information from a variety of sources demonstrates your breadth of research and settles any ethical disputes over how you derived your conclusions. A case against a national medical care plan, for example, should include more information than that provided solely by the American Medical Association. The use of a variety of sources tends to generate higher credibility.

Give Credit to Your Sources

Mentioning your sources will engender some confidence in your information. The sources must, of course, be credible. If you are not considered an authority on the subject, then you will be expected to give considerable credit to your sources. Audiences will expect it. Moreover, you have an ethical obligation to mention the author you have quoted.

Eliminate Spurious Sources

A spurious source is one that is false, counterfeit, and not genuine. It is also one that assumes a position of authority it has no right to assume. National scandal newspapers and magazines are among the most flagrant examples of spurious sources. The use of one spurious source, if detected, can destroy your credibility entirely.

Avoid Oversimplification

Oversimplified conclusions drawn from complex information can be meaningless as well as unethical. Basically, the sin of oversimplification is committed when you draw conclusions without looking at other aspects of the information. The person who looks at the many conflicts in the world and says, "We are headed for a third world war," is oversimplifying a problem that deserves closer analysis and a more qualified conclusion.

Demonstrate Respect For Your Listeners

The person who underrates the intelligence of his listeners may have considerable trouble in establishing credibility. If you are talking to a group of women's clothing designers, you would not start by defining a shirtwaist or by talking about the basics of cutting and fitting. Too many speakers use great amounts of the obvious. The effect paralyzes an audience with boredom while eroding credibility. Show respect for your audience by including new, yet comprehensible, information.

Know Your Information

An audience may sense whether or not you are at ease with your information. An understanding and command of what you are saying will create greater credibility.

EVIDENCE AND THE ESTABLISHING OF PROBABILITY

The goals of evidence are to clarify, amplify, and prove. The result is the establishment of probability, which is, in effect, the creation of a reason for an audience to believe that what you say is true.

Through information, you attempt either to represent the truth or to predict the likelihood of an occurrence. If you are demonstrating how to ski, or if you are presenting information about the Civil War, or if you are predicting better health through a national health plan, you are using probability.

It is probable *that after your demonstration speech, your listeners will know something about skiing. It is not certain that they will have learned how to ski.*

It is probable *that a talk on the Civil War will clarify some of the causes and events, but it is not certain that you will have presented all the truth.*

It is probable that evidence about the needs for a national health plan will indicate some reason for its adoption, but its success is not certain.

In other words, the quantity and the appropriateness of the evidence will determine the extent to which probability will be established. Evidence, therefore, advances an idea from the level of possibility to a level of probability.

You cannot expect, however, that all listeners will understand, believe, or act on your ideas as you present them. Your objective, therefore, should be to move the audience along a continuum toward what you believe to be the most accurate or most believable message. Accuracy is the function of the informative message. Believability is the function of the persuasive message. Evidence, through the vehicle of probability, is the means by which both are established.

One can diagram the continuum accordingly:

Impossibility   **Certainty**
└────────────────→ **Probability** ────────────────→

Along the continuum, and between what is impossible and what is certain, there are other gradations:

The possible
The plausible but uncertain
The possible but not probable
The possible but not likely
The possible and probable
The probable but not assured
The probable

Keep in mind when we consider the various forms of evidence that its function is to establish probability. When things are absolutely true or false, the communicator is faced with few problems in communication. In the more common realm of probability the communicator must put his tools of rationality to their best use.

THE FORMS AND TESTS OF EVIDENCE

We have discussed the purposes and functions of evidence. Our next concern will be with the *types* of evidence. What form does evidence take? How do we analyze its effectiveness, validity, or usefulness?

Five different forms of evidence will be presented. It is critically important that you recognize that one form can interrelate with another, or with all others. We are making distinctions only for the purpose of understanding. Notice, for example, that two of the categories are evidence by authority and evidence by statistics. Keep in mind that the authority might have been the source of the statistics. Both are therefore interrelated, and so both tests ought to be applied.

The five forms of evidence are:

Evidence by example
Evidence by statistics
Evidence by comparisons
Evidence by authority
Evidence by observers

Evidence by Example

Perhaps the most frequently used form of evidence is the example. It is, simply, a specific case or illustration that is used to support a contention. You might say:

Contention: The lack of exercise is dangerous to one's health.
Example: Stan Walker never exercised. He died at age 35.

There are, however, many questions that can be asked to establish the validity or usefulness of an example. Some are included below.

1. *Are the examples representative of the class?* "Tall men make good basketball players. Take Kareem Jabbar for example." From this statement, you see that Kareem is certainly a good basketball player but is he representative of tall men? Tall men may be generally uncoordinated and Kareem may be an atypical example.

2. *Are there negative instances to counteract our examples?* The negative instances of the many tall "giants" who were extremely uncoordinated would counteract the example of Jabbar. Negative instances or examples reduce the effectiveness of the positive instance or example.

3. *Are the examples complete?* You might point to the government postal system as a sample of the government's inefficiency by showing how long it takes for the mail to be delivered over a short distance. If you do not point out that the

failure of people to use zip codes is partially responsible, then the example is incomplete—and to some extent erroneous.

Evidence by Statistics

To support a contention or establish a position, you may wish to use statistics. Statistics are numerical devices for establishing probability.

Contention: The lack of exercise is dangerous to one's health.
Statistics: Eighty-eight percent of those who did not participate in a sport, or exercise regularly, had heart trouble before the age of forty.

On the surface, information stated in statistics appears to contain less subjectivity than other forms of evidence. Such is not always the case. What is empirical in appearance may be deceptive in implication. Several questions may be asked of statistics.

1. *Do the statistics represent an accurate sampling?* Statistical surveys are usually based on data taken from sample groups ostensibly representative of larger groups. You are familiar with those used for rating television programs or predicting the success of a particular political candidate. The population surveyed is actually quite small, yet the conclusions about the larger population are frequently valid. However, the *sampling must be representative of the larger group.* A sampling of Illinois Republicans may be insufficiently representative of the Republican Party. Likewise, a rating of ABC or NBC news programs based on a sampling of college professors would be equally misleading.

2. *Are the statistical units accurately identified?* If you are speaking about housing, then you must define—precisely—what a housing unit is. Consider several questions that could be asked. Were the housing units cited in the argument permanently fixed units? Did they exclude mobile homes? Did they exclude apartment units? Did they exclude summer homes? Obviously, then, figures can vary according to the definition of the unit. The implications of the evidence could be misleading.

3. *Are the statistical units comparable?* Comparisons are generally used to shed some light on the extent of a problem. If you were to talk of the poverty of one country by comparing its wages to those of another, you may be distorting the picture if the wage units are not comparable. The figures may

have to be translated into purchasing power in order to create a clearer picture of the hourly wage units being compared. Consider the following chart:

	Hourly wage	Wage units needed to purchase pair of shoes.
Country X	$1.00	4
Country Y	$2.50	4

A conclusion suggesting that Country X was more impoverished than Country Y, therefore, would have been erroneous (assuming that the wage rate was the only basis of the argument).

4. *By whom was the information collected?* The source of statistical information may indicate its objectivity or subjectivity. Information collected by independently funded research agencies on the quality of a product is likely to be more valuable than information gathered by the product's manufacturer. Consider how statistics on automobile safety gathered by automobile manufacturers have been subject to greater doubt than the more acceptable statistics of the government.

5. *Are the differences significant?* Of general interest to the population during this decade has been the question of which automobile gets better mileage. The communicator who contends that his make gets better mileage than another ought to answer whether the difference is one-half mile per gallon, or a more significant difference.

6. *Are the correct statistical terms used?* Three common statistical terms are: mode, mean, and median. Misunderstanding may arise when these terms are misused to explain central tendency and probability. Consider how an average derived from the following five salaries could be misleading:

	Income
A	$500
B	$500
C	$1000
D	$2000
E	$10,000

The mean, or *average,* is $2800. The mode, or *the wage received by the greatest number of persons,* is $500. The median, or *half-way point,* is $1000. A reference to the "mode" as an implied average could be deceiving to the uninitiated.

In summary, the following questions are useful in evaluating statistical evidence.

1. Do the statistics represent an accurate sampling?
2. Are the units accurately identified?
3. Are the units comparable?
4. By whom was the information collected?
5. Are the differences significant?
6. Are the correct statistical terms used?

Evidence by Comparisons (Analogies)

Comparisons can either be *literal* forms of evidence or *figurative* forms. A literal comparison, or analogy, is one that compares two examples or things that have similar characteristics. You could compare United States foreign policy toward Germany and France. A figurative comparison is one that involves two examples that are unlike. A comparison of Hitler's voice to a clap of thunder would draw an interesting parallel, but it would be a figurative comparison—two things that are not *actually* alike. As we point out elsewhere, the function of the figurative comparison is actually more useful as a device of clarification than as a device of proof. So let us consider here the questions that you should be asked of a literal comparison.

1. *Do the points of likeness outweigh the differences?* For a comparison to be useful as evidence, it ought to have many points of likeness. You could, for example, compare the United States involvement in Vietnam with that of the French in the 1950s.

2. *Are there fundamental differences in the objects to be compared?* If you wish to compare the economic growth of two countries, you need to consider the point of time when both countries began industrialization. If it is different, then your comparison might be weak. In an argument concerning the relative intelligence of boys and girls at certain age levels, you would make a fundamental mistake to ignore the difference in maturation rates of the two groups.

3. *Do additional comparisons support the same premise?* A comparison is stronger if several instances support the same point. If you are to show that the sales tax should be adopted in state X, you might point to state Y for comparison. Your case would be strengthened if you could point to several other states as well. In other words the single comparison can be

strengthened if you can find additional comparisons to support your point.

4. *Is the figurative comparison used as proof?* You are all familiar with the statement, "Don't change horses in the middle of the stream." Certainly this is a dangerous place to change horses. However, you should not use this as proof for the opposition to changing presidents in wartime. The figurative analogy may be used as explanation but should not be used as logical proof.

Evidence by Authority

A common form of evidential support is the testimony of authorities or observers. The opinion of an authority or observer ostensibly establishes the validity of the message. Although it is necessary as a device of reinforcement, and frequently it may be the only evidence available, the opinion of others is subject to many questions.

Some guidelines for questioning authoritative evidence are:

1. *Is the authority an expert in the specific field?* Authorities in one field of expertise are frequently called on for their opinions on subjects not related to their profession. Athletes, especially, are paid salaries in excess of their annual income from their sport to testify in behalf of products. Obviously, their background does not qualify them as experts on automobiles. Even Dr. Jones—a noted expert in biochemistry— may not be prepared to make valid judgments about cigarette smoking if his area of expertise is nutrients and vitamins.

2. *Is the authority free of hidden bias?* A member of a congressional committee investigating the role of the Navy in the age of the rocket might call on both the rocket and Navy expert for positional statements. Both authorities are likely to have considerable interest in establishing rocketry in the Navy and thus their bias would have to be recognized. Similarly, the bias of the American Medical Association would have to be understood in relation to the issue of a national health care program. Many experts do, in fact, have biases; determining the extent to which their predisposition affects their judgment is at times difficult.

3. *Is the authority well known?* In general, the well-known authority can be expected to be more reliable than lesser known authorities unless, of course, his popularity was attained in

ways not directly related to his specialization. You have to avoid the premise that *all* well-known authorities are reliable.

4. *Is the authority well regarded by other experts?* A critical test of an authority is whether or not he is respected by his peers. Respect can be determined in several ways. Consider, first, publications. In most cases, manuscripts of articles and books are evaluated by experts prior to publication. If the material is published, then the author must have a degree of respect among experts in his field. Second, an elected office in a professional organization can likewise indicate some recognition and respect for the authority. Third, winning special awards may indicate special recognition for outstanding contributions to the profession.

5. *Has the authority had recent experience with the subject under discussion?* Some experts are outdated. In an age of rapid change, you must question the recent experiences of the expert. In most of the sciences, for example, some information is subject to change about every six months. Thus, this test of authority is most important in those fields where change occurs regularly.

6. *Is the authority morally acceptable?* Does the expert have a reputation for honesty and integrity? The testimony of the expert may be weakened by exposure of his or her background. The good character of the expert is important for acceptance of his testimony.

Evidence by Observers

The observer is one who is called on to support an issue or premise because of his physical proximity to an event under discussion. In the case of an automobile accident, the observer may be a person in one of the cars involved, or in a car near the accident, or a pedestrian. If the issue involves the influence of alcohol, the observer might be a bartender. Pedestrians who observed the behavior of the accused at the scene of the accident could be asked to report on his behavior.

The following guidelines can be used to test the testimony of the observers:

1. *Is the observer biased?* The testimony of a person's brother-in-law is liable to be more biased as that of a nonrelative. If the observer has anything to gain by his testimony, it may be open to question.

2. *Is the observer physically capable?* Observers who are color blind should not be used to testify on the lights at the intersection where an accident occurred. Observers who have limitations that may interfere with their abilities to observe or hear should be used with caution.
3. *Was the observer in a position where he could observe?* Perhaps the witness is called on to identify a person who was some distance away. You could raise questions concerning his testimony if there were obstructions in the way.
4. *Is the observer morally acceptable?* Observers with questionable reputations are not reliable especially if they have been known to lie about matters related to the subject at hand.

Summary of the Tests of Evidence

Evidence by Example

1. Are the examples representative of the class?
2. Are there negative instances to counteract the examples?
3. Are the examples complete?

Evidence by Statistics

1. Do the statistics represent an accurate sampling?
2. Are the statistical units accurately identified?
3. Are the statistical units comparable?
4. By whom was the information collected?
5. Are the differences significant?
6. Are the correct statistical terms used?

Evidence by Comparisons

1. Do the points of likeness outweigh the differences?
2. Are there fundamental differences in the objects to be compared?
3. Do additional comparisons support the same premise?
4. Is a figurative comparison used as proof?

Evidence by Authority

1. Is the authority an expert in the field?
2. Is the authority free of hidden bias?
3. Is the authority well known?
4. Is the authority well regarded by other experts?
5. Has the authority had recent experiences with the subject under discussion?
6. Is the authority morally acceptable?

Evidence by Observers

1. Is the observer biased?
2. Is the observer physically capable?
3. Was the observer in a position where he could observe?
4. Is the observer morally acceptable?

The Newman Tests of Evidence

The validity and usefulness of evidence can be seen from a number of perspectives. In their book *Evidence,* Robert P. Newman and Dale Newman provide some interesting tests for evidence.[5] They are:

Situational Tests

1. Tension. The lower the tension associated with an event, the higher the credibility of reports about it.
2. Accessibility. The more accessible the situation being reported on, both to the reporters and their audience, the more credible the reports.
3. Freedom to report—absence of gag rule. The more freedom a witness has to report things as he sees them, the greater his credibility.

Documentary Tests

4. Authenticity. The greater the presumption of authenticity, the higher the credibility of a document.
5. Internal consistency. The higher the internal consistency of an author, the more credible his testimony.
6. Carefulness of generalization. The more careful the generalizations of a writer, the higher the credibility of his testimony.
7. Reluctance. The greater the damage of his own testimony to a witness, the more credible it is.

Characteristics of the Writer

8. Expertise. The greater the relevant expertise of an author, the higher his credibility.
9. Objectivity. The greater the objectivity of an author, the more credible his testimony.
10. Accuracy record. The more accurate the description and pre-

diction record of a source, the higher the credibility of his testimony in general.

Tests of Primary Authorities

11. Eyewitness principle. The greater a witness's personal observation of a matter to which he testifies, the higher his credibility.

12. Contemporaneity. The more contemporaneous the report of a witness, the more credible his testimony.

13. Selection of primary sources. The more discerning a writer's selection of primary sources, the more credible his testimony.

14. Accuracy of citation. The more accurate the citations of a writer, the more credible his testimony.

SUMMARY

Evidence is used to clarify, amplify, and prove ideas. Clarification helps to make ideas understandable. Amplification illustrates and expands an idea. Proof brings information into position to make conclusions apparent.

"Facts" may be subjected to questions. You should be ultracritical of evidence that is falsified, exaggerated, or distorted. Avoid incomplete research, omission of evidence, and irrelevant evidence. In using evidence, draw from various sources, give credit to sources, eliminate weak sources, and don't oversimplify. Carefully examine your evidence to establish the validity, usefulness, subjectivity, and quality of sources.

Review and Exercises

---

1. Applying the tests of evidence, evaluate a political speech, an editorial, and an advertisement.

2. Find what you would consider good pieces of evidence in the following categories: example, statistics, comparison, authority, and observers.

3. Who would you consider good authorities on political questions, sports questions, and ethical questions?

4. Find what research has been done on the unreliability of eyewitnesses.

5. Examine a famous trial. How was evidence used to prove the guilt or innocence of the person on trial?

Additional Readings

Bradley, Bert E., *Fundamentals of Speech Communication: The Credibility of Ideas,* William C. Brown, Dubuque, Iowa, 1974.

Ehninger, Douglas, and Brockriede, Wayne, *Decision By Debate,* Dodd, Mead, New York, 1963.

Hart, Roderick P., Friedrich, Gustav W., and Brooks, William D., *Public Communication,* Harper and Row, New York, 1975.

Rieke, Richard D., and Sillars, Malcolm O., *Argumentation and the Decision Making Process,* Wiley, New York, 1975.

Wattenberg, Ben J., *The Real America,* Doubleday, Garden City, N.Y., 1974.

Footnotes

[1] William R. Dresser, "The Impact of Evidence on Decision Making," *Concepts in Communication,* edited by Jimmie D. Trent, Judith S. Trent, and Daniel J. O'Neill (Boston: Allyn and Bacon, Inc., 1973), p. 164.

[2] James C. McCroskey, "A Summary of Experimental Research on the Effects of Evidence in Persuasive Communication," *Concepts in Communication* (Boston: Allyn and Bacon, Inc., 1973), p. 172.

[3] *Ibid.,* p. 176.

[4] Hugh Sidey, *Time* (November 18, 1974), p. 15. Reprinted by permission from *Time,* the Weekly News Magazine; Copyright © Time Inc.

[5] Robert P. Newman and Dale Newman, *Evidence* (Boston: Houghton Mifflin, 1969), pp. 87–88. Reprinted by permission of the publisher.

CHAPTER 6 STRUCTURING THE MESSAGE: THE INFORMATIVE OPTION

CHAPTER 6 STRUCTURING THE MESSAGE: THE INFORMATIVE OPTION

The process of selecting the subject of your message requires you to analyze your *intent* and your *audience*. What is it that you want to say? Do you simply want to present information? Or do you want to do something with the information? Demonstrate it? Interpret it? Convince someone of its truth? Convince people to take a course of action?

Some clear thinking about your overriding intent will largely determine the style and form of your speech. In this chapter we are assuming that you do not desire to shake up, undo, or modify the beliefs of your audience. Rather, you are choosing to remain on neutral ground by presenting information. You have not yet chosen to advance toward a position.

The option before you, therefore, is characteristically *informative*. It is an option that, although it contains many of the same elements of other options, is aimed primarily toward the clarity of presentation.

RATIONALE FOR THE INFORMATIVE OPTION

The question before you is what paths toward effective communication do you take?

Make a few assumptions. You can assume that the persons with whom you are communicating wish to listen to you either because (1) they are not fully knowledgeable about the information you are about to present, or (2) they have not considered the perspective from which you will presenting the information. Obviously, some of your listeners will know more than others, but you can safely assume that your task will be to fill in the gaps in their knowledge. The data you present will be "new"—that is to say, previously unknown to them. You will also be showing relationships they have not yet considered.

If your audience is totally aware of the information, there is no point in choosing the informative option. You might agree with Anatol Rapoport who states: "In *any* situation, information about something we already know is worthless as information."[1] In other words, your listeners are not likely to want a rehash of obvious and common truth. It is the information that you possess that makes you worth listening to.

The process of making unknown information comprehensible to your listeners calls for the informative message to have clarity, interest, and understandability. There are different levels of complexity each of which places greater demands upon your ability to clarify information. First, realize that the level of complexity will be determined by how much information is required for an audience to understand a single concept or to perform a single task. The less information and the fewer steps involved, the simpler the speech will be. However, *do not confuse simplicity with clarity*. The statement, "You can tune an automobile by changing the points and plugs," is simple but not necessarily clear. Those who know nothing about changing points and plugs will be just as much in the dark as they were before.

Second, realize that clarity can be determined by how well you show the relationship of one piece of information to another. This process of *synthesizing* places an important burden on you as the communicator.

Third, realize that clarity can be determined by the information you choose to discard. Perhaps the most difficult task of all is to know what information is irrelevant to understanding the message. Too much information can overload the attention of your listeners.

DEFINING THE INFORMATIVE APPROACH

A word should be said about the natural attempt to draw a distinction between the informative and persuasive types of messages. It is nearly impossible. And most contemporary authors agree. The elements of the informative speech are used in a persuasive speech, and vice versa. We will shortly be discussing the techniques of attention and introduction, for example. You use the same techniques in the persuasive speech—perhaps with some variations.

In designing an informative message you make the distinction only so that you exclude those pigments that color it "persuasive." Much of this process is determined by your intent in communication. The authors agree with James McCroskey who states: "A communicator with persuasive intent has a conscious desire to influence the attitudes of his audience. A communicator with informative intent consciously rejects the desire to influence his audience's attitudes."[2] One short example will illustrate the point. Consider the intent of the person who makes the following statements:

Informative Statement
It is raining.
INTENT:
Merely to convey information. The statement remains informative unless your intent is to discourage a friend from going out.

Informative Statement Which Leans Toward Persuasion
It is raining very heavily.
INTENT:
The intent of stating "very heavily" may be informative, but its effect is likely to have a greater impact on the behavior of the listener.

Persuasive Statement
It is raining so heavily that you ought to stay home.
INTENT:
The intent of this statement is a clear attempt to modify the behavior of the listener.

The intent of the audience may also influence the informative or persuasive nature of your message. Your intent might be purely informative; however, your listener may use the information to determine what he will do.

Informative Intent   Listener's Interpretation
It is raining.   Hmm, I guess I won't go out today.

Likewise, your intent might be persuasive, but your listener might be interested only in the factual data that you are presenting. Thus, we may conclude that to the extent that your objective is informative, and to the extent that your audience will interpret it in that light, it can be said that your approach will be informative.

Let us assume that your intent is informative. The situations, types, and reasons for selecting the informative option are numerous. Basically, we see two main types: (1) the "how to" message, and (2) the message "about" something.

The "how to" approach can include definitions, descriptions, explanations, and instructional methods in such a way as to make your listeners understand *and perform* a task or activity. With the present-day high cost of automobile repairs, a speech on *how to* fix some common problems might be welcome.

The message "about" something also involves the same methods, but it does not require that the listener perform anything. It imparts knowledge to clarify understanding, but its purpose ends at this function.

"How to" approach:	I want to tell you how you can repair your car.
"About" approach:	I want to tell you something about the history of the automobile.

A combination of the two approaches is not uncommon. It is necessary to make the distinction only from the point of view of determining the extent to which you will present straight information and the extent to which you will demonstrate how that information operates.

CONSTRUCTING AN INFORMATIVE PATTERN

A clear idea of your purpose ought to help you determine the broad pattern of your message. By "pattern" we mean the overall structure—the major steps and segments of your speech.

Of the various patterns described below, none may serve the specific requirements of the occasion or the topic. It may be necessary for you to tailor your own pattern from a combination of the elements of different patterns. The following descriptions are put forth so that you may have a rational choice. Each pattern has its limitations. *It is your task to select the options and by doing so mold a pattern that is dynamic and useful. Predictable formulas tend to be boring. Inject the unsuspected. Draw on your originality.*

Consider the following patterns either in their entirety or in part.

Step One: Patterns for Introductions

The major functions of an introduction are to (1) capture attention and (2) focus on the topic.

Assuming that you have researched your subject fully and that you are prepared to speak on it with confidence, you may, nevertheless, find yourself struggling for a way to begin. Many good speeches have been severely weakened by vague, apologetic, or ill-planned openings. Much can be accomplished with a good opening. Along with attention and focus, your audience might also grant you some respect and open-mindedness. The psychological processes of how and why this occurs are considered elsewhere in this book. Here we are reporting the most common time-tested methods of opening a speech. The several options available to you are:

INTRODUCTIONS
    Statement of the Subject
    Statement about Yourself
    Reference to the Audience or Occasion
    The Questioning Process
    The Quotation
    The Startling Statement
    The Use of Humor
    The Presummary

Statement of the Subject

At some point in the introduction your subject should be stated. If a minute or two passes without some reference to the subject, you may confuse or lose your listeners.

Sometimes it is quite appropriate to begin your remarks with a simple, declarative statement of the subject. This approach can be very effective especially if your audience expects you to get right to the point. Your subject may have built-in interest value to your audience. Consider that you are an officer of a company, and your audience is composed of the hierarchy of the company. You could begin your speech by stating: "The cost of energy has reduced our profit margin." You must, however, be certain that the audience has some sort of expectation about the nature of your subject. Otherwise those who were inattentive to your first sentence could lose the focus of your remarks.

Statement About Yourself

The self-conscious cliché, "Unaccustomed as I am to public speaking," is both dull and uninspiring. Excessive egotism can likewise undermine your intent. Tactfully handled, however, a statement about yourself can be extremely effective for establishing ethos and focusing on the subject. You can (1) tell an incident about yourself as it relates to the topic, (2) tell how you came to be interested in the topic, or (3) tell how you met someone who is an authority on the topic.

Consider how the following statement can capture interest, state the topic, establish ethos, and add a touch of humility:

> *No doubt you've seen many commercials in which a mechanic, dressed in a bristling white uniform, claims that Brand Name stations are both friendly and competent. Well, having worked as a mechanic for ten years in a uniform, which I might add, was never clean, I can honestly say that the quality of service has declined drastically.*

Reference to the Audience or Occasion

The purpose of the gathering may be an occasion that, in and of itself, determines the theme of your speech. Assume for a moment that you are a scientist attending a conference on the uses of solar energy. A reference to the interests of the audience or the goals of the conference ought to set in motion your speech. You might state:

> In an age when our very existence depends on the creativity we put forth, the significance of this conference has broad and far-reaching implications.

The device of complimenting an audience, though frequently used and sometimes overworked, can have a pleasant and congenial effect. President John F. Kennedy was particularly adept at this type of introduction. While serving as senator from Massachusetts, he spoke in Puerto Rico:

> It is an impressive experience to come from historic Massachusetts to historic Puerto Rico. Much is different—but much is the same. We occupy a beachhead on the cold North Atlantic—you are an island in the sunny Caribbean. We represent one of the oldest bases in our nation's economy— you represent one of the newest. We battle snow and sleet— your antagonist is more often sun and heat.[3]

The Questioning Process

It is not uncommon to begin a speech with a question or a series of questions. The questioning process may be rhetorical—that is to say, it may call forth an answer in the audience's mind rather than an actual response. In many informative settings, however, the technique of eliciting an actual verbal or hand-raising response may be useful— especially if your message is demonstrative. The automobile mechanic might ask the rhetorical question:

> Have you ever been in a rush to get somewhere when your car won't start? It's a helpless feeling, isn't it? Well, I think I can help you with some information about a few simple techniques of automobile repair.

The Quotation

An effective device for both catching attention and focusing on the theme is the use of the quotation. It need not be well known, but it should be from a person of quotable status. What is the purpose of using another person's words if it does not signal a reference to the context in which you are speaking? Opening quotations should not be too long. In a speech about the uses and importance of time in our everyday lives, you might start with a quotation from Edward T. Hall:

People of the Western world, particularly Americans, tend to think of time as something fixed in nature, something around us and from which we cannot escape; an ever-present part of the environment, just like the air we breath.[4]

The Startling Statement

Unquestionably, the impact of a statement that startles an audience—or even comes as a mild surprise—is quite useful. Startling statements immediately capture attention, but selecting one may not be as simple as presumed. For one thing, some judgment needs to be made as to what the audience knows and doesn't know. An audience that is unaware of the economic impact of the motion picture industry abroad might find the following statement startling: "Film in the 1960's claimed a weekly audience of 376 million equal to one-eighth the world population."[5] But an audience of motion picture experts may not be surprised at all. Some discrimination also needs to be made concerning the appropriateness of the startling statement. A repulsive description of open-heart surgery may not only be in poor taste before a group of children but be so potent as to deter from the main point of your message that might involve instruction about the basics of the human circulatory system.

The Use of Humor

Whether or not you choose to use humor in your introduction should depend on how appropriate it is to the subject and the occasion. Most informative subjects carry with them some opportunity for humor unless, of course, the subject involves a contemporary and tragic event. In creating humor, attempt to be original. Do not be intimidated by the thought that you have no talent for humor.

If your choice is the humorous opening, try to avoid some basic pitfalls. Unless you are extremely adept at timing, or you have the best joke of the decade in your pocket, do not use humor that relies solely on the impact of a punch line. Failure to evoke laughter may result in the loss of credibility and attention. Similarly, do not string jokes together one after another. Your intent is to generate attention—but you want your humor to point in a direction. Random jokes rarely accomplish that intent.

Avoid the temptation to signal that you are trying to be funny. It is best to use surprise. Charles Mudd and Malcolm Sillars state: "There is no joke that has to work so hard for a laugh as the one that is introduced with the suggestion that it is intended to be funny."[6]

For the speaker who is just beginning to learn his craft, we suggest that the safest form of humor is that which does not work for side-splitting laughter. A story or incident that is light and entertaining, one that does not rely on laughter but seeks out enjoyment, is the best type of humorous opening. How to make humor effective can be the study of a lifetime, but some basic principles are:

1. Use tact and good taste.
2. Avoid sarcasm.
3. A humorous opening should not be long.
4. Use the humor to make a point.

The Presummary
An opening that generates interest is good, but one that sets forth the objectives of the message is ideal. Because the informative message relies on clarity for its success, an introduction that not only states the subject but clarifies it in terms of its parts will establish a mood of receptivity in the minds of the audience. In opening a speech on energy, you might say:

There have been several advances in the economizing of energy. Consider three categories: heating, driving, and cooking.

Step Two: Patterns for the Body

The main part of the message may be referred to as the body. It is the essence, the substance, of what you say. The most appropriate organization pattern for the body is that which fits the nature of the subject the best. The patterns that we will consider are:

The Body

The Chronological Pattern
The Spatial Pattern
The Topical Pattern
The Process-Demonstration Pattern
The Demonstration-Instruction Pattern
The Two-Sided Pattern
The Narrative Pattern

The Chronological Pattern
If, in selecting your topic, you decide that the development of the main theme depends primarily on discussing *events*, then you are likely to use the chronological pattern. Catastrophic events such as

Pearl Harbor, the assassination of President Kennedy, or the Chicago Fire may be best organized according to a time sequence.

The pattern is simple. You begin by relating an event, which is then followed by subsequent events. A chronological pattern employing a date sequence is as follows:

Topic: The History of Elmore College
    I.   Founded in 1822
    II.   Accepted women in 1879
    III.   Became a state polytechnic college in 1915
    IV.   Became a state college in 1939

Or, you could use the time of a clock to establish a sequence of events:

    I.   At about 7:45 A.M., the fog began to roll off the ocean onto the freeway.
    II.   At 8:10, it was impossible to see more than thirty feet ahead of you.
    III.   Suddenly, at 8:17, a deafening noise was heard.
    IV.   For the next thirty seconds one crash was heard after another.
    V.   A minute later, the largest traffic accident in the history of California had occurred.

Or you could also use a sequence that presents periods of time:

I would like to discuss three major periods of American history:
    I.   The Depression
    II.   World War II
    III.   The Korean War

The effectiveness of the chronological pattern depends on making the sequence of events easy to remember. If the order is logical, with one event following or caused by the previous event, it can also be quite effective as an attention-getting climactic device. Notice how, in the clock-time sequence, each event may move toward a climax.

LIMITATIONS. Make certain to place your topic in a specific time frame. The use of too many events or a vague period of time can confuse listeners. A five- to seven-minute speech should not include more events than those that can be described in segments of thirty seconds each.

The Spatial Pattern

If, in examining your topic, you expect to answer such questions as where to go, where something is, how something is structured, and how something is planned, you will find the *spatial pattern* an effective device. Such topics as traveling abroad, weather patterns, or a proposal for a new university are ones that can be developed according to physical placement.

The effectiveness of the spatial pattern depends on how well you can describe where things are in relationship to one another. You can do so by using geography to divide your subject: north, south, west, east. Things can likewise be described from left to right, inside to outside, or top to bottom. A speech on Switzerland might be discussed accordingly:

    I.   The Northern Section: Near Germany
    II.   The Southern Section: Near Italy
    III. The Western Section: Near France
    IV. The Eastern Section: Near Austria

To describe a refrigerator, you might say:

    1.   On the left is the main section.
    II.   On the right is the freezer.
    III. The top is for larger items.
    IV. The bottom is for smaller items.

LIMITATIONS. It is not difficult for an audience to get disoriented if the spatial relationships are too complicated. The more relationships there are, the more confusing your message is likely to become. In this case, you may wish to employ the use of a diagram or map.

The Topical Pattern

A very flexible organizational pattern is the topical pattern, which arranges the message according to its natural, or inherent, parts. A discussion about trees would include a discussion of roots, the trunk, branches, bark, and leaves. Similarly, a speech about American defense would include air defense, land defense, and naval defense. The topic is already categorized for you according to its basic structure or components.

A topical outline about the economic tools for combating inflation might include:

ECONOMIC TOOLS AGAINST INFLATION
    I.   Government Spending
    II.   Interest Rates
    III. Construction
    IV. Price Controls
    V.   Public Works Policies

LIMITATIONS.   Some communicators are inclined to move back and forth from one subtopic to another. It is important, therefore, to include all information under its most pertinent and appropriate heading. It is also important to spend relatively equal time discussing each of the main headings. A speech about the university's athletic program might be designed accordingly:

The physical plant
The intramural program
The intercollegiate program
The physical education program

You may be inclined to speak more heavily about the intercollegiate program. If the intercollegiate program is to be the main part of the message, then it ought to be divided according to its subtopics: football, basketball, and so forth.

Another problem of the topical pattern can be the breadth of subtopics. Subtopics that are too broad will produce a disorganized effect. A speech about Texas might be designed according to its politics, economics, and social structure. However, if each section is not internally well designed, the effect will be confusing. How easy it would be, for example, to intermingle the social and economic structure of the state.

The Process-Demonstration Pattern

A useful pattern for making understood the theory and function of how something works is the process-demonstration pattern. A decision needs first to be made concerning what it is that you wish to explain. Then you need to outline, step by step, how each function affects the next function. If the procedures are clear, with each step explained in detail, the process-demonstration pattern will operate to provide the clarity.

You may find two steps particularly useful. First, define the parts. Second, show the relationship of the parts to one another. In speaking about a stereo system, you might point out.

There are three basic parts:

1. Receiver-Amplifier (definition) (relationship)
2. Turntable (relationship)
3. Speakers (effect—sound)

The purpose of demonstration is to illuminate, educate, and make understandable. It is dependent on making theory understandable, pictorially and by analogy. Unless you are training people to repair stereos, your speech will merely attempt to show the theory of operation.

LIMITATIONS. The process-demonstration pattern depends on clear definitions of each part and each step. You cannot assume that an audience will know technical or specialized terms. Their misunderstanding of one of the steps, or parts, can cloud the entire impact of your message. Internal summaries and repetition are therefore important.

The Demonstration-Instruction Pattern

You should distinguish the demonstration-instruction pattern from the process-demonstration pattern previously discussed because the objectives are somewhat different. Whereas the intent of the process-demonstration pattern is to make theory understandable, the purpose of the demonstration-instruction pattern is to teach, or to show how to put theory into practice. You are setting before your listeners certain objectives that they are expected to perform either immediately after your presentation or later. Your message might involve a mental task, such as how to plan an informative speech, or a physical task, such as how to ski.

A step should, therefore, be built into your message that encourages some degree of participation by your audience. Participation can take the form of discussion or the actual performance of the task.

LIMITATIONS. In the demonstration-instruction pattern, time must be allowed for questions. And because of the chance of error, more time must be allowed for repetition. Short speeches, therefore, may not be best suited for the instructional situation.

The Two-Sided Pattern

As we have said, it is difficult to talk about a subject without interpreting it, evaluating it, or modifying audience beliefs. Because it is the intent of the informative option to stay neutral, you ought to have a pattern that can be used when the subject matter lends itself to controversy. The two-sided pattern, which can easily be converted into a multisided pattern, is one way of dealing with various interpretations of a controversial subject. This can be done by establishing categories such as:

Agreement	Disagreement
Advantages	Disadvantages
Pros	Cons

LIMITATIONS. It is not easy to approach a two-sided question with total objectivity. It is best, therefore, to stress the *facts* of both sides rather than the *interpretations* of both sides. Frequently, the two-sided pattern is an excellent device for one section of a speech rather than the entire speech.

The Narrative Pattern

Certain situations call for telling a story, incident, extended example, or personal experience. The narrative pattern is one that does not follow a specific format but allows for extended descriptions of events, people, scenery, and so on. The most effective form of narration is that which comes from your own particular view of the things that you are reporting. To that extent, it is very important to infuse this pattern with as much originality and freshness of thought as possible.

Originality is a quality that should permeate all your messages. It does not mean, however, that you should appear either an eccentric or a nonconformist. Rather, it is a way of looking at things—a fresh interpretation of incidents and facts.

LIMITATIONS. The purpose of narration is not so much to instruct as it is to make incidents memorable. It can be extremely effective if you place some limitations on yourself. The selection of an incident—its time, place, and characters—is very important. Your story must have a clear opening and a closing that either draws things to a climax or makes a point. Although the expression, "the moral to this story," is too much of a cliché to use, you should nevertheless keep in mind that an informative speech does seek to make a point.

Step Three: Patterns for Conclusions

Among beginning communicators, the person who concludes his speech by shrugging his shoulders and saying, "Well, I guess that's it," is not uncommon. Abrupt or dangling conclusions can ruin a well-prepared message, so you ought to be prepared for what you can do at the end.

Some methods for ending a speech are similar to those that you can use for introductions: statements about yourself, the subject, the audience and occasion, the questioning process, the quotation, the startling statement, the use of humor, or the summary. Most common is the latter—the summary.

The summary need not be long. It simply needs to be a short restatement of the major points in the speech. On a speech about automobile and driving safety, you could conclude by saying, "Remember, two things are important: (1) the regular checking of tires and brakes, and (2) an attitude of defensive driving—looking out for the other person."

Whatever option you choose for the conclusion, keep in mind that the most critical feature is a restatement of the essence of your subject matter.

Step Four: Checking Your Transitions

We have discussed patterns as devices for organizing and presenting subject matter. The pattern is important because it sets a direction. For the audience, it provides a sense of orientation, or predictability, to what the communicator is trying to put across. For the speaker, it is a method of determining what is most appropriate for inclusion in the speech. A pattern tells the communicator what to select and what to discard. Moreover, it is a useful device for remembering the main elements of the message.

Properly designed, a pattern should also infuse your speech with a most important dimension: impact. Impact means the registering of the strongest impression possible with the available information. It does not mean a constant barrage of explosive statements. Rather, the intent of impact is to leave the audience with meaningful understanding and retention of as much of the information as possible.

How impact is achieved can be a mystery. Albert Mehrabian suggests that in an interaction between people, only 7 percent of the impact results from what is said; 38 percent from how it is said; and 55 percent from how the person looks while saying it.[7]

It is our contention that one of the ways in which impact is achieved is by channeling audience attention toward the center of what you say. Whatever you say must, therefore, be related to your central theme. You thus lessen the likelihood of your listeners' focusing on irrelevant and diversionary elements.

Such channeling is achieved by paying close attention to your use of transitions. They tie your ideas together. Good transitions prevent minds from wandering as you move from point to point. Excellent transitions compel your listeners to anticipate the next part of your message. There is no formula for the ideal transition, but an understanding of what constitutes unity, coherence, and emphasis will help.

Unity is the quality of always keeping things in focus—within the limitations of your central theme. If your theme involves the workings of an automobile motor, avoid the temptation to talk about the time your car broke down or about the conveniences of reclining seats. The concept of the motor must dominate the speech; all else must be related to it.

Coherence is the quality of linking ideas together in either subtle or obvious ways. A common practice is that of enumerating ideas. You may say, "There are three parts of this motor: 1 ..., 2 ..., and 3 ...." Neither clever nor original, enumeration does nevertheless achieve a quality of coherence by establishing the connection between the most important ideas. Key words that begin with the same letter or sound alike can also provide useful transitions. You might state, "The three T's of good manners are: timing, tact, and taste."

Coherence also comes from clear causal relationships that we will discuss in Chapter 8. Rhetorical questions such as, "What causes pollution?" set the audience's minds toward listening to your answers. Coherence is, therefore, getting the audience to expect or know what will come next.

Emphasis is the quality of dramatizing the most important aspect of your message. There are many devices for achieving emphasis: strong language, highly emotive appeals, and even the pounding of your fist on the table. Here we are concerned with organizational devices. Four useful considerations are: timing, selection, climactic order, and anticlimactic order.

Timing can be used by waiting until the right moment to mention key ideas. In other words, it involves presenting ideas when the audience is most attentive. Or it can be a designed plan of waiting until the end to present the most important idea. Or it can be a method of giving more time to main ideas and less time to the least important ones. Timing achieves emphasis.

Selection is the method of choosing those elements that are likely to give your speech its greatest impact. A speech about Moscow is likely to reach its high point in mentioning the secret activities in the Kremlin, for example.

Climactic order is the device of designing a speech so that the most critical event is near the end of the speech. It is a process of setting up a chain of events, each of which induces expectation of a forthcoming event. The revealing of clues, or of incomplete pieces of information, much as in a mystery movie, is an effective technique. Not only does this provide for natural transitions, but it intensifies interest as well.

Anticlimactic order presents the conclusion, or main theme, first. It then proceeds to discuss the events or factors that led up to the conclusion. It is the reverse of the climactic pattern.

Finally, it is important to understand that transitions are the result of good design. Attention to the qualities of unity, coherence, and emphasis will help tie together your message.

THE VISUAL DIMENSION

Whether your information is complex or simple, the use of visual aids can enhance the impact of your speech. Donis A. Dondis, the author of *A Primer of Visual Literacy,* comments: "We seek visual reinforcement of our knowledge for many reasons, but primary among them is the directness of the information, the closeness to the real experience."[8] McCroskey has stated, "The employment of visual aids in conjunction with verbal messages designed to increase understanding by the audience significantly increases the amount of learning on its part."[9] The use of visual aids can also affect the persuasive speech. William J. Seiler reports that "visual aids designed to supplement and clarify a persuasive message can affect attitude change and speaker credibility."[10]

As an accessory to communication, the visual aid functions as reinforcement. It is not your obligation to create an artistic product, but you should consider the option of using whatever reproductions, art forms, or photographs are available. Visual aids such as charts, graphs, flannel boards, strip charts, blackboards, objects, models, specimens, slides, motion pictures, and technical aids are easily obtained.

Your subject matter will suggest to you what is most useful in the form of visual support. Some subjects require higher levels of visual support than others. Visual communication can take place on four levels.

The first level is *actual reality.* The actual object under discussion can sometimes be brought in, examined, and demonstrated before a group. The advantage of showing "the real thing" is obvious, but sometimes it is impossible—if the object is too large, or if your subject matter is abstract.

The second level is *pseudo reality.* Because buildings, automobiles, and space craft present a physical problem for the speaker, you may select operational models to demonstrate your point. Whenever your subject matter involves complex three-dimensional objects, it is profitable to have some sort of visual representation.

The third level is *pictorial realism.* This is the technique of demonstrating various interpretations, or angles, of your subject matter by means of photographs. A picture of a hungry child may have more impact than descriptions of hunger.

The fourth level is *pictorial symbolism.* This is the technique of taking an object, or information, and abstracting it into a visual form that closely represents a picture of the object.

Rationale for the Visual Option

Why employ the visual dimension?
The communicator's message can often be complicated by

extended verbal explanation and description. Visual aids can be employed to ensure clarity and, hence, better comprehension. All learning is, after all, the result of sensory experiences. When the number of senses involved increases, the learning process is expedited. The person not only *hears* but *sees*. Knowledge intake is accelerated.

The receiver will experience other advantages by viewing. First, his attention is focused on the object; hence, attention is sustained over a greater period of time. Second, the monotony of a single system of communication,—that is, the verbal approach—is broken with a visual stimulus that provides a greater psychological interest factor. Third, retention is aided with the assistance of visual images. Fourth, the listener is able to conceptualize with greater accuracy. And fifth, relationships are indicated with greater clarity.

Operational Principles

Successful implementation of visual support requires attention to a few simple but vital operational details. Clumsy handling of visual materials, for example, obstructs the communicative process by drawing the listener's attention to irrelevant activity. Below is a list of basic reminders.

1. *Anticipate difficulties.* A chart might appear simple enough to handle, for example, but the clip to which it is to be attached could malfunction—an embarrassing and awkward moment.
2. *Remove distractions.* An exceptionally well-designed graph can be disrupted by a flickering light in the background.
3. *Rehearse.* A brief rehearsal of handling a model might eliminate fumbling at a crucial point in a speech.
4. *Be brief.* Plan for a short demonstration with visual aids. Do not leave charts hanging while moving on to a new subject.
5. *Explain with clarity.* Nothing is more tedious and counter-productive to the communicative process than a detailed chart that requires a long and random explanation. Divide your presentation into a few basic steps.
6. *Plan appropriate placement.* Place the object in a spot that allows for the best viewing by all receivers.

Basic Visual Systems

Numerous visual systems are available for the communicator. More can be created from combinations of others, but we will be concerned with a few basic and commonly accepted devices.

Graphs

BAR GRAPHS. Bar graphs are functional in demonstrating a quantitative analysis and comparison of given statistics. Their purpose is not to demonstrate details but to condense data into an immediately visible chart.

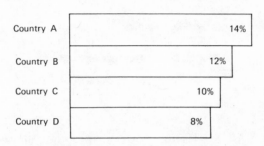

Crime rate in the world

PIE GRAPH. The pie graph is especially useful for the communicator who wishes to demonstrate the proportions of each part in relation to each other and to the whole. You could examine, for example, the cost of running a college's athletic program in comparison with instructional costs.

LINE GRAPH. The line graph is specifically designed to demonstrate fluctuations during a specific time period.

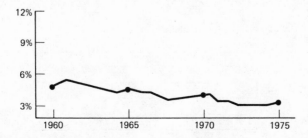

Chronological-factual descriptions can be extremely tedious and time-consuming if you must rely on verbal explanation. A quick visual glance at a line graph can immediately register the vital information.

PICTOGRAPH.   The pictograph also is a device for showing a quantitative analysis. It differs only in its utilization of pictorial figures to represent numerical figures.

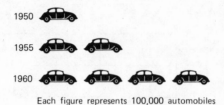

Each figure represents 100,000 automobiles

Charts

FLOW CHARTS.   Useful in demonstrating relationships is the flow chart. This visual system demonstrates how one entity depends on another. Consider the typical business chart.

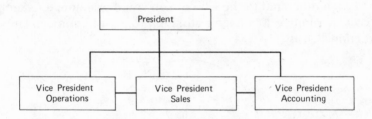

FLANNEL BOARD AND STRIP CHARTS.   The purpose of these two chart-type devices is to allow flexibility in demonstrating material at the appropriate time, in other words, to show one step first without the confusion of the following steps appearing simultaneously.

The flannel board is board covered with flannel; the material to be placed on the board also has a flannel backing. At any time, you may place a strip with printing on the board.

1.   Announcing candidacy

2.   Delivering the platform

3.

4.

5.

The strip chart is similar except that information is placed on the board with a blank strip covering the print. At an emphatic point in the speech, you remove the strip from the board thus revealing your subject matter.

DATA CHART. The data chart is a mere listing of the subheadings of a given subject. The headings are printed clearly on a stable board. The data chart is generally used as a means of reinforcing the verbal content of a speech for the purpose of retention.

A Professional Football Team is a Large Organization
   1. Eleven offensive players.
   2. Eleven defensive players.
   3. Eleven to fifteen special players, for example, punters, kick-off return specialists, and so forth.
   4. Five to seven coaches
   5. A taxi squad
   6. A general manager
   7. A publicity manager (department)
   8. A medical staff
   9. A manager
   10. A president.

OTHER CHARTS. Other charts available to you are:

1. Schematic chart—designed to demonstrate how mechanisms operate.
2. Diagramatic chart—designed to demonstrate connections or a system of operation.
3. Phantom-view chart—a picture of, say, a motor with no covering or a fully exposed larynx.
4. A multiple leaf chart or a notebook—demonstrating a sequence of items related to a whole.

Blackboard
The many uses of the blackboard are familiar. However, careless use of the blackboard can create serious breakdowns in communication. For example, you should never overuse this system nor should you turn your back to the audience for an extended time, nor should

Picture of
blackboard

you clutter the board with random information, nor should you talk to the board.

Remember:

1. Print clearly.
2. Organize materials.
3. Use only for description and emphasis.
4. Continue speaking to the audience.

Objects and Models

For the description of three-dimensional objects unfamiliar to the listeners, the use of the actual object or a model is recommended. In demonstrating the repair of a television set, for example, nothing is more useful than performing the task with the actual object. This is likewise true for many problems.

However, you should be aware of the problems. More often than not, the actual object is too small for adequate viewing by the entire audience. Adjustment of the wiring in a telephone, for example, is sure to be missed.

Quality Control

Prior to making the decision to employ visual aids, you should carefully examine the quality of the object and its specific uses. Effective visual support is not a haphazard process. Review its basic qualities whether it be a chart, graph, blackboard, photograph, or model.

1. Is its size large enough for optimum visibility?
2. Is the lettering clear, neat, precise, and simple?
3. Are colors used to enhance sensory perception?
4. Are the materials durable and unlikely to fail in the communicative situation?
5. Is good workmanship obvious?
6. Is the visual aid performing a specific task in the communicative act?

SUMMARY

Clarity is the essential element of the informative option. You can improve clarity by adjusting the level of complexity, by showing relationships, and by uncluttering, or streamlining, ideas. Your introduction may capture attention, focus on the content, relate the topic to the specific audience, limit the scope, or outline the major units of the presentation. You need a specific pattern to give an appropriate structure to your message. Your conclusion should highlight, relate, and review ideas.

Transitions help to create unity, coherence, and emphasis.

Finally, you should consider the importance of the visual dimension. Visual aids can help to focus the attention of the listener, provide variety, retain ideas, improve conceptualization, and clarify relationships. In using visuals, be careful that they do not become distractions. Plan their use carefully.

Review and Exercises

1. Many authors claim that all information exchange is persuasive in nature. Do you agree or disagree?
2. Design three different introductions for the same topic. Show adaptation to three different audiences.
3. Design a list of specific topics that fit into the chronological pattern, the spatial pattern, and the process-demonstration pattern.
4. Write out a list of transitional phrases. Check your own speaking to see which ones you use on a regular basis.
5. Look through a current magazine to see which visuals catch your attention. Identify the specific factors that worked to get your attention.
6. Design a clear message that does not need verbal explanation.
7. Design a visual message that could be used universally to identify the following: danger, food, exit, and restrooms.

Additional Readings

Hackett, Herbert, Andersen, Martin, Fessenden, Seth, and Hagen, Leslie Lee, *Understanding and Being Understood*, Longmans, Green and Co., New York, 1957.

Makay, John J., and Sawyer, Thomas C., *Speech Communication Now! An Introduction to Rhetorical Influences*, Charles Merrill, Columbus, Ohio, 1973.

Olbricht, Thomas S., *Informative Speaking*, Scott, Foresman, Glenview, Illinois, 1968.

Petrie, C. R., Jr., "Informative Speaking: A Summary and Bibliography of Related Research," *Speech Monographs*, **XXX,** 1963.

Footnotes

[1] Anatol Rapoport, "What is Information," *Communication and Culture* edited by Alfred G. Smith (New York: Holt, Rinehart and Winston, 1966), p. 42.

[2] James C. McCroskey, *An Introduction to Rhetorical Communication*, 2nd edition (Englewood Cliffs, N.J.: Prentice-Hall, Inc., 1972) p. 207.

[3] John F. Kennedy, Unpublished Remarks at a Democratic Dinner, San Juan, Puerto Rico (December 15, 1958), p. 1.

[4] Edward T. Hall, *The Silent Language*, (New York: Doubleday, 1959). Copyright © 1959 by Edward T. Hall. Reprinted by permission of Doubleday & Company, Inc.

[5] *World Communication* (New York: UNESCO Publishing Center, 1964), p. 41.

[6] Charles S. Mudd and Malcolm O. Sillars, *Speech: Content and Communication*, second edition (Scranton, Pa.: Chandler Publishing Company, 1969), p. 287. Copyright © 1962, 1969 by Chandler Publishing Company. Copyright © 1975 by Thomas Y. Crowell Company. Reprinted by permission of Thomas Y. Crowell Company.

[7] Albert Mehrabian, "Communication Without Words," *Psychology Today*, **II** (September, 1968), p. 53.

[8] Donis A. Dondis, *A Primer of Visual Literacy* (Cambridge, Mass.: The MIT Press, 1973), p. 2. Reprinted by permission of the MIT Press, Cambridge, Mass.

[9] McCroskey, *An Introduction to Rhetorical Communication*, p. 218.

[10] William J. Seiler, "The Effects of Visual Materials on Attitudes, Credibility, and Retention," *Speech Monographs*, **XXXVIII** (November, 1971), p. 334.

CHAPTER 7 APPROACHING THE PERSUASIVE OPTION: ESTABLISHING A POSITION

RATIONALE FOR THE PERSUASIVE OPTION
LOCATING THE POINTS OF CONTROVERSY
FRAMING AND WORDING YOUR PROPOSITION
    Proposition of Fact
    Proposition of Definition
    Proposition of Value
    Proposition of Policy
    Guidelines For Framing a Proposition
CONSTRUCTING A PERSUASIVE PATTERN: OPTIONAL
SEQUENCING
    Step one: Patterns for Introductions
        Attention
        Presenting the Proposition With Clarification
            Options
    Step two: Elements of the Problem Area
        The Need Approach
        The Advantages Approach
    Step three: Elements of the Solution Area
        Is it a panacea?
        Is it practical?
        Is it workable?
        Does it solve the need or produce the advantage?
    Step Four: Patterns For Conclusions
        The Summary
        Emphasis of One Need or Advantage
        Emphasis of the Solution's Practicality
        Call for Action
        Repetition of the Introduction

CHAPTER 7 APPROACHING THE PERSUASIVE OPTION: ESTABLISHING A POSITION

RATIONALE FOR THE PERSUASIVE OPTION

In approaching the persuasive option, you may have made a choice. On a subject that contains different sides, or interpretations, you may have selected a stand. In taking a stand, you may be assuming the role of advocate—one who is seeking to influence, modify, or change beliefs. You may be attempting to win support.

The extent to which you will be able to modify beliefs will be difficult to gauge. Some listeners will be favorable to you—for them, you will be putting their own beliefs into words and solutions. Others will be adamantly opposed. You may experience extreme difficulty in making the slightest modification in their beliefs.

More often than not you may be talking to listeners whose feelings are not strong in either direction, and who have not been inclined to make up their minds. The public may believe something should be done about inflation, but they may not have a concept of a solution. The persuasive message could gain support. Government agencies, certain businesses, and judges are parties who are seeking to make rational choices. The persuader-communicator provides the arguments from which such groups make decisions.

There are many elements that constitute the act of persuasion; some of them we have already discussed. In the next four chapters, we will be discussing the aspects of establishing a position, the logical option, the psychological option, and the response. In this chapter we will consider:

☐ Locating the points of controversy
☐ Framing and wording your position
☐ Constructing a persuasive pattern

LOCATING THE POINTS OF CONTROVERSY

Much confusion may be inherent in any given topic. You may agree with certain aspects of one side of the question and, at the same time, disagree with other elements of the same side. Ideas will come from everywhere—from your research as well as from those with whom you talk. So your first task is to find out what the sides are so that you may frame your position. The essential part of this task is to find out what, precisely, the points of controversy are likely to be. What are the areas of disagreement, if any? This is the first step in establishing your objectives pertinent to where you stand and what you will need to say to convince your listeners of its worth. This will require a look at how to explore for issues in any subject. In the next few pages we will diagram some basic techniques.

Consider in the following illustration how you can clarify the process of finding issues. In complicated and more developed questions the discovery of issues will go beyond the simplicity of these illustrations, but the process is basically the same.

Here are two people engaged in a conversation. The argumentative sides represented by each person, however, represent the makings of any persuasive situation.

Barbara: You stole my hat.
Stan: Yes, I did.

In this exchange between Barbara and Stan, there is a potential argument. Barbara has contended that Stan stole her hat, but Stan has agreed with her, so there is no argument—hence, no grounds for persuasion.

In each persuasive situation, there will be a subject area and issues acceptable to both sides. To belabor these issues without clarification of the fact that they *are* areas of agreement can obscure the communication process. You should first distinguish and clarify these areas from those involving disagreement. Let us call these agreed-on areas "nonissues."

In the second situation, we can see the development of an issue from the flat opposition of statements.

Barbara: You stole my hat.→•
Stan: No, I did not.

The conflict has created two obvious stands. Either one could be subscribed to by an audience. Belief in who is right will be dependent on the presentation of evidence and other forms of communication. As it now stands, the flow of the controversy can be seen as a movement from one point to another with each canceling out the other until a new dimension, or new statement, is introduced. The argument has turned at the issue of affirmation and negation. It is, therefore, a question of *fact*.

However, Stan could have taken a number of options each of which would have established new issues, new turning points in the argument, and new areas of disagreement. The point at which the argument turns, therefore, sets the stage for different modes of persuasion. Notice the following:

Barbara: You stole my hat.
Stan: No, I did not; I borrowed it.

The line of argument has moved to a new level. Diagramed, the turning point of the argument rests as follows:

You **stole** my hat.
                        No, I **borrowed** it.

Here, Barbara and Stan have created the basis of an argument of *definition*. Should the act be considered one of "stealing" or one of "borrowing"? How each party seeks to establish why his or her definition is valid becomes, therefore, the critical issue and the grounds for persuasion.

Another change of direction may be produced by a totally different response to Barbara's statement. Consider:

Barbara: You stole my hat.
Stan: Yes, I did, but it was a good thing that I did.

The turning point becomes one that considers the appropriateness of the action. In effect, it is a question of *value* as to whether the stealing in this case was a good action or a bad action.

To introduce one final dimension to the argument, Stan might advocate a course of action. He might state:

Stan: We should all borrow hats.

Here the issue becomes one of *policy*. In other words, Stan is recommending that some sort of policy be adopted that would encourage, or make lawful, the borrowing of hats. The issue may turn on its subsequent advantages: The borrowing of hats will promote brotherhood and sisterhood.

The diagrams above will aid you in locating the key issue in the controversy. Where does the argument turn? At what point is there disagreement? Once you have discovered the key issue, you are prepared to incorporate it into your stand.

FRAMING AND WORDING YOUR POSITION

With your topic selected and your key issue determined, you should be ready to frame your position in a clearly worded statement. This statement, which we shall call a *proposition,* becomes the focal point of your persuasive objective. It reflects your stand. It refines, restricts, and limits your point of view to a manageable area.

From our discussion of locating issues, we can suggest a choice of four different types of propositions. They are:
- ☐ Proposition of Fact
- ☐ Proposition of Definition
- ☐ Proposition of Value
- ☐ Proposition of Policy

Proposition of Fact

The proposition of *fact* is a method of wording your position so that it is concerned with establishing the truth or falsity of a contention. In other words, it is a statement that says what happened, or what did not happen; what is, or what is not. A good proposition of fact has no ambiguity. Some examples are:
- ☐ The Kennedy assassination was not the result of a conspiracy.
- ☐ The I.R.A. bombed Belfast.
- ☐ The accident took place on January 12.

Proposition of Definition

The proposition of definition includes elements of both fact and value. It seeks to assign a category, description, or *definition* to something. It does, nevertheless, allow for interpretation. Consider the following:
- ☐ This chair is an antique.
- ☐ Smith's actions should be classified as treason.
- ☐ Drama is a fine art.

Proposition of Value

The proposition of value depends on a judgment determining the worth, or value, of something. Although it is sometimes difficult to distinguish from a fact or definition, it is the type of proposition that can never be fully determined by factual evidence. It may sometimes relate to taste or aesthetics or morality. Absolute principles of judgment can never be used. Consider:

- ☐ United States foreign policy has worked for the benefit of mankind.
- ☐ Vasarely is a great artist.
- ☐ Music is good for the soul.

Proposition of Policy

Facts, definitions, and value judgments all play a role in the establishment of a proposition of policy. Basically, the above calls for the adoption of a course of action in the form of an on-going policy. Often the proposition of policy has attached to it the particular body that will implement the policy—such as the government or the courts. Examples of the proposition of policy are:

- ☐ We should reinstate capital punishment.
- ☐ We should adopt a national sales tax.
- ☐ We should legalize prostitution.

Guidelines for Framing A Proposition

Your proposition reflects you. Your thinking and rationality are seen by the care you give to forming a clear and reasonable position. To prevent meaningless quibbles over your definitions, to prevent your listener from interpreting your position in vague and confusing ways, and to make your position worth considering, you ought to follow some basic guidelines in wording your proposition.

The Proposition Should Have At Least Two Sides
A nondebatable proposition does not usually lend itself to persuasion. Recall that the objective is to modify beliefs, and so there ought to be beliefs that are at least modifiable. You would hardly advocate the proposition that "the earth revolves around the sun."

The Proposition Must be Limited in Scope
As we indicated earlier, the selection of a topic that is too broad allows for too much flexibility. A detailed analysis of specific points becomes quite difficult. It is important, therefore, to limit it in scope so as to allow time for complete analysis and support.

When considering the following propositions, ask yourself how much time would be required for adequate presentation:

- ☐ The United Nations should be changed into a form of world government.
- ☐ The United States should adopt a new constitution.
- ☐ The grading of this course is unfair.

A topic limited and adapted to the allotted time ought to provide a more productive experience for the communicator and audience.

The Proposition Should be Specific

We have talked about making ideas specific; the same applies to propositions. Many poor propositions are phrased in vague and broad terms: Consider:

(poor)   I think we should do something about this situation.
(poor)   Let's stop all our arguments and get something done.

Notice how the proposition can be improved by converting a broad subject into a more specific one:

(broad)   Compulsory arbitration is desirable.
(specific)   The automotive industry ought to adopt compulsory arbitration.

The Proposition Should be Unbiased

You should be careful not to inject unsupported biases into your proposition. Naturally a proposition establishes a side, but it does not do so with biased terminology. Notice how bias is used in the following cases:

We should abolish the *dangerous* game of football.
We should withdraw support from *irresponsible* allies.
This *unfair* policy should be abolished.

The Proposition Should Contain One Central Idea.

The proposition should be limited to a single major idea avoiding the suggestion of multiple points. The following propositions contain multiple points:

We should withdraw from the United Nations and increase the size of our armed forces.
We should adopt either a sales tax or increase our income tax.

The Proposition Should Be Clear

In general, you should avoid terms that are vague and open to various interpretations. Many propositions never focus on real issues but bog down on definitions of unclear terms. Consider the problems of clarity in this proposition: "We should punish wrongdoers." Certainly we would have many different concepts of "punishment" and "wrong doers." Perhaps a clearer proposition might be: "Massachusetts should use public lashings for husbands who desert their families."

Notice the improvement in clarity in the following rewritten propositions:

(Unclear) *Pressure groups* should have *some kind* of *restriction.*

(Clear) State lobbyists should be required to register with the secretary of state.

(Unclear) We need to improve our schools.

(Clear) Public school teachers should receive a minimum yearly wage of $10,000.

The Proposition Should Be Relevant

The topic should be "alive" rather than one merely selected for "practice." For suggestions of live topics examine contemporary printed materials, listen to current problems on radio, watch and listen to issues discussed on television. If you can find a topic that crosses the interest lines of both communicator and listeners, you should have a relevant area for a proposition. The following resolution might have great relevance for the citizens of Dade County but little for others: Dade County should have an air pollution control officer.

In reviewing and analyzing your proposition, ask the following questions:

1. Does the proposition suggest that there are two sides to the question?
2. Is it limited in scope? In time?
3. Is the proposition specific? Is it in exact language?
4. Is the proposition unbiased? Does it contain slanted words?
5. Is the proposition limited to a single theme? Might it be split into two themes?
6. Is the proposition clear? Is it free from words that are ambiguous?
7. Is the proposition relevant? Is it of interest to the communicator and the listeners?

CONSTRUCTING A PERSUASIVE PATTERN: OPTIONAL SEQUENCING

In the following section, we will be presenting the basic building blocks for the construction of a persuasive pattern. Some components will be necessary; others will not. It is your choice. What you select will depend on your proposition, situation, and audience. It is essential that you consider the following as options. Let us call it the *principle of optional sequencing.*

Basically, we will be dealing with four steps, each of which contains its own options. They are:

Step One: Patterns for Introductions
Step Two: Elements of the Problem Area
Step Three: Elements of the Solution Area
Step Three: Patterns for Conclusions

Step One: Patterns for Introductions

The function of an introduction to a persuasive message is (1) to capture attention, (2) to present the proposition, and (3) to clarify your proposition.

Attention
The process of capturing attention is a on-going process and the function of all forms of communication. There are certain steps that you can take in the introduction both to capture attention and to introduce the subject area. Many of these we have discussed in the chapter on the informative option (Chapter 6). You may turn back for a discussion for each. In review, the ones most appropriate for persuasion are:

Example—actual or hypothetical—that focuses on the topic:
Statement of the Subject
Statement about Yourself
Reference to the Audience or Occasion
The Questioning Process
The Quotation
The Startling Statement
The Use of Humor

Presenting the Proposition With Clarification Options
Essential to the introduction is a statement of the proposition either before, within, after, or as a part of an attention device. You might state: The United States should adopt a comprehensive national health plan.

Following the proposition, you may wish to provide additional clarification or information about the subject area. Depending on the necessity of each, you could employ the following options.

DEFINITION OF TERMS. If several national health plans have been the subject of recent discussion, it may be necessary for you to define your subject matter so as to avoid any misinterpretation of your position. Frequently the proposition of policy has terms that can be defined. You might say: By "comprehensive national health plan" I mean one that covers all costs of medical care from cradle to grave.

RELEVANT HISTORY. If you spend too much time on background information, you may be taking something away from the central thrust of your speech—which is to discuss the need for such a plan. However, some brief history may help your audience to place the subject in perspective. With respect to your proposal for a comprehensive national health plan, you may wish to refer to:

☐ Background about social security
☐ Background about Medicare and Medicaid
☐ Background about Workmen's Compensation
☐ Background about other social legislation

STATEMENT OF GOALS AND ASSUMPTIONS. The issues in your message may call for a statement of certain goals and assumptions. To opponents of comprehensive health care, it might be necessary to mention that equal health care has been a goal of all previous legislation and that, moreover, the United States desires a system of health protection that surpasses those of the rest of the world.

LIMITATIONS OF THE PROPOSITION. To avoid fears and controversy over irrelevant or specific issues, it may also be necessary to suggest that your concern is not with some of these issues. You might state:

Although I am interested in a national health plan, I am not advocating that the government provide the cost of all drugs, aid for cosmetic surgery, and the cost of medical aids such as glasses, crutches, and so forth.

PRESUMMARY OF THE ISSUES. You may also wish to employ a presummary of the issues that you will be covering. On the topic of medical care, you might say:

Basically, I see three areas of concern:

1. The rising cost of medical care.
2. The ineffectiveness of private health insurance.
3. The inadequacy of our present hospital system.

Step Two: Elements of the Problem Area

Your central concern in the persuasive message will be to establish a reason why your audience should find your point of view, or proposal, acceptable. The substance of the problem area may draw on patterns mentioned in the chapter on the informative option, namely, the chronological, spatial, and topical pattern. It is essential to establish your subissues as reasons. To that extent, we will be concerned with setting up two types of reasons: the need and the advantage.

The Need Approach

The basic concept of the need approach is to demonstrate that there are serious problems in the present system that call for a change. The approach can also apply to human problems as well as to governmental ones:

You need to exercise to preserve your health.
The United States needs to adopt a comprehensive national health plan.

Organizationally, the need approach is set up by establishing one or several reasons for the acceptance of your proposition.

Proposition: Americans should purchase smaller cars.
Need: Large cars consume too much gasoline.
Need: The shortage of gasoline causes higher prices, hence, greater inflation.

Each need *stresses a reason*. And it does so by amplifying and developing that reason. Reasons should not be stated and dropped: They must be evidenced and discussed. Consider the pattern and how it can draw on options from other chapters.

Proposition: Americans should purchase smaller cars.
Need: Large cars consume too much gasoline.
    EVIDENCE: Statistics about the relationship between large cars and the consumption of gasoline.
    EXPLANATION: Inductive logic (see Chapter 8) to indicate that continuance of the situation will have severe ramifications in the future.

APPEAL: Psychological option (see Chapter 9) to indicate that inaction could produce a shortage of heat for the listener's home.

Notice that the need approach outlined above has impact because it is statistically evident and psychologically compeling. These features add depth to the need area. Further methods of evidencing should be used such as:

Evidence by example
Evidence by statistics
Evidence by comparisons
Evidence by authority
Evidence by observers

In addition to the various devices of communication that can be used to develop the need area, there is one consideration that can lend greater depth and strength to the need. You need to ask, "Is the issue *inherent?*"

Inherency is a term that is used to determine whether or not the need arises out of a *structural deficiency*. It is a way of examining whether or not the problem is serious enough to call for a new program—or replacement. If you are advocating that certain buildings be torn down in your city, you would *not* be presenting inherent reasons if you said:

They need new paint.
They need new windows.
They need better plumbing.

These are reasons that call for some repair; they do not call for tearing down the buildings. If, however, you said:

The recent fire destroyed several roofs.

Water damage has caused severe defects in the walls and floors
you have established *inherent* reasons—in other words, problems that cannot be solved except by means of your solution. The inherent reason creates, therefore, a more rational and compeling reason to change. You ought to consider it in the development of your need approach.

The Advantages Approach

The persuasive goal of the advantages approach is similar to the need approach: to convince your listeners that you have good reasons for advocating your position. However, the approach is somewhat different. The concept establishes that problems, or needs, are already apparent. The solution advocated by you will produce some advantages that the present system cannot produce. The approach therefore hinges on the future; it is a *prediction* that a new solution can do a better job than a past solution.

Structurally, the advantage approach is useful because contemporary issues and problems are relative—rarely do we argue for or against federal supremacy versus states' rights in absolute "either-or" or "black and white" terms. One is not rejected in favor of another. We seek, rather, to find either a middle position or to decide where one should *dominate,* not replace, the other. Each side has its advantages; each side has its disadvantages. The solution of the problem of juvenile delinquency, for example, is an accepted need. What should be done to *handle* the problem is open to debate, discussion, and relative judgment. You might decide it is advantageous to provide more vocational training and more jobs; others may contend that a strict disciplinary system under the status quo is more realistic. Complex problems such as these have given rise to the advantages approach, essentially for three reasons.

First, the advantages approach is designed to present a *relative* solution to a *relative* problem. It is an *adjustment* in the status quo rather than a major change.

A. You accept the problem of the status quo but usually maintain that the problem is somewhat greater than the status quo recognizes.
B. You maintain that new legislation would serve to solve the problem "somewhat better" than the status quo is presently doing.

Second, the advantages approach is designed to expose *how* a new solution would work better than the status quo. Unlike the need approach, the advantages approach *begins* with a statement of the plan, then proceeds to discuss why such a plan is:

A. More workable or flexible than the status quo.
B. More advantageous than the status quo.

Third, this method is designed to add something to the present system rather than to take away from it. Generally, the advantages approach recognizes that the present system is acceptable but incapable of handling a large problem. Some changes are therefore necessary to make it capable of adjusting to new problems. If you argue that all United States citizens should have a minimum annual income, you may recognize that welfare and retraining programs are doing only a partly adequate job of managing the problems of the poor. A new federal program, you contend, would *add* to existing programs and thereby improve them.

Consider the three principles in the following outline of the advantage approach:

Introduction:	Juvenile delinquency is on the rise.
Solution:	We want to continue present systems but also add a large-scale program of vocational training and job placement for delinquents.
Advantages:	This system would solve the problem *better than* the present system because

      1. *More* direction will be provided to unemployed youths.

      2. *More* earning power will reduce need to commit crime.

      3. *More* involvement in programs will reduce time spent doing nothing.

Note the three principles.

1. This approach does not spend time developing the need area. It suggests there are *more* advantages.
2. This approach discusses specifically *how* a new plan will produce those advantages.
3. This approach adds to the status quo by suggesting vocational training and job placement.

Several criteria should apply in developing the advantages approach:

1. Your position should not significantly deviate from the goals of the status quo. In other words, you should in no way attempt to change the *goals* of the present policy. You might advocate that we withdraw troops and bases from abroad, but in a comparative advantage case you do not recommend that we neglect our treaties.
2. The plan should be detailed and explained so as to demonstrate logically that it will produce the *alleged advantages*. The more significant the cause–effect relationship between the plan and advantages, the more effective your position is likely to be.
3. The plan should prove that the goals of the status quo will be accomplished significantly better than under the *present policy*. Here, you should compare the status quo with your suggested plan or alteration in the status quo.

4. Finally, you must maintain that your plan is likely to achieve the goals better than any other *alternate policy.*

Step Three: Elements of the Solution Area

Whether presented before or after the problem area, the solution should be stated in relatively brief terms. The central part of your message is the need–advantage area. The function of the solution is to give some indication of what can be done to solve the problem. By showing a practical solution, you place your message in a realistic perspective.

The solution is not intended to be a detailed and extended statement that, like a congressional bill, seeks to provide specific criteria and solutions to all aspects of the problem. It is, merely, a basic structure. An example of a relatively simple solution for a speech advocating a comprehensive health plan might be as follows:

1. A new agency will be established under Social Security.
2. The function of the agency will be to set criteria and establish prices for medical care.
3. All medical bills of all United States citizens will be paid by the agency.
4. The program will be financed by new taxes.
5. The agency will promote the development of new medical facilities and new medical schools.

In analyzing and constructing your solution, you should consider several questions and criteria:

Is it a Panacea (a Plan Designed to Eliminate All Problems)?

If it is, reject it. You can never solve all the problems associated with a given proposition. Your purpose is only to change opinions by making your subject believable. Exorbitant government spending and utopian plans will only suggest to your listeners that you are unrealistic.

Is it Practical?

If it is, accept it. You should attempt to demonstrate that your solution can accomplish significant results without drastic changes and drastic spending. A typical approach to large problems such as medical care is to suggest that the money be obtained from cuts in spending in other less useful areas.

Is it Workable?

Is it a plan that can function without cumbersome administration and complex variables? If you, the communicator, have to design the administration of an entirely new program, you are likely to raise questions about operations. It is best to suggest that it be operated in a way that is similar to the operation of an analogous program.

Does it Solve the Need or Produce the Advantage?

The area most likely to raise questions in the minds of your listeners is whether your solution actually solves the problem. If you paint a very glum picture of the slum conditions in North America, and then proceed to talk about spending $100 million a year, your plan will not, in all likelihood, begin to approach meeting the need.

Step Four: Patterns for Conclusions

Your concluding remarks need to reiterate, in someway, the substance of your message. A positive thought needs to be emphasized. Whereas the purpose of the conclusion in the informative option is to ensure *retention* of the content of your message, its purpose is to *convince* in the persuasive message. This may be done in several ways.

The Summary

You may present a summary of all the major points in the message with particular reference to key elements of the problem and solution areas.

Emphasis of One Need or Advantage

You may choose to select the most important issue in your entire presentation for the conclusion. Repetition of the most critical issue and exclusion of the rest of your message can have a dramatic impact.

Emphasis of the Solution's Practicality

Often, the only issue between the audience's accepting your remarks and rejecting them will be the element of practicality. Can it really be accomplished? By anticipating this issue and the relative importance it plays in the minds of the audience, you may bolster your chances of influencing beliefs.

Call for Action

Perhaps the most difficult conclusion to present is the call for action. Here, you are obliging your audience to do something—either immediately or in the not-too-distant future. The suggestion that they write their congressmen is overworked and sometimes a flat way of concluding. However, in larger issues such as health care, it may be one of the most important things that your audience can do. Attempt to think of original ways of eliciting audience involvement.

Repetition of the Introduction

If you chose a startling statement or, perhaps, a quotation for your opening, you might also find it appropriate to end with the same statement. This method can be effective as a device that gives a sense of unity to your entire message.

SUMMARY

Once you have taken a stand or position on an issue, you may choose to assume the role of an advocate. In this role, you will attempt to influence, modify, or change the beliefs of others. You should, first, locate the points of agreement and disagreement. This step is essential to rational persuasion.

Your position should then be framed into a clearly worded statement, called a proposition. The next step involves the construction of a persuasive pattern. The introduction to your persuasive message should gain attention and clarify your position. The message should then build on the needs for change or the advantages of your position. Your solution should be presented with logical support and statements concerning its workability. Finally, you need to select a conclusion which is most appropriate to your message. Your options are: the summary, the highlighting of a key issue, the stress on the solution's practicality, the call for action, or the repetition of the introduction.

SUMMARY

THE PERSUASIVE OPTION: REVIEWING OPTIONAL SEQUENCING

   I.   Locate the points of controversy.
  II.   Frame and word your position.
      A.   Types of Propositions
          1.   Proposition of fact

2. Proposition of definition
3. Proposition of value
4. Proposition of policy
B. Criteria for Propositions
1. At least two sides.
2. Limited in scope.
3. Be specific.
4. Be unbiased.
5. One central idea.
6. Be clear.
7. Be relevant.
III. Constructing a persuasive pattern.
A. Step one: Patterns for Introductions
1. Attention
2. Present proposition.
B. Step two: Elements of the problem area
1. The need approach.
2. The advantages approach.
C. Step three: Elements of the solution area
1. Panacea?
2. Practical?
3. Workable?
4. Does it solve the problem?
D. Step four: Patterns for conclusions
1. The summary
2. One need or advantage
3. Solution's practicality
4. Call for action
5. Repetition of introduction

Review and Exercises

1. What is the difference, if any, between persuasion and manipulation?
2. What are the issues in the current controversies over abortion, busing, and equal rights for women?
3. Write out propositions of fact, definition, value, and policy.
4. Prepare an introduction to a persuasive speech in which you accomplish the following objectives: attention, clarification of terms, relevant history, and statement of goals.

5. What is the difference between the needs approach and the advantages approach?
6. Design practical solutions for relatively short speeches on inflation, traffic deaths, and pollution.

Additional Readings

Johannesen, Richard L., *Ethics and Persuasion: Selected Readings,* Random House, New York, 1967.

Lerbinger, Otto, *Designs For Persuasive Communication,* Prentice-Hall, Englewood Cliffs, N.J., 1972.

McBath, James H., and Fisher, Walter R., "Persuasion in Presidential Campaign Communication," *Quarterly Journal of Speech,* **55,** February, 1969.

McGinniss, Joe, *The Selling of the President 1968,* Trident Press, New York, 1969.

Scheidel, Thomas M., *Persuasive Speaking,* Scott, Foresman, Glenview, Ill., 1967.

Simons, Herbert W., "Requirements, Problems, and Strategies: A Theory of Persuasion for Social Movements," *Quarterly Journal of Speech,* **56,** February, 1970.

CHAPTER 8 STRUCTURING THE MESSAGE: THE LOGICAL OPTION

RATIONALE FOR THE LOGICAL OPTION
DEFINING THE LOGICAL OPTION
CONNECTIONS: THE ESSENCE OF LOGIC (TOULMIN MODEL)
    The Claim
    Evidence
    Warrant
    Backing for the Warrant
    Qualifier
    Reservation
THE UNITS OF LOGIC
    Inductive Reasoning
    Deductive Reasoning
    Causal Reasoning
STRATEGIES FOR THE LOGICAL OPTION
A SITUATIONAL ANALYSIS OF THE LOGICAL OPTION

CHAPTER 8 STRUCTURING THE MESSAGE: THE LOGICAL OPTION

RATIONALE FOR THE LOGICAL OPTION

You have selected your position. You have framed it into a proposition and outlined your persuasive approach. Now you will begin to concentrate on filling in the structure. You will phrase ideas. You will develop them. You will attempt to draw from your listeners either agreement or rational response. In this chapter we will present the option that establishes the rationality and logic of your position.

The situations for which you draw substantially on the elements of logical structure are usually those that carry some controversy. A national or local crisis may have generated public and private dialogue. Heated opinions may have been exchanged. Editorials may have appeared in the media. Those communicators who, during the confusion, can sort out and clarify issues will in all likelihood gain respect. The logical position will stand as the one to be taken: It will promote further inquiry, rational options, and judicious decisions.

The communicator who chooses the logical option can accomplish some additional results. First, this person can demonstrate a command of the issues, thus enhancing his credibility. Second, his preparation and structured approach ought to provide guidance for those who wish to make decisions after considering the full ramifications of the topic. Third, the analysis will, by drawing together related issues, produce conclusions not seen before.

DEFINING THE LOGICAL OPTION

The term *logic* (from the Greek, "logos") denotes "correct reasoning or valid thought." To rhetoricians it holds some broader, perhaps more confusing, implications. Logic implies more of a "style" of rationality, because speakers do not present ideas in formulas that can be considered traditional logic. Logic formulas, wherever they are used, serve more as a test of the reasoning process involved in communication.

There does not appear to be any way of separating what is logical from what is emotional. We have chosen to discuss logical and psychological options in different chapters only for the sake of allowing a discussion of the different methodologies. Any distinction that is apparent should pose more of an *objective* rather than an *actual* distinction. How an idea will affect a listener is beyond your control. You can only anticipate that the listener's mind might experience certain processes while you are presenting your ideas.

The listener could react strongly and immediately, positively or negatively, to what you say. Or the subject matter will involve enough options and doubts so that your listeners are more prone to weigh and consider the pros and cons of what you say. The logical option can service either frame of mind: giving reasonableness to strong feelings and giving options to uncertain feelings. In either case, the logical option will contain a number of levels, or issues, for consideration.

In other words, the function of the logical option is *analytical*. Its purpose is to break the subject matter up into its parts so that it may be seen, weighed, and understood. The parts will be then connected in such ways as to permit the listener to draw conclusions. You can say that the psychological option is more reflexive. The impact of the message is instantaneous and without need for prolonged analysis.

How the logical option will determine your approach depends on the situation, topic, and audience. Consider the subject of gun control, for example. Following the assassinations of John and Robert Kennedy and Martin Luther King, there were strong outcries for gun control. The nation seemed predisposed toward accepting it. Surveys reflected the national attitude. The examples of the assassination were strong, potent, and emotional. Consideration of many points of analysis was unnecessary. As a speaker, you could have drawn heavily from the elements of the psychological approach and won favor with an audience.

However, as the months passed, many editorials appeared about the right to bear arms, the crime rate, and the need for self-protection. The advocate of gun control found it necessary not only to present the examples of the assassinations, but to answer those considerations. This approach took on more elements of weighing, evaluating, analyzing—in other words, the features of the logical option. Notice that both situations employed both approaches: logical and psychological.

CONNECTIONS: THE ESSENCE OF LOGIC

When one conclusion interferes with another, doubt is raised. Decisions are harder to reach, and confusion predominates. The controversial situation subsequently sets the scene for the logical option.

The primary purpose for using the logical option—either in planning, structuring, or evaluating—is to provide ways of *seeing or drawing connections from idea to idea and from idea to conclusion*. The logical option provides the connecting link. It is the element that makes conclusions drawn from a combination of ideas believable. As a communicator, you will be constantly involved in drawing together ideas and structuring units.

In recent years, the name of Stephen Toulmin has become popular among textbook authors. Toulmin wrote a book, *The Uses of Argument*,[1] which provides models for examining logical structure. The Toulmin Model, as we will call it in our own adapted form, has been widely used in argumentation and speech-communication texts.[2]

There are some differences of opinion as to why and how the Toulmin model of analysis is useful. Bradley states that it "allows the speaker to state the *degree* of certainty or probability."[3] The pattern allows us, according to Ehninger and Brockriede to see "a *dynamic* relationship between evidence and claim."[4] And Albert Lewis has stated.

> By putting an argument into proper form, one creates a context in which rational questions can be asked. Toulmin is thus shifting the focus of his logical model from that of judgment to one of formulation—i.e., the clear statement of argument—and for substantial arguments, at least, leaving the tools for judgment to be formed by field, situation, and audience.[5]

The key words that describe the Toulmin Model are: "degree of probability," "dynamic relationship," and "formulation." Each suggests that the process involves a connection between information and idea. As a communicator, you should be concerned with *using* connections—they serve to explain and prove the worth of what you say. As a listener, you may want to analyze connections for weaknesses and deficiencies.

The Toulmin Model is an excellent approach for understanding both *how to use* and *how to analyze* connections. To understand the model, we need first to define its six parts: claim, evidence, warrant, backing for the warrant, qualifier, and reservation.

The Claim

The claim can be a statement, conclusion, proposition, contention, or assertion. "Beverly stole my hat" is a claim. So is, "We should adopt a world monetary system." The claim should carry with it, initially, a ring of believability or probability. It is not expected, in other words, that your claim will be, "The moon is made of green cheese," unless, of course, you have the evidence to suggest that it is.

Evidence

We have discussed evidence in Chapter 5. It is the data, or information, used to make the claim acceptable and believable. Some will accept your evidence; others will not. It is your obligation to present evidence that will increase the probability of its being accepted. Consider how the following evidence supports the claim, "Rocktown should have a new hospital."

Evidence ⟵————————⟶ **Claim**

Statistics show that
more people need
medical services in
Rocktown.

Rocktown should
have a new hospital.

Warrant

An understanding of the warrant is essential to understanding the usefulness of the Toulmin Model. The warrant is the connector between the evidence and the claim. It shows *why* the evidence is pertinent to the claim. It validates the use of the evidence to support the claim. Notice how the warrant works to make the claim.

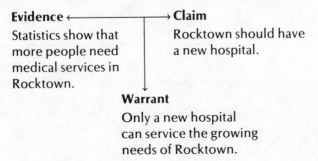

Evidence ⟵————————⟶ **Claim**

Statistics show that
more people need
medical services in
Rocktown.

Rocktown should have
a new hospital.

Warrant
Only a new hospital
can service the growing
needs of Rocktown.

Backing for the Warrant

Because the warrant is pivotal for connecting the evidence and claim, it may need to be strengthened and supported. The warrant must be acceptable to the audience in order for them to draw the same conclusions as yourself. You may ensure this by presenting backing and support for the warrant.

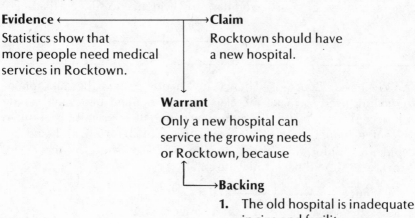

Evidence
Statistics show that more people need medical services in Rocktown.

Claim
Rocktown should have a new hospital.

Warrant
Only a new hospital can service the growing needs or Rocktown, because

Backing
1. The old hospital is inadequate in size and facility.
2. The population of Rocktown is growing.

There are two additional elements of the Toulmin Model that aid in understanding and measuring the degree of probability established between the evidence and the claim. If there are doubts or items of information that throw some question on the claim, they should be acknowledged. The two elements of the model that allow for this are called the *qualifier* and the *reservation*.

Qualifier

The qualifier is simply a device for modifying, or qualifying, the claim. It designates other possibilities and contingencies. When there is a high degree of certainty, it is unnecessary; but if there is uncertainty, you should use the qualifier. Words and phrases such as "It has become apparent" or "probably" or "should consider the possibility of" or "in the future," are qualifying expressions.

Claim

Rocktown should
have a new hospital.

Claim with Qualifier

(It is apparent) that Rocktown
should have a new hospital.
Rocktown should (probably)
have a new hospital.
Rocktown should consider (the
possibility of) building a new
hospital.

Reservation

The reservation is the element that gives substance to, or a reason for, the qualifier. Why should you use "probably" or "it is apparent"? Simply because there might be some information that reduces the probability of the claim. Consider for example:

Qualified Claim

Rocktown should probably
have a new hospital.

Reservation

1. Unless the new hospital
   in Chadwick can service the
   needs of Rocktown.
2. Unless a new addition can
   improve the old hospital.

Remember, that the Toulmin Model is a dynamic device. Each aspect affects the other—determining the extent to which it should be used or developed. As well as making connections, it is meant to "see" connections and perhaps to raise questions. By understanding all the influencing and counteracting forces in all arguments, you will understand the options. Consideration of all options should give your message a higher level of analysis and subsequently a higher level of credibility.

THE UNITS OF LOGIC

Language is a device for expressing our thoughts. Spontaneous impressions and random thoughts take form in ideas that we express in words and syntax. And from our language, we attempt to construct larger thought patterns that reflect the reality of events and time.

Without systems of thought that are consistent with reality and tell us something about our past, present, and future, our thoughts and actions become aimless. Without some usable and reliable thought patterns, we are likely to build convictions on insufficient data, myths, and the words of others. Our perceptions of reality become clouded and our communication is less credible.

As human beings, therefore, we have devised systems of logic that serve as devices for formulating our own thoughts, as means of structuring and communicating ideas, and as ways of validating all ideas—our own or those of others. The uses of logic are functional at all levels of communication whether it be in the larger design of an entire speech or the development of concise and miniscule arguments. Logic systems do not provide recipes from which messages can be instantly structured. Their uses are perceptual and functional in maintaining rationalism within the sender–speaker, the message–speech, and the receiver–audience.

Over the centuries, three patterns of reasoning have emerged from the writings of logicians, philosophers, and rhetoricians. They are systems of reasoning that have evolved out of man's natural thinking process; they are not merely devices for categorizing ideas. Properly used and clearly presented, they are the most fundamental and effective means for building arguments. These logic systems are inductive reasoning, deductive reasoning, and causal reasoning.

Inductive Reasoning

The lessons of experience and life itself are the bases of the inductive pattern of reasoning. As children, we learn that hot stoves burn us when we touch them. If we go beyond the ropes at a pond and cannot touch ground with our feet, there is a moment of desperation. The lesson teaches us to be careful the *next time*. If we are watching a baseball game and are hit by a foul ball, we learn to protect ourselves better at the next game. The individual who determines the quality of all automobiles made by a certain company from his experience with one or two of its automobiles has also used inductive logic.

The inductive process, therefore, employs the method of reasoning from the *specific,* or *specifics,* to the *general.* Diagrammatically, this process appears as follows:

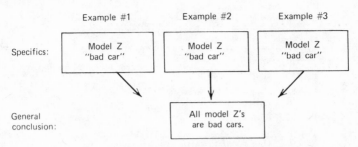

The pattern of reasoning from specific to general is, therefore, a natural thought process. One bad experience tells us to beware the next time. The use of inductive reasoning carries with it some hazards that we will discuss later, but it is well to keep in mind that *its primary function is to establish probability.*

Probability is employed to construct, first, *arguments that predict negative consequences.*

If you are to support the continued ban on nuclear testing, for example, you would maintain that lifting the ban would result in (negative consequence) a health hazard. You would *predict* this hazard on the basis of (specifics) the effects on the people of the Pacific Islands, effects on fish, and effects on water pollution. Your argument would appear as follows: We should not allow nuclear testing because of its effect on:

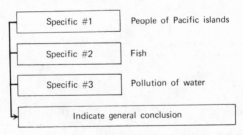

Nuclear testing is a health hazard.

Because nuclear testing is a health hazard in these cases, you have established the *probability* that it will happen again if nuclear testing is resumed.

Second, inductive organization may be employed *to predict positive consequences.* Generally, this structure is used when you advocate a course of action prior to presenting supportive arguments. You might refer to this as the *advantages approach.* The pattern is structured as follows: Massachusetts should adopt the New York system of criminal rehabilitation for the following reasons:

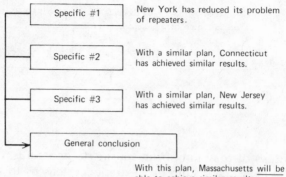

Specific #1	New York has reduced its problem of repeaters.
Specific #2	With a similar plan, Connecticut has achieved similar results.
Specific #3	With a similar plan, New Jersey has achieved similar results.
General conclusion	

With this plan, Massachusetts will be able to achieve similar results.

A third system of inductive reasoning employs *specifics to establish the extent and significance of a problem.* This pattern is structured as follows: The United States should set up a national board to investigate the problems of delinquency among persons under sixteen.

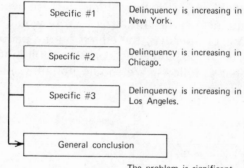

Specific #1	Delinquency is increasing in New York.
Specific #2	Delinquency is increasing in Chicago.
Specific #3	Delinquency is increasing in Los Angeles.
General conclusion	

The problem is significant enough to warrant the national investigative board.

In short, inductive reasoning may be used to:

1. Predict negative consequences.
2. Predict positive consequences.
3. Establish the significance of a problem.

In all situations, the process of induction operates on the principle of *specific to general,* and in all cases, the process of induction involves the *criterion of establishing probability.*

To test the validity of inductive reasoning, you ought to ask several questions:

1. Are there enough specifics to prove the truth of the conclusion?

2. Are there negative cases, or specifics, that are contrary to your conclusion?
3. Are the specific cases typical?

Deductive Reasoning

The opposite of the inductive pattern is deductive reasoning, or reasoning from *the general to the specific*. In the inductive process, general truth is established by a collection of specific data—data that are sufficient and representative enough to establish probability. In deductive reasoning, however, you assume a general truth and apply this truth to particular cases. Consider the most familiar of all deductive syllogisms:

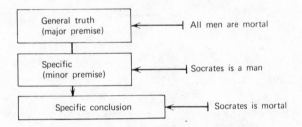

The validity of the reasoning was established simply by connecting the truth of man's mortality to the specific case of Socrates. Notice two things about the general truth, however. First, the word "all" allows the premise to include every man. It is *all inclusive*; no particular is left out and no qualification is considered. Second, the truth is an *absolute*. The fact that all men die is unquestioned; the establishment of probability is unnecessary.

Because the criterion of "all-or-nothing-at-all" is applied to the formal deductive syllogism, its usefulness to you as the speaker can be limited. More often than not, you as a communicator speak on topics that are relative. You attempt to establish the strength of your position by marshaling and presenting the strongest and most probable arguments. If a topic were black or white, true or false, absolute or not absolute, then it would probably exclude the necessity of dialogue.

We will not, therefore, slavishly adhere to the criterion of *absolute truth*; rather, we will require our general, or major, premises to be *accepted truths*. The premise that "all men are created equal," for example, is an *accepted truth*. Although you might find contestable issues within the statement, it is, among democratic societies, a presupposition of all human rights. Structured deductively, it would appear as follows:

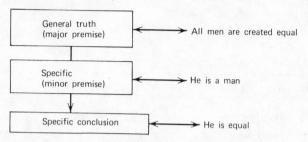

You might extend the argument accordingly: "Because he is equal, he should be accorded an equal opportunity for higher education."

Another *accepted* truth is that "All persons who drive while heavily intoxicated are accident prone." Consider the following structure:

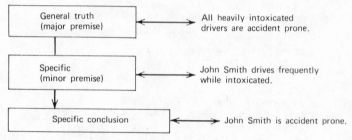

There are three forms of deductive reasoning: the categorical deduction, the hypothetical deduction, and the disjunctive syllogism. Each has a unique type of usefulness in developing the rational message.

Categorical Deduction

The deductive forms illustrated above are categorical in nature. Each begins with a major premise, which is followed by a minor premise, and concludes with a statement connecting the minor premise to the major premise. Hence, we have:

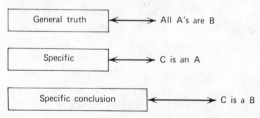

How might you apply this pattern or arrangement in a communication situation? If you were to advocate stricter narcotics laws in

Massachusetts, you might argue:

General Truth:	Narcotics breed crime.
Specific:	Massachusetts has a serious narcotics problem.
Conclusion:	Therefore, narcotics is breeding crime in Massachusetts.

Hypothetical Deduction

The hypothetical syllogistic form follows essentially the same pattern as the categorical syllogism: A general truth is followed by a specific conclusion. It differs, however, in that it contains an "if" clause. The function of the minor premise is to deny or affirm the hypothetical premise. Denying the hypothetical premise would appear as follows:

Major Premise:	(General Truth) If capital punishment is a deterrence to crime, then the crime rate should decrease where capital punishment is used.
Minor Premise:	(Specific) Crime is continuing to rise in country A, a capital punishment country.
Therefore:	Capital punishment is not a deterrent to crime.

Essentially, the speaker is advocating that capital punishment not be reinstated. He realizes that one of the strongest arguments *for* capital punishment is as a deterrent,—the crime rate should decrease or, at least, remain static. Proof to the contrary—the form of the minor premise (the specific)—that crime is continuing to rise in country A in spite of capital punishment—*negates* the validity of the general truth.

Disjunctive Syllogism

Although it follows the same pattern of general-to-the-specific, the disjunctive syllogism differs from the categorical and hypothetical syllogisms in that it contains an "either-or" proposition. The purpose of the disjunctive pattern is to put forth two alternatives from which the communicator may establish his contention. The alternatives are usually opposites, and therefore the negation or affirmation of one alternative subsequently affects the other. An argument stated in disjunctive form would appear as follows:

Major Premise: (general truth)	Either the Federal government cuts back its military aid to the Middle East, or it must raise taxes.

| Minor Premise:
(specific) | Since a cut back in commitments
will affect the diplomatic relations. Then, |
| Conclusion: | The government must raise taxes. |

Causal Reasoning

We have examined how inductive and deductive reasoning may be used as patterns of arrangement and as devices for determining validity in arguments. A third form of logic is referred to as causal reasoning. Essentially, causal reasoning appears to some extent in all forms of logic, for its purpose is to establish causation. Every incident, every sample, every solution, is traceable to one or several causes. When we spoke of *inductive* reasoning, we concluded: "Nuclear testing is hazardous to health." The underlying element of causation is obvious:

nuclear testing ←——————→ health hazard
(CAUSE)   (EFFECT)

In speaking of *deductive* reasoning, we employed the example of "Narcotics breeds crime." Again, we find an element of causal reasoning:

narcotics ←——————→ crime
(CAUSE)   (EFFECT)

Thus, causal reasoning is universal to all forms of logic. At some level there must be a cause and an effect.

Why, then, do we isolate causal reasoning and speak of it as a separate form of reasoning to be distinguished from inductive and deductive logic? The purpose is simple. Causation does appear *within* most forms of reasoning; yet, arguments are not always structured on a causal pattern. Compare the following two patterns to distinguish the difference between inductive and causal reasoning:

Example A	**Example B**
Inductive	*Causal Reasoning*
1. People on pacific islands	1. Chemical *A* in nuclear explosions
2. Fish	2. Chemical *B* in nuclear explosions
3. Water pollution	3. Chemical *C* in nuclear explosions
Indicate:	*Cause:*
Nuclear testing is a health hazard.	A health hazard.

Both conclusions have underlying causal reasoning, but only Example *B* employs causal reasoning as a *general pattern,* or *structural system,* for arriving at that conclusion.

How, then, is deductive reasoning to be distinguished from causal reasoning? The deductive syllogism that began with the major premise "Narcotics breed crime" appears obviously to be based on the *causative* premise that narcotics is the *cause* of crime. Again, the essential difference lies in the structure of the reasoning. The major premise was used to establish a general truth that would subsequently call for stricter narcotics laws to check the spread of crime in Massachusetts. The *primary emphasis,* therefore, was not to establish the fact that Massachusetts *has* a serious narcotics problem. The argument did not present *how and why* narcotics causes crime. The fact that it causes crime *is taken for granted* in the major premise. The structure of the argument is designed to lead you to the need for legislation in Massachusetts. Consider the differences in the two following examples:

Example A	**Example B**
Deductive Reasoning	*Causal Reasoning*
1. Narcotics breed crime.	1. Psychological problems
2. Massachusetts has a narcotics problem.	2. Economic problems
	3. Racial problems
3. To check crime, Massachusetts needs narcotics laws.	*Cause:*
	Dope addiction
	Solution:
	Problems to Alleviate:
	1. Psychological problems
	2. Economic problems
	3. Racial problems.

The purpose of the causal reasoning, therefore, is to analyze and present the causes or effects of a given problem and subsequently to focus on the remedies that can eliminate the problem. Diagrammatically, it appears as follows:

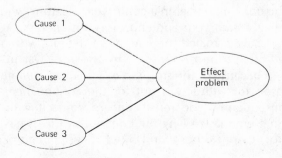

Or, conversely, the causal system might be employed to demonstrate that the problem (*effect*) will produce *causes* to other problems.

To test the validity of causal reasoning, you can ask the following questions:

1. Is the cause the actual cause of the effect, or are there other more significant causes?
2. Is there a counteracting factor that breaks the relationship between the cause and the effect?
3. Is the cause significant enough to produce the alleged effect?

STRATEGIES FOR THE LOGICAL OPTION

Before setting down the basic structure of a message, you ought to consider several questions.

First, *what organizational pattern will best fit a given topic?* Too often, those who are conscious of organization strive rather painfully to fit ideas into patterns rather than allowing the natural order of the idea to mold the pattern. The effect is usually awkward and contrived. Just as the architecture of a residence cannot serve the purposes of an air terminal, certain organizational structures do not fit all topics.

The purpose of the logical pattern is to stress the reasons and support for a particular course of action. You should not stop with arranging ideas merely for clarity alone (although that is an important consideration) but you must also realize that no assertion can stand alone, naked, in the midst of controversy. The process of integrating ideas into structures that stress their validity is important.

Consider, for example, the question of whether or not the United States should withdraw its military commitments to Western Europe. You might select a chronological pattern to develop the subcontention that *over the years,* the military threat of communism has diminished and that it is time for a reappraisal of United States commitments. In a speech delivered to a sympathetic audience, the pattern might be quite effective. In a controversial setting where negative response is likely from your audience, it is not enough. A description of events that have signaled the coming of detente with communism might not withstand the response, "The threat of war in Europe has been lessened because of the strength of American commitments; this is not a reason for withdrawal but for the continuance of commitments." Consequently, you must concern yourself with structuring arguments that emphasize *why* the communist threat has diminished (ostensibly for reasons other than United States commitments, such as the growing economic strength of Western European nations). The design, in other words, must fit the topic.

Indispensable to the preparation of the well-structured address is a second consideration: *Which issues deserve prominence?* The main issues in a controversy are usually apparent. The questions of how, when, and where to place major issues in the speech involve a consideration of what order is most likely to draw listeners into supporting your position.

Research on this subject has produced some findings that are reported by Loren Anderson. He states:

> *Cohen reported that a message was more effective if need arousal preceded, rather than followed need satisfaction. . . . Gulley and Berlo compared the effectiveness of three orders: anti-climax, climax, and pyramidal. In the pyramidal arrangement the most important material is placed in the middle of the message. Both the climax and anti-climax speeches were more effective than the pyramidal order. This study suggests that the most important material should be placed either first or last in the message.*
>
> *One variable which may influence the choice of a climax or anti-climax organization is subject interest. Anti-climax order may be useful in arousing the attention of a disinterested audience while a climax order may be preferable if the audience is already interested in the source's topic.*[6]

Ordinarily, you can apply the following advice:

1. Place your strongest arguments first.
2. Select two to four subordinate, yet important, issues to support your major contentions.
3. Never omit a point that deals with the opposition's strongest argument.
4. If the audience is not aware of the significance of the problem, discuss the problem first and your solution second.
5. If the audience is aware of the problem and its significance, discuss your solution first and present advantages second.

A third basic consideration is: *which combination of arguments has cumulative force, or which arguments best compliment one another?* No pattern of organization, no matter how well designed, will have logical strength if the major issues are not supportive of one another. Unrelated and isolated points tend to distract from the rational address. Consider, for example, how you might design a speech advocating a further strengthening of diplomatic relations with Red China. It might be tempting to conjecture about the implications of

Sino-Soviet relation or the cultural revolution, but a speech that deals directly with the defining characteristics of diplomacy—that is, with the military, economic, and political relationships between the two countries—is likely to be more effective. By splitting the concept of diplomacy into three distinct parts, the speech is simple yet forceful. To achieve the cumulative force of which we spoke, remember to *avoid the temptation to include points that, although interesting, may distract from the central purpose.*

A fourth consideration is: *What is an appropriate number of major issues?* Success in communication is often measured by the listeners retention, and thus you ought to limit your speech to a few meaningful points—points that the listener is likely to recall. Assuming a short period of time, you ought to limit yourself to *no more than four basic areas.* Even four can be cumbersome. Some speakers assume that by presenting many points they will win over opposing views through the use of quantity alone. The result is confusion. Some persons are likely to think of the speaker's weakest point, reduce it to the absurd in their minds (or openly) and by doing so conclude that the speaker's reasoning is flimsy.

In summary, some basic considerations of message construction are: (1) select a pattern to fit the topic; (2) decide which issues deserve prominence; (3) combine and relate arguments to one another; and (4) decide on the most manageable number of points.

A SITUATIONAL ANALYSIS OF THE LOGICAL OPTION

The intent of the logical option is to create an atmosphere of rationality—one that is less likely to inflame emotions. Consider how the elements of the preceding chapter, "Approaching the Persuasive Option," and this chapter can determine the level of rationality in a message. We will analyze the comments of three different speakers indicating the various levels of rationality.

Irrational Speaker

1. Something has to be done about delinquency.
2. Today's youth is getting away with murder.
3. They are all pot-heads—they rob, rape, and menace the population.
4. One of the nicest boys I know got caught up in a robbery.

5. Parents are simply not watching their children.
6. I suggest we double the police force and throw them in jail or something.

You might have found the irrational speaker's ideas interesting, but you should also realize that he explained nothing and offered no solutions. His speech was simply the complaint of an irate citizen; every statement is sweepingly broad and bears no relevance to its preceding statement. You might listen and conclude: "Yes, there is a problem." But nothing that explains the phenomenon of the problem is available for reflection and consideration.

The next speaker, whom we shall call more rational than the first, presents a more organized message. The gist of his argument is as follows:

MORE RATIONAL SPEAKER

I. The problem of delinquency is most complex. Several problems are apparent.
  A. Economics and inflation.
  B. Social and psychological factors.
  C. Problems of drug addiction.
  D. Racial prejudice.
II. The number of delinquents who repeat crimes is great. In New York alone there was a 70 percent rate of recidivism.
III. Legislation is needed to revise the rehabilitation systems.
  A. The social conditions of the prisons place the delinquent in the environment of the hardened criminal.
  B. There is a lack of guidance and counseling.
  C. Vocational training programs are lacking in the prisons.

Compared with the first speaker, the second speaker has a clearer concept of what he wishes to say. He focuses on the aspect of rehabilitation, he analyzes the problem and examines its causes, and he supports his major points with subpoints. The listener learns of the importance of doing something about the problems of our penal systems.

Yet this speaker's pattern of development has some confusing features. It could, for example, fail to convince the listener that the problem, recidivism, is caused by the failures of the rehabilitation system. The speaker clearly presents ideas, but he does little to show relationships. Let us be more specific.

His opening is good. He states that the problem is "complex," and he then proceeds to amplify its causes. In Step II, however, he does nothing to demonstrate a direct relationship between recidivism and the problems of Step I. The necessity for rehabilitation is mentioned in Step III, but his suggestion does not establish poor rehabilitation as the *cause* of recidivism. The *connection* is made only by implication, not by rhetorical proof or logical organization. His subsequent three statements aptly describe the conditions of prison, but again no apparent connections are drawn to the previous viewpoint.

The third speaker, whom we shall call the most rational of the three, presents a case similar to the second speaker. However, he is able to assemble his arguments into a tighter and more compelling pattern of analysis. His arguments are clearer; his reasoning is easier to accept.

Most Rational Speaker

I.   Delinquency is *caused* by many factors.
    A.   Economics.
    B.   Social and psychological problems.
    C.   Problems of drug addiction.
    D.   Racial prejudice.
    E.   Rehabilitation.
II. Consider one of the most critical problems—rehabilitation.
    A.   The percentage of repeaters is great.
        1.   A national average of 70 percent.
        2.   In New York, for example, 70 percent.
    B.   This problem is *caused* by the social conditions of the prisons.
        1.   Delinquents serve with hardened criminals.
        2.   Prisons lack guidance and counseling facilities.
        3.   Prisons lack vocational training.
III. To eliminate this one cause of delinquency, the country ought to revise its penal system.

The third speaker's arguments are clearer for several reasons. His transition statement not only limits his topic to one phase of the problem, rehabilitation, but serves to signpost his direction in the speech. He deals with the effects of the present problem by indicating the number of delinquents who are not rehabilitated. Because evidence is stated after the contention, there is no confusion as to what it supports. Following the description of the problem, the speaker then examines its causes in Step B, that is, the social conditions of the prisons. The order is logical and rational. Finally, in Step III, he presents a solution—legislation to revise the rehabilitation system. A description of the specific legislative bills could be elaborated on under Step III.

In short, the speaker employs logical organization to clarify issues, support contentions, and show connections between ideas. His logical message is subsequently forged into a single unit that is forceful, weighty, and vigorous.

SUMMARY

The logical option is primarily the analytical aspect of message construction. You employ the logical option to clarify issues and to see and make connections between information and ideas. The Toulmin Model provides a pattern for showing relationships between evidence, claim, and warrant. Inductive reasoning is the method of moving from specific illustration to general conclusion. Deductive reasoning is the reverse: from general to specific. Causal reasoning demonstrates the cause of an event or problem. All three patterns must be checked for defects.

Finally, you should select the appropriate number of issues, highlight the ones that deserve prominence, and then select a pattern that fits the specific topic.

Review and Exercises

1. Using the Toulmin Model, design one basic issue on the topic of handguns, a national health care plan, or the waste of energy.
2. Discuss the function of the "warrant" in the Toulmin approach.
3. Present illustrations of inductive, deductive, and causal reasoning. Present the tests of each so as to indicate the validity or invalidity of your examples.
4. Select a topic. Make a statement as to how logical strategy could be used to develop that specific topic.
5. Select a political speech or an editorial. Do a logical analysis of the issues.

Additional Readings

Dye, Robert D., *Conflict Among Humans,* Springer Publishing, New York, 1973.

Freeley, Austin J., *Argumentation and Debate,* second edition, Wadsworth, Belmont, Calif., 1966.

Jandt, Fred E., editor, *Conflict Resolution Through Communication,* Harper and Row, New York, 1973.

Mills, Glen E., *Reason in Controversy,* Allyn and Bacon, Boston, 1964.

Footnotes

[1] Stephen Toulmin, *The Uses of Argument* (Cambridge: Cambridge University Press, 1958).

[2] See footnotes below.

[3] Bert E. Bradley, *Fundamentals of Speech Communication: The Credibility of Ideas* (Dubuque, Iowa: Wm. C. Brown Company Publishers, 1974), p. 133. Reprinted by permission of the publishers.

[4] Douglas Ehninger and Wayne Brockriede, *Decision By Debate* (New York: Dodd, Mead & Company, 1963), pp. 98–99.

[5] Albert Lewis, "Stephen Toulmin: A Reappraisal," *Central States Speech Journal,* **XXIII** (Spring 1972), p. 54.

[6] Loren J. Anderson, "A Summary of Research on Order Effects in Communication," *Concepts in Communication,* edited by Jimmie D. Trent, Judith S. Trent, and Daniel J. O'Neill (Boston: Allyn and Bacon, Inc., 1973), pp. 130–131.

CHAPTER 9 STRUCTURING THE MESSAGE: THE PSYCHOLOGICAL OPTION

CHAPTER 9 STRUCTURING THE MESSAGE: THE PSYCHOLOGICAL OPTION

RATIONALE FOR THE PSYCHOLOGICAL OPTION

All communication is integrated with human behavior, and to that extent, everything you say will have psychological impact. It is important to isolate and discuss some of the pertinent elements of human psychology to see how they pertain to communication and, specifically, to see how they can influence the construction of a message.

Ethics: A Primary Consideration

To apply what *it is that you know* about human behavior *to influencing* human behavior poses an ethical question—one that we raised with regard to evidence. There is a distinction of a sort between *motivation* and *manipulation,* but the specific differences between the two are impossible to isolate. The distinction provides, therefore, an attitudinal choice on your part. Will you use psychological information for good or bad purposes? Each situation will be unique—but you should approach each with some sense of how and why you are persuading.

It has been said that persuasion is a tool, just as the hammer is a tool. The hammer has both constructive and destructive purposes. How it is used will depend on your choice. Doctors use persuasion to influence patients to take certain precautions concerning their health. Lawyers use persuasion to gain acceptance of the innocence of their clients. Factory supervisors use persuasion to encourage workers to make their quotas with high levels of quality worksmanship.

The insights into psychological behavior will not necessarily convert you into a "master persuader." Some people are very difficult to move from already established positions. So the psychological option may be used only to gain a hearing—to get persons to be at least attentive to your reasoning.

It is important also to consider how the psychological option can influence you as a listener. Understanding your own need systems will enable you to function more rationally when others try to exploit you for their own purposes.

Let us now proceed to gain a perspective of how the psychological option is used in communication.

The Development of Attitudes

Human beings have needs. Around these needs, they build feelings, attitudes, and behaviors. When we say hello to someone, there is an expressed need to make contact with other human beings. The simple word "hello" carries with it other additional levels of meaning. Consider from the following simple illustration how feelings, moods, and attitudes are worked into this transaction between two persons.

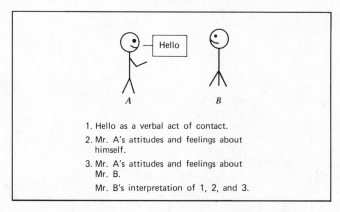

1. Hello as a verbal act of contact.
2. Mr. A's attitudes and feelings about himself.
3. Mr. A's attitudes and feelings about Mr. B.
   Mr. B's interpretation of 1, 2, and 3.

From saying hello, Mr. A may try to enlarge the conversation with the expression "Cigarette?" (asked as a way of making contact and saying hello). This relatively simple act of human contact begins to bring into play a much more complex series of attitudes and feelings. If Mr. B is a person who has strong feelings against smoking, he will interpret and react quite differently than if he wanted a cigarette.

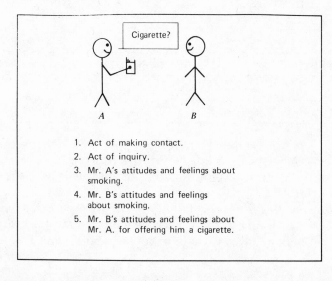

1. Act of making contact.
2. Act of inquiry.
3. Mr. A's attitudes and feelings about smoking.
4. Mr. B's attitudes and feelings about smoking.
5. Mr. B's attitudes and feelings about Mr. A. for offering him a cigarette.

Consider, finally, what would happen if the message were changed to, "You should quit smoking." Here you can see an increase in the problems of attitudes and feelings. "Who are you to tell me what to do?" may be one response. "You know, I think you're right," might be another. There are countless other possibilities that could evolve from this interaction. Try to discover a few.

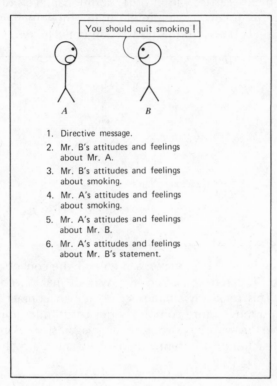

1. Directive message.
2. Mr. B's attitudes and feelings about Mr. A.
3. Mr. B's attitudes and feelings about smoking.
4. Mr. A's attitudes and feelings about smoking.
5. Mr. A's attitudes and feelings about Mr. B.
6. Mr. A's attitudes and feelings about Mr. B's statement.

APPLYING ATTITUDES TO MESSAGE CONSTRUCTION

Attitudes: A Reappraisal

In Chapter 3, we discussed how attitudes influence the communicative act. Understanding how you begin to work the attitudes of an audience into message construction—or into what you say—is our next concern.

However, this is no easy task. Even when you understand the attitudes of your listeners, there is no guarantee that what you say will influence them in any way. And, of course, you cannot think in terms of adjusting all your views to the particular biases of a group. We suggest, therefore, that you think mainly in terms of developing a *sensitivity* for audience concerns. The integration of audience attitudes into your message will show concern for their background and their views. It is the sensitivity that is most important.

We should say a few more things about attitudes—both in review and in expansion of what was previously discussed. How might you, for example, look at the various forms of attitudes? Consider some key words and concepts.

Feelings are emotions that people have acquired through their interaction with other persons, situations, experiences, and ideas. *Opinions* are the verbalizations that people make openly and publicly to others; they reflect a composite view of their value systems. *Values* are somewhat different—and considerably deeper—than opinions. They have a strong social and cultural base.

And beliefs touch on all areas. Milton Rokeach suggests that beliefs come from many sources.[1] They may result from direct experience: We know that rain is wet and snow is cold. Or beliefs may or may not be confirmed by friends and relationships. You may think, for example, that a new style of shoe is appropriate for you and ask for the confirmation of others. You may also receive beliefs from teachers and parents. In the same manner, they may come from persons to whom you assign high levels of credibility such as medical doctors. These beliefs help you to establish your own identities as well as those of others. Understanding the similarities will make it possible for you to build ideas on certain assumptions.

Perceptions

Having some information about, or sensitivity to, how people *perceive* things is equally important to communication.

It is important to know that people respond in differing ways to physical stimuli. Physical *filters* such as hearing, sight, touch, taste, and smell may vary. The degree to which they vary may create distortions or misperceptions of what is being communicated.

Environment may also distort perception: the size of a room, its heating, the number of people in it, and any number of other factors. Past experiences will affect perceptions. So will hunger, visual patterns, sex, and other motivational factors.

Many studies have been done on how different people perceive different events. And, of course, you are familiar with the typical distortions and misperceptions of witnesses who have viewed the same crime. Some consideration therefore should be given to perception and its role in how you develop your message. Certain ideas, for example, may have to be presented in two or three different ways to assure an accurate *perception* of the concept.

Empathy

Empathy is essential to message construction for it is the process of reaching out into the feelings of your listeners. It is the act of projecting yourself into the feelings of another person with the intention of seeing things from his point of view.

In programs of police training, the problems brought on by the lack of empathy between two groups has been most acute. To the policeman's adversary, the term "police" itself is "dirty" implying "establishment," "brutality," or "pig." To the police, the terms "hippie," "communist," and "anarchist" are used to describe the enemy. Neither group, by using these terms, demonstrates empathy. When groups have been brought together for open talks, the lines of communication have been opened and empathy has begun to emerge.

Role playing is one device by which one person can develop insight into another person's perceptions. In the classroom, you might be asked to illustrate the role of the teacher. There is a dual value involved. On one hand, the teacher can see how he appears to others—because his role is being performed by someone else. On the other hand, you can acquire empathy by assuming the motives and personality of another individual. Salespersons, for example, are often trained to role-play the feelings and attitudes of certain types of customers.

Finally, let us consider some additional principles that may be useful in understanding attitudes, perceptions, and the uses of empathy.

1. People tend to evaluate things according to simple "either-or" categories.
2. People attempt to see things consistently and to build stable frames of reference.
3. People tend to limit and adjust their perceptions according to what is agreeable to their needs and values.
4. People's frames of reference tend to emphasize similarities and ignore differences.
5. People tend to see only certain principles in things.
6. People tend to ignore relationships that are not contiguous in space and time.

Attitude Modification

Is it advantageous to modify attitudes? Can it be done? The answer is a qualified yes. To do so, you need an approach—one that is based on an objective and a measurement. You need to decide how strong the attitude is; you need also to decide how far you expect to move that attitude in a different direction.

Four approaches can be used. For one, you can attempt to develop an attitude if none currently exists. Some groups are neutral on certain subjects. Conservationists are trying to develop a "conservation" attitude, for example. The establishment of a new attitude is, therefore, one way to approach the problem.

Second, you can try to attach an attitude to another attitude. If your listeners have positive attitudes about good health, then it makes sense to try to transfer that attitude to the problem of smoking. In this way you are changing the attitude by attaching it to an already accepted attitude.

Third, you can change the direction of an attitude from pro to con or from con to pro. This process requires a sense of gradation. Few rigid supporters of gun control are likely to shift to being avid peddlers of guns. Those who believe strongly in the right to bear arms, however, might be convinced to accept a law licensing hand guns. The gradation of the attitude change is less severe, hence, easier to deal with. A sense of gradual shift is important to attitude modification.

Fourth, you can increase the strength of an attitude. Consider how weight watchers need to have their attitudes strengthened periodically. The strengthening of attitudes is also seen in fund-raising campaigns. Usually the audience (if made up of supporters) is in favor of the cause or candidate, but their attitudes may have lessened in intensity. The approach is to reaffirm their beliefs, and in doing so to change their attitude.

These are but a few approaches to attitude modification. We will examine other ways in the following two sections.

APPLYING APPEALS TO NEEDS: ANOTHER DIMENSION

Because all human beings have needs, you can adapt messages accordingly. You can direct your appeals toward two of the most basic of needs (the need for air and water) by, say, developing a message on pollution and environmental control.

The classification of needs has engaged the attention of many psychologists. Many of the lists have been disputed, revised, and reviewed. One of the most popular methods of grouping and categorizing human needs is that of Abraham Maslow, a well-known psychologist.[2] He states that human needs rank in the following manner:

Physiological needs
Safety needs
Belonging and having needs
Esteem needs
Self-actualization needs

The physiological needs are basic to survival: water, food, sleep, oxygen. They rank highest in priority.

The safety needs provide a belief in those things that appeal to a sense of security. Everyone wishes to be safe in his home and on the street, and thus subjects such as crime protection have strong appeal.

The belonging and having needs include the need for attention, friendship, identification, and love. We have a need to be a part of a group—to be included, recognized, and wanted.

Similarly, we have esteem needs. We need to be respected. We need to know that we are successful. We need to have our achievements noticed and acknowledged.

Finally, we have self-actualizing needs. When the other needs have been satisfied, we are ready to pursue the need for personal achievement. The self-actualized person shows acceptance of self, of others, and of nature. And the self-actualized person is not threatened by the unknown. He is spontaneous, and he is comfortable when alone.

Everett L. Shostrom has produced an interesting chart showing how non-self-actualizing types can move into self-actualizing types. The first chart describes the characteristics of each type. The second shows how one can become self-actualized.[3] Shostrom characterizes the self-actualizing person as one who trusts his feelings, communicates his needs and preferences, admits to desires and misbehavior, enjoys a worthy foe, offers real help when needed, and is honestly and constructively aggressive. (See figures 1 and 2.)

Applying Appeals to Needs: A Specific Case

As we have said, the categorization of appeals and needs can be broad. In the book, *Human Behavior: An Inventory of Scientific Find-*

Figure 1
The Manipulative Type
From Man, The Manipulator, by Everett Shostrom. Copyright © 1967 by Abingdon Press.

ings, Bernard Berelson and Gary A. Steiner have produced a list of twenty-eight *social* needs including such needs as retention, play, and construction.[4] Lists of human wants frequently include such items as conformity, sympathy, adventure, loyalty, curiosity, fair play, property, sexual attractiveness, reputation, and physical enjoyment. Consider how this list of needs might be converted into specific appeals.

Figure 2
The Actualizing Types
From Man, The Manipulator, by Everett Shostrom. Copyright © by the Abingdon Press.

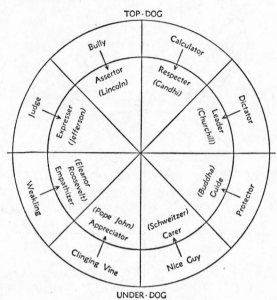

You are delivering a speech to a young couples group on the subject of a long-range investment program. Some of the appeals might be as follows:

Need-Appeal	Statement
Conformity	Other people of your age have found this program useful.
Sympathy	I'm sure you have sympathy for old people living on bare subsistence.
Adventure	You'll be able to take a trip to South America.
Loyalty	By investing in this, you are also investing in America.
Curiosity	Have you ever thought of how millionaires get rich?
Fair Play	You wouldn't want others to support you.
Property	This plan can pay off mortgages and buy a second home in Hawaii.
Sexual Attraction	Wealthy people can afford to keep themselves well-tanned and in sexually attractive physical condition.

Reputation	You will be known as one of the fortunate few with enough funds for a productive retirement.
Physical Enjoyment	Can't you see yourself in a warm climate away from the cold?

STRATEGY OF THE PSYCHOLOGICAL MESSAGE

Attention Reconsidered

We have talked about attention as a device for the opening, or introduction, to a speech. It is important that listeners be attentive throughout your entire message. Attention is difficult to hold, and most of us have a limited ability to sustain it for long periods of time. Distractions, such as people entering a room, may disrupt the flow of your message.

What works to hold attention? Consider first how you can gain attention by shifting sensory channels. The change from one appeal to another, or the change from a verbal presentation to a visual presentation, can shift and refocus the attention of the audience.

Or you can gain and sustain attention by activity. When things are on display in, say, a department store window, notice how our attention is drawn toward the things that are animated—the things that move. Similarly, you can move your body. By coming closer to the audience or by the use of gestures, you can capture attention.

Attention can be obtained with strong statements: "Your cells are dying at the rate of 10,000 a minute!" Or with effective comparisons: "The virus is so small that the average size human cell can hold 60 million polio viruses."

Proximity is the word for the method of showing that the problem is close to the interests of the audience. If your message is about the need for greater security, you might say, "Just two blocks away your neighbor, Ethel, had her television stolen." To the audience, this event is close and emphatic.

Selecting Objectives

It is important, as a psychological strategy, to select clear objectives. An objective that is improperly selected can be disastrous to the intent of what you say. For some groups, your objective may be to acquaint your listeners with the scope of a problem. However, scope and information may not be the interest of another group.

You can set an objective by deciding, for example, that you are going to focus on the problem from your point of view. You may admit that your thoughts are to be considered only "from your viewpoint" and that you have no intent to tempt them to consider otherwise.

The selection of an objective will determine the strategy, or slant, that you will take. The objective in itself will have psychological impact.

Identification

Another option in the strategy of the psychological message is the device of identifying with the beliefs of your audience. This method is called identification. A group that believes strongly in the preservation of individual freedoms may be convinced of the desirability a public nonsmoking law by the use of the following statement:

> You are, certainly, in favor of individual freedoms. I'm simply asking that you extend that thought to the freedom of the nonsmoker. She should be free to breathe air that is unpolluted by the smoker. She should be free from the fears of cancer. And she should be free from persistent irritations to her eyes.

Likewise, a business group that strongly supports free enterprise and capitalism might be led to identify with the speaker by the use of information that confirms their thoughts about the economic system.

Common Ground and Credibility

The use of the common ground approach indicates to an audience that those things that are similar in your background and theirs somehow binds you together. And it does. Sales groups who are told that you too have sold things may tend to accept your observations more readily than those of a nonsalesperson.

However, the establishment of credibility has to go somewhat above the I'm-like-you-so-believe-what-I-say approach. Your general knowledge, reputation, sincerity, and good will toward the audience will help establish credibility—or *ethos.* If reputation is particularly important in getting your audience to believe your information, you may include statements about your background. "When I was in Texas," you might say, "I got to observe the drilling for oil firsthand."

Another way to establish credibility is to reveal your position. Alan C. Elms suggests that you should consider admitting, as opposed to disguising, your intent.[5] If the audience hears you state your intention in the speech, there is a greater likelihood for trust to arise.

Repetition and Restatement

There is evidence that, when advertisements are repeated constantly and frequently, there is a strong psychological effect. Consider how those messages stick with us. Fill in the blanks: "Things go better with _____," "You've come a long way, _____". You will not be able to repeat key ideas a hundred times in a short speech, but consider that the principle of repetition, used judiciously, can greatly enhance the psychological impact of your message.[6]

Visualization

Visualization is simply the process of getting persons, by means of their imaginations, to place themselves in a situation. It is a you-are-there approach in which you describe the surroundings, noises, sights, and smells of a particular event or situation. If your topic is the need for better housing, you might attempt to visualize for your listeners how decrepit slums look and smell to the visitor.

Visualization is also the means by which you can predict the outcome of a particular solution that you are recommending. "If we develop solar energy," you might say, "you can look forward to a better standard of living at a lower cost." Similarly, you can use visualization to predict a negative consequence if your plan is not adopted.

SUMMARY

The psychological approaches to understanding human behavior are important to developing a communicative climate as well as an effective message. You must understand that perceptions will distort, focus, and change things according to the uniqueness of each individual in your audience. Attitudes and values provide a base from which you can develop views, and the needs of your listeners can aid in designing your appeals.

You can gain and sustain attention by shifting sensory channels, by activity, by proximity, and by suspense. Selecting objectives is critical because communication must be related to knowledge and attitude levels. Finally, you may wish to select one or more of the following psychological options to enhance your message: identification, common ground and credibility, repetition and restatement, admission of position, and visualization.

Review and Exercises

1. What is the function of ethics in persuasion?
2. Select one of your strong attitudes and describe how and why it was developed.
3. List your key beliefs. Compare your list to that of another classmate.
4. Recall an incident where your perception and biases may have misled you. How could you have prevented that misperception?
5. Select one typical appeal for five human needs from a speech or editorial.
6. Design a speech for a specific audience that stresses one major appeal.
7. Select one idea and repeat it in four different and interesting ways.
8. Present three examples of identification.

Additional Readings

Broadbent, D. E., *Perception and Communication,* Pergamon, London, 1958.

Holtzman, Paul D., *The Psychology of Speakers' Audiences,* Scott Foresman, Glenview, Ill., 1970.

Insko, Chester A., *Theories of Attitude Change,* Appleton-Century-Crofts, New York, 1967.

Nimmo, Dan, *The Political Persuaders,* Prentice-Hall, Englewood Cliffs, N.J., 1970.

Segall, M. H., and Campbell, D. T., and Herskovits, M. G., *The Influence of Culture on Visual Perception,* Bobbs-Merrill, Indianapolis, 1966.

Summers, Gene F., editor, *Attitude Measurement,* Rand McNally, Chicago, 1970.

Footnotes

[1] Milton Rokeach, *Beliefs, Attitudes, and Values* (San Francisco: Jossey-Bass, 1968), p. 1–12.

[2] Abraham H. Maslow, *Motivation and Personality* (New York: Harper and Row, 1954), pp. 80–92. Reprinted by permission of the publisher.

[3] Everett L. Shostrom, *Man, The Manipulator* (New York: Abingdon Press, 1967), pp. 37, 55. Copyright © 1967 by Abingdon Press. Reprinted with permission of the publisher.

[4] Bernard Berelson and Gary A. Steiner, *Human Behavior: An Inventory of Scientific Findings* (New York: Harcourt, Brace and World, Inc., 1964), pp. 257–258.

[5] Alan Elms, *Social Psychology and Social Relevance* (Boston: Little Brown, 1972), p. 177.

[6] Carl Hovland, Irving L. Janis, and Harold H. Kelley, *Communication and Persuasion* (New Haven: Yale University Press, 1953).

CHAPTER 10   THE RATIONAL EVALUATION

RATIONAL LISTENING
  The Importance of Rational Listening
UNDERSTANDING LISTENING
THE TYPES OF LISTENING
  Discriminatory Listening
  Evaluative Listening
  Appreciatory Listening
OBSTRUCTIONS TO RATIONAL LISTENING
  Memorization
  Casual Attention
  Uninteresting Subjects
  Distractions
  Your Background as an Obstruction
  The Speaker as an Obstruction
  Some Basics for Better Listening
RATIONAL ANALYSIS
  Discovering Fallacies
THE RATIONAL RESPONSE
  Organizing a Response
  Refutational Strategies

CHAPTER 10 THE RATIONAL EVALUATION

In your role as communicator, you have been made aware of the two-way process of communication. Many of the techniques you have applied in the construction of a message will likewise apply in the evaluation of what is being said. In this chapter we will explore some additional considerations that will promote a sense of objectivity, a willingness to weigh ideas against other ideas, and a judicious ability to distinguish between the probable and the improbable. For the next few pages, we will assume that you are the receiver of messages—one who has the option of responding to what has been said. Your function will be primarily that of an evaluator—one who listens, analyzes, and responds.

Evaluation does not always mean criticism, however. Anyone who enters all communication settings with a frown and a pessimistic ear can find grounds for rejecting anything. We assume that you will be *empathic.* That is to say, you will be willing to try to understand the meaning of what is being said before you proceed to analyze and criticize. No listener–receiver ought to close off those elements of conjecture that might lead to fresh ideas and better understanding. Acceptance of what *might be* true may establish a continuing and productive line of communication.

Your task, then, is to determine the line at which the message either becomes, or ceases to be, rational. The three processes we will discuss are listening, analysis, and response.

RATIONAL LISTENING

The principles of rational communication should not be seen solely from the point of view of the source, the sender, and the message. They apply to the listener as well. It is the speaker's task to structure a message that is stimulating and meaningful, but it is the listener's equal obligation to understand and evaluate what is being said. As a voter and participant in the democratic process, you ought to consider your role as that of an educated citizen. As an advocate, you ought to know the strengths and defects of opposing viewpoints.

When receivers neglect their role in the communicative act, they contribute to the obstruction of the communication process. Unfortunately, many of us do this. We listen only to that which we enjoy, or agree with. We do not try to distinguish the important from the unimportant. We are more impressed by the speaker's importance than by the value of what he or she may say. Many listeners are simply indifferent.

The Importance of Rational Listening

Rational listening is important to our personal lives as well as to civilization. It provides enrichment, knowledge, cooperation, and understanding. Its importance may be underscored by the fact that over 45 percent of our time is spent in listening. As members of society, we function intellectually primarily as listeners. Listening is, in fact, a basis of a child's learning process—through auditory stimuli he collects data, imitates words and syntax, and subsequently learns to communicate. Listening is also the means by which we can foster effective human relations. The family, business, labor union, politician, and reporter who avoid the obligations of listening contribute to misunderstanding. Our right of free speech carries with it an equal obligation of responsible listening.

For the college student, listening can have some additional and very pragmatic advantages. Your facility for language can be improved with some concentration on the words of public communicators. Examinations are easily passed if you substitute listening for daydreaming. Moreover, you can acquire knowledge more rapidly and efficiently if you not only hear but absorb.

UNDERSTANDING LISTENING

Before you seek to improve your listening skills, you should eliminate any misconceptions you might have about the process. Remember that you are in control of your own mechanism.

One common misconception is the belief that poor listeners generally lack intelligence. Perhaps—in some cases. But most people are able to increase their listening and retention ability considerably.

A second view is that listening cannot be improved. Some authors make a distinction between hearing and listening. Hearing is auditory reception, but listening involves the dimension of understanding and remaining attentive to what is being said. Just as the mind is capable of growth through education, listening can be improved by concentration and practice.

A third fallacy is that reading will provide you with the techniques for listening. Although it is true that reading may provide you with the background necessary for understanding, it does not necessarily improve listening techniques. Reading, unlike listening, does not usually take place in a social setting where variables may influence your intake. Unlike the reader, the listener must set his attention to the speaking rate of the communicator.

THE TYPES OF LISTENING

The listener's first task is to determine what *type* of listening is applicable to a given situation. Confusion about the various listening roles can lead to nearly as many problems as not listening at all.

Basically, most listening can be categorized as: (1) discriminatory listening; (2) evaluative listening, and (3) appreciative listening.

Discriminatory Listening

Discriminatory listening requires the receiver to understand, remember, and comprehend the integral parts of an idea or object. It may involve learning statistics, the parts of a machine, or the steps in driving a car. Its basic function is the learning process, or the cognitive activity to restructure what has been said into areas or categories.

Evaluative Listening

Evaluative listening involves the process not only of conceptualizing and understanding a subject but of making a *judgment concerning the value* of an idea. Its function is critical and evaluative, as in the case of weighing relative ideas in politics, philosophy, and other humanistic areas. The listener who, for example, must make decisions in elections must employ this variety of listening during the heat of the campaign.

Appreciative Listening

At times, the listener may choose not to challenge or remember the contents of a speech but simply to *enjoy* or *appreciate* what is be-

ing said. Because the speech may deal with something with which he is already familiar, he may choose to enjoy its style and delivery and pay little attention to content. If he views the message to be one of entertainment, then his listening is said to be appreciative.

OBSTRUCTIONS TO RATIONAL LISTENING

Rational listening requires attention, comprehension, and retention. There are many factors that can present barriers to any of these three elements. Some of them are as follows.

Memorization

In the first place, you should not be overly eager about concentrating on the subject matter so that you may memorize its contents. The intent is noble, but the effect is not so good. If you are concerned with memorizing, you may be frustrated. No one can remember everything.

Allow what is being said to be said. Understand the basic ideas. If you are concerned with remembering details, devise an effective note-taking system.

Casual Attention

Having spent five to six hours a day for twelve years in the public school system, some students tend to develop what are called systems of *false attention,* which include eye contact with the speaker, an occasional nod of the head, and perhaps a smile or frown. But these are devices that only cover up casual or no, attention.

If you have gotten into the habit of false attention, you may begin convincing yourself that you are actually listening. Avoid deluding yourself; listen.

Uninteresting Subjects

There is little you can do to protect yourself against the countless number of boring speeches on uninteresting topics. However, do not prejudge the content of the speech before you hear its development. Wait and listen—the subject may get increasingly interesting. You may wish to seek answers to certain questions about the subject. This concern will increase your attention.

Distractions

The greatest enemy of rational listening is the distraction: someone entering the room, a flickering light, or a noise. You cannot protect yourself against major distractions, but often minor ones can send your attention in different directions. Do not let minor irritations become major ones.

Your Background as an Obstruction

There may be certain aspects about your background that create what appears to be a considerable distance between you and the speaker. Biases and personal beliefs derived over a long time from being a northerner, a card-carrying vegetarian, or whatever may unconsciously set up obstructions in the listening process. If your background and beliefs are different from the speaker's, attempt to keep an open mind to his side of the world. The concepts being discussed may be unique to you, so be prepared to establish empathy, or an understanding, for another point of view.

The Speaker as an Obstruction

If a speaker has not learned the rudiments of effective delivery or if he seems to you to be physically unattractive, you should not allow your attention to be impaired. His message may be of vital concern.

Conversely, a speaker's charisma should not be a reason for concentrating on his "presence" or the aura he exudes. Even if his reputation is to be highly respected, a speaker will often tread into areas where he has little expertise. You ought to discriminate what you choose to accept.

Some Basics for Better Listening

1. Set your mind for listening. Don't let obstructions impair concentration.
2. Establish a motivation, or a desire, to listen.
3. Establish empathy for the speaker's position.
4. Establish certain questions in your mind about the nature of the subject. Bring to the listening situation some background.
5. Don't let your background and personal biases cloud your point of view about the content of the speaker's message.
6. Learn to recognize central ideas. Don't be compelled to remember all the speaker says.
7. Develop, if necessary, an efficient note-taking system.

RATIONAL ANALYSIS

In the following pages we will be concerned with understanding when it is that a message ceases to be rational. It is a difficult line to draw. Part of it might be determined by all the methods we have already discussed relative to evidence—the position, the logical option, and the psychological option. Some additional insights into reasoning, provided below, ought to sharpen your perspective even further. Keep in mind, however, that one flaw in a person's reasoning may reveal little about the worth of his position, but a conspicuous pattern of poor information, fallacious reasoning, and propagandized rhetoric will reveal much about his motives. The following tools will provide you with the options of rejection and response.

Discovering Fallacies

Fallacies can be either the product of intended deception by a communicator or the result of his misanalysis. In either case, the fallacy ought to be recognized because its effect on rational communication is cancerous. Based on irrelevant premises and appeals to hot emotions, it misleads audiences into accepting appearance for reality. Its impact is so strong that it has misguided nations into committing irrational acts because, disguised as logic, it creates an aura of truth without acknowledging all the facts, or the facts at all.

The fallacy usually functions as a device that shifts the focus of the audience from central issues, or logical dialogue, to *irrelevant* matters. Sometimes a fallacy is easily detected, but often it is insidious and subtle. Once accepted, a fallacy will subvert the entire communication process. The analytical listener, speaker, lawyer, politician, or college student should, therefore, shield himself from its manipulative effects.

The ways and means of distorting the truth are innumerable. A slight shift in meaning, a condescending inflection of voice, or a raised eyebrow may imply—without logic—that a legitimate argument deserves no serious attention. With some meticulous listening and basic training, you ought to recognize, instantly, three fundamental types of fallacies: (1) begging the question, (2) the *non sequitur,* and (3) material irrelevancies.

The Fallacy of Begging the Question

The fallacy of begging the question may appear in several disguises, but it is recognizable in any form of reasoning that is premised on *unproven assumptions.* The unproven assumption is subsequently substituted for the truth. It might be argued, for example, "We ought to depose the government of Country A because it is controlled by a dictator and dictators, as we all know, are tyrants." Only the statement, "as we all know," establishes the assumption that "all dictators are tyrants"—nothing else. Another speaker might ask casually, "Who can believe politicians nowadays?" Based on a popular notion about politicians, the question relegates all political views to lies—without proof to the contrary.

More precisely, begging the question can be discovered in four forms:

THE CIRCULAR ARGUMENT (TAUTOLOGY). Communicators sometimes repeat premises, or restate them in different wording, as a devious method of avoiding the obligation of proof and support. The mother who demands that her adolescent son not stay out late with the statement, "Don't argue with me; it just isn't right, that's all," has committed the error of tautology. With no reasons, she has simply repeated her opinion about late hours in a different variation: "You shouldn't stay out so late. It just isn't right."

THE HIDDEN JUDGMENT. Another method of suggesting that an idea is true without proving that it is true is by means of the *hidden judgment.* The speaker uses this method by tinging his arguments with subtle coloring and innuendo. Hidden judgment can appear in a myriad of ways but the most familiar, and most frequently used, is the derogatory adjective. He might discredit a plan for social legislation by suggesting: "We should not accept this *unrealistic* idea for several reasons: 1, 2, and 3."

An uncritical listener may be unconsciously biased by such an adjective that has been slipped into the context of what appears to be a logical argument. The use, for example, of highly charged terms such as "communistic," "socialistic," "fascistic," and "capitalistic" are examples of implicit value judgments that may have little or no bearing on the contention. Many speakers are known to color their *own* point of view with words such as, "Let us consider some *objective* solutions."

THE SUGGESTIVE QUESTION. When the speaker seeks a positive response to a biased question, he has employed the suggestive question. The question itself is, in actuality, an assertion or conclusion. The speaker who asks, "Are you going to accept the lies of communists as proof of their desire for peace?" has told his audience that communists lie.

In the heat of political controversy, the suggestive question is often used to discredit the course of action prescribed by the opposition. Consider the question, "How can you guarantee that this program will not be extremely costly?" For one thing, it is difficult to *guarantee* anything; for another, the term "costly" can be applied to any financial amount. The classic example of the suggestive question is the lawyer who asks, "Have you stopped beating your wife?" The suggestion is that *you once did* beat your wife.

POISONING THE WELLS. Poisoning the wells is simply expressive terminology for another underhanded way of "sneaking in" an assumption. Through this technique, the communicator intentionally discredits the position of his opposition *before* it has been presented. A statement such as, "I suppose he will answer me with that old-fashioned nonsense about . . .", is typical of this fallacy. "I may not be as gifted a speaker as my opponent, but I am not so naive as to suggest, as I am sure he will, the business about . . ." is another example of this rhetorical trick. Let us assume that you are an advocate of a national health plan, and your opposition anticipates your plan, which he guesses will be under the auspices of the Social Security system. He states, "I suppose my friend will offer you what *sounds like* a practical plan to be set up under the Social Security." His innuendo in the form of words such as "suppose" and "sounds like" can weaken your position.

The Non Sequitur Fallacy

Literally translated, *non sequitur* means *it does not follow*. As a term of logic, it describes all those forms of reasoning in which there is no connection between assumption and fact, or between premise and conclusion. This fallacy is recognizable in the formal patterns of deductive, inductive, and causal reasoning, but the term is usually applied to those irrelevancies beyond the periphery of formal logic.

Consider the illogic of the following *non sequiturs*:

Example 1: The football team at X College is great; therefore, the school must be excellent.

Example 2: It's a beautiful day—surely it won't rain.

The *non sequitur* fallacy is identifiable in eight forms:

THE POST HOC FALLACY. The terms of the *post hoc* fallacy are derived from the Latin phrase, *post hoc ergo propter hoc,* which means *after this, therefore on account of this.* It occurs as a fallacy when one assumes that one event was the cause of another simply because the events followed one another in time. It is a fallacy because the time factor may be irrelevant to the argument. You might take an aspirin, for example, and feel better in one hour. You obviously assume that the aspirin was the reason, but it is also possible that rest, or some other factor, accounts for the better feelings. Herbert Hoover, for example, was blamed for the Great Depression because it followed shortly after he assumed the office of president. The reasons for the depression were complex, and you cannot blame Hoover solely.

The *post hoc* fallacy is usually the basis of myths such as voodoo. The pin is stuck into the head of a doll and a person dies shortly thereafter. The connection is at least questionable. There are many variations of the fallacy but it should be easily recognized. When it is clothed in sophisticated language, it can be deceptive.

THE FALLACY OF COMPOSITION. The fallacy of composition describes a form of reasoning which that that *what is true of the parts must also be true of the whole.* You might argue that because all ears in a crop of corn were good, the crop must have been good. Perhaps, but not necessarily. The crop may have yielded very few ears of corn. Consider some other examples:

Example 1:   The acting, lighting, staging, and directing of the play were excellent. The play must be excellent. (Perhaps it was poorly written.)

Example 2:   All the players on the team are excellent. The team must also be excellent. (As a team, they may not function at all.)

THE FALLACY OF DIVISION. The fallacy of division is the converse of the fallacy of composition. In other words, it assumes that *what is true of the whole is true of the parts.* Consider the reverse of example No. 2 above.

Example 1:   The team is a championship team. Therefore, all its members must be all-stars. (Several collegiate and professional teams have disproved this theory.)

Example 2:   The major network on Channel 12 is an excellent network. Therefore, all its programs must be excellent. (We know better.)

THE FALLACY OF ACCIDENT. Another common type of *non sequitur* is the fallacy of accident that suggests that *what is true in an unusual situation is also true in an ordinary situation.* A lie might be justifiably used to avoid causing a panic in an airplane. However, the situation, which may involve the collapse of a defective part, is unusual and is not a rationale for telling lies. Consider another example:

Citizens deserve the protection of the law. Jennifer should have received more protection. (Not if she is committing a criminal act.)

THE FALLACY OF EQUIVOCATION. A fifth *non sequitur* is known as the fallacy of equivocation. It occurs when it is assumed that *the meaning of a word applicable to one situation is similar to the same word used in a different situation.* Radical groups frequently use the following rationale for their actions: "Our forefathers revolted to throw off the tyranny of an oppressive government. We should, therefore, revolt to throw off the tyranny of an oppressive federal government." The two words are equivocated in the preceding statement: "tyranny" and "oppressive." In the first sense, "tyranny" and "oppressive" have militant connotation: the Revolutionary War. In the second sense, the words have different meanings that are derived from the political views of the radical groups. Notice also the equivocated meaning in the following sentence: "Marriage is a wonderful *institution,* but who wants to live in an *institution?*" Here, "institution" is used both as a conventional activity and as a physical place.

THE BLACK OR WHITE FALLACY. The black or white fallacy occurs when a communicator develops an argument by *dividing it into a choice between two extremes.* By asking the audience to choose between two extremes, the speaker excludes other options that listeners may have considered. In the 1950s it was common for speakers to use the following reasoning: "If we adopt this *social legislation,* we are promoting communism, and if we do not adopt it, we are preserving capitalism and the free enterprise system." Such a division is unwarranted because the mere passage of one form of social legislation does not mean the United States will be adopting communism *in toto.* The principle of the black or white fallacy is applicable to any type of division of a problem into extreme parts: good or bad, all or nothing, religious or sacriligious, expensive or cheap, and dishonest or honest. Is the following questioning unfair?

Question:	"Are you honest or dishonest?"
Answer:	"Honest."
Question:	"Have you ever lied?"
Answer:	"Yes."
Conclusion:	"You are dishonest."

THE FALLACY OF MISUSING THE MEAN. The opposite of the black or white fallacy is the fallacy of misusing the mean. Here the assumption is that any problem, whether it be complex or simple, can be reduced to an average or a central point between two extremes. You might argue, for example, that we should adopt socialism because it is half-way between the two extremes of democracy and communism. You attempt to decide the issue from logic and evidence, not mathematics.

Example 1:	The owner wants to give the workers $2.50 an hour, and the workers want $3.50 an hour. Therefore, they should get $3.00 an hour. *Note:* Perhaps, but not if the owner can afford considerably more, or if $3.00 will put him out of business.
Example 2:	Because one-half of country *A* is communistic and the other half is democratic, each half should have fifty representatives. *Note:* Such a deadlock might be disastrous for the country.

FALLACY OF REASONING FROM A CLICHÉ. Reasoning from a cliché is the process of applying a well-known saying, epigram, metaphor, or quotation to a premise or conclusion in an argument. Usually the saying is hackneyed, one that has been used countless times, and subsequently it is intended to lend an aura of truth to the argument. Clichés are rarely worth much and should be exposed as such. Consider the following:

Example: Still waters run deep; therefore, it is likely that quiet individuals are deep thinkers. (Perhaps they have nothing to say.)

Material Irrelevancies

All fallacies are fraudulent and irrelevant but some appear to be more irrelevant than others. The material irrelevancy is a form of transference that involves the process of making the audience consider an issue that is totally irrelevant to the one at hand. A *non sequitur* fallacy develops similarly; however, when one says that a team must be good because all its players are good (fallacy of composition), there is some *relevance*. Good players do equal good teams in many instances. A *material irrelevancy*, however, has no conceivable relevance to the conclusion. Various types of irrelevancies are:

THE ARGUMENTUM AD HOMINEM FALLACY. Translated, *argumentum ad hominem* means "argument to the man," or simply, "name calling." By discrediting the character of the man, the speaker expects to discredit his argument. Although such reasoning is flagrantly erroneous and unfair, it is used perhaps more frequently than any other fallacious rhetorical device. Some examples are:

Example 1:   How can we accept the word of union leaders? They are all criminals.

Example 2:   No wonder he supports abortion. He is insane.

THE FALLACY OF ARGUMENTUM AD POPULUM. A second type of material irrelevancy is *argumentum ad populum,* which literally translated means "argument to the people." This fallacy is committed by speakers who promote arguments based purely on the fact that "the people" are for it. Popularity is rarely the ultimate test of truth. Consider:

Example 1:   Grant was an excellent president. *Many people* voted for him.

Example 2:   *Everyone* said that the *Titanic* would not sink.

Essentially, we have discussed three basic types of fallacies: begging the question, *non sequitur,* and material irrelevancies. The list is not complete; fallacies appear in many forms and nuances. See what type of fallacies you can discover.

THE RATIONAL RESPONSE

Certain communication settings, especially those involving public debate, will allow for or promote responses by participants and listeners. The television editorial that usually allows time for a citizen's rebuttal is one example of the many opportunities that you may have to voice an opinion.

The levels of participation can range from asking a simple question to a highly developed and lengthy response. In either case, you will be employing all the devices of message analysis and construction that we have discussed in all previous chapters.

Organizing a Response

In addition to whatever organizational options you will choose, you need to consider several principles that will aid you in focusing and clarifying whatever lines of argument have developed. These methods include:

1. Restate the issue under consideration. If, for example, the opposing viewpoint contains several issues, you will need to state specifically the issue that you are about to challenge, or analyze.
2. Avoid distorting your adversary's position. It is both unfair and unethical to alter the meaning of the issue under consideration.
3. Consider stating the importance of the argument. Although many issues may have been presented, the entire position of your opposition may rest on one key point. If so, designate it as such.
4. Refute the argument. Use all the forms of message analysis and construction previously discussed.
5. Build your position. It is not enough simply to challenge an issue. You must build up your own point of view as well.
6. Consider the option of concluding with a restatement of your position and how it affects the validity of the opposing viewpoint.

Refutational Strategies

The following strategies are helpful in constructing an opposing viewpoint.

1. Turning the tables.
2. *Reductio ad absurdum.*
3. The dilemma.
4. Refutation by overwhelming counterproof.
5. The method of residues
6. Exposing irrelevant arguments.

Turning the Tables

An effective form of refutation is the technique of using the opponent's evidence to draw a completely opposite conclusion than was originally intended by him. Suppose, for example, an advocate were to say that a professional team ought to move to another city. He states: "On November 29, 1975, there were only 15,000 persons watching the game."

You could turn the tables if you responded: "That was good attendance considering the circumstances. On that day, there was a severe blizzard and very hazardous road conditions. Moreover, the subway system was not operating."

Or, suppose an advocate were to state that "New Hampshire should pass extensive welfare legislation because its welfare payments are the lowest in the nation." You could answer, "Yes, but New Hampshire has the lowest payments because its welfare problems are the lowest in the nation. Extensive legislation is not required."

The process of turning the tables can be extremely devastating and also enjoyable for the listener.

Reductio Ad Absurdum

A device similar to turning the tables is the process of reducing an argument to the absurd. Here the speaker must take a basic assumption of his opposition and extend it to the point of absurdity.

An advocate of national health insurance might maintain that only a small percentage of society is covered by any form of private health insurance plan. You could reply, "If you are suggesting that the government pass national health insurance legislation simply because people do not have private health insurance, then I assume you would suggest that the government also extend fire insurance, life insurance, and automobile insurance to all citizens."

The method is an effective device for exposing the absurdity of a basic premise, but it must be employed carefully. Its process is that of extending the assumptions of one argument to the assumptions of another, more extreme situation. In other words, the argument is similar to the analogy, that is, fire insurance compared to health insurance, or a painful arm compared to a terminal disease. As a form of analogy, it is subject to all the hazards of analogous reasoning.

The Dilemma

The purpose of the dilemma is to place the opposition in a situation in which he must select one of two alternatives, both of which are destructive to his basic position.

A classic dilemma that has been passed down from ancient rhetoricans involved a teacher of law and his pupil. The teacher accepted the pupil with the understanding that the pupil pay for his lessons when he had won his first case in court, but after the student had received his instruction he did not plead a case. This prompted the teacher to sue him. In court, the teacher presented the following dilemma:

> My pupil must pay me the tuition because he will win or lose his first case in court. If he wins, he must pay in order to fulfill our contract. If he loses, then he must pay because the court decides in my favor.

The student, however, retorted with an equally effective dilemma:

> I should not pay the tuition because if I win, then the court has decided in my favor. But if I lose, then I will not pay according to the terms of the contract.

Refutation by Overwhelming Counterproof

At times, the opposition may build an issue on a stack of statistical data, testimony, examples, and analogies. The task of examining all the forms of proof in order to construct an attack may be impossible. Moreover, if you attack the evidence of a case built on so much evidence, then it is likely that the opposition will merely pull out more proof. One of the best approaches to the issue built out of much evidence is to present overwhelming counterproof that will make dubious the conclusions of the issue.

The Method of Residues

In any form of oral discourse, the presentation or recognition of a need or problem requires a subsequent stand on a solution to that problem.

In analyzing a solution you might use the method of residues. The process involves reducing the situation to a specific number of solutions and then proceeding to eliminate all but one as a valid solution. Diagrammatically, such an analysis would appear as follows:

SOLUTIONS
A. Excluded. Not practical.
B. Excluded. Too expensive.
C. Excluded. Won't solve the problem.
D. Excluded. Will offend other interests or groups.
E. Accepted. Best solution to the problem.

The procedure is an effective one for establishing a strong case in your favor. It is usually employed *in anticipation* of what the opposition will say. At the turn of the century, the suffragettes in England were engaged in a bitter struggle for voting rights. The opposition to the militant suffragettes generally took the position that the women would attempt to win their rights by passive constitutional means. In public debates, the suffragettes anticipated that this would be the response of their opponents, and they outlined their refutation accordingly.

We have been attempting to win votes for women for over fifty years.

A. We have used petitions. It has failed.
B. We have lobbied in Parliament. That has failed.
C. We have used pressure at the polls. That was unsuccessful.
D. We have paraded in the streets. That was unsuccessful.
E. Now we are using destructive means, and it is acquiring the attention the movement needs.

The method of residues guides the listener into rejecting all but one of the possible solutions. As with all refutational strategies, the device also has a weakness. If your opponent is able to find *another* solution or is able to point out that one of the solutions has or can be effective, then he will be able to damage your point of view.

Exposing Irrelevant Arguments
Speakers frequently present more issues than they can prove. Anything that is unproven and irrelevant should be exposed as such. As a device of refutation, it can drain the vigor out of the opposition. Nothing is quite so effective as excluding an entire argument as an irrelevancy.

SUMMARY

Rational listening can be difficult. Many of us are trained to be either indifferent or critical listeners. Rational listening calls for the selection of the right option: discriminatory, evaluative, or appreciative listening. Listening skills can be improved by developing motivation, increasing concentration, empathizing with the speaker, minimizing personal biases, looking for central themes, and improving note taking.

Messages ought to be examined closely for truth and validity. The discovery of fallacies is one approach. You may choose, then, to respond. If so, be aware of the various response options available to you.

Review and Exercises

1. Analyze your own listening skills. Under what conditions do you listen most effectively? Under what conditions do you listen most ineffectively?
2. Observe an audience and write a profile of high and low listening points. What factors contributed to these differences?
3. Under what conditions should you shift from evaluative to appreciative listening?
4. From newspapers, television, and magazines collect samples of the fallacies discussed in this section.
5. State a position and then respond to it from the opposing side.

Additional Readings

Barker, Larry L., *Listening Behavior,* Prentice-Hall, Englewood Cliffs, N.J., 1971.

Fearnside, W. Ward, and Holther, William B., *Fallacy: The Counterfeit of Argument,* Prentice-Hall, Englewood Cliffs, N.J., 1959.

Nichols, Ralph, and Steven, Leonard A., *Are You Listening?,* McGraw Hill, New York, 1957.

Weaver, Carl H., *Human Listening: Process and Behavior,* Bobbs-Merrill, Indianapolis, 1972.

CHAPTER 11   THE RATIONAL DECISION

DECISION-MAKING: THE DEMOCRATIC SAFETY
VALVE
    Discussion: The Tool of Decision-Making
    The Purposes of Discussion
    Approaching the Discussion Process
    Format of the Discussion Process
PROBLEM-SOLVING: THE FUNCTION OF RATIONAL
DECISION-MAKING
    Step one: Recognizing the Problem
    Step two: Describing the Problem
    Step three: Considering the Various Solutions to the
        Problem
    Step four: Selecting the Best Solution to the Problem
    Step five: Acting Upon the Solution
THE FUNCTION OF LEADERSHIP
    The Topical Elements of Leadership
    The Interactional Elements of Leadership
PARTICIPATING AS A GROUP MEMBER
CRITERIA FOR EVALUATING GROUPS

CHAPTER 11 THE RATIONAL DECISION

DECISION-MAKING: THE DEMOCRATIC SAFETY VALVE

Where there is a need to resolve conflict and to explore problems as they affect two or more persons, there will be a need for the methodology of the decision-making process. In some cases, the process will be simple. When the subject grows in complexity—affecting, as it often does, many persons in many ways—the process will require full understanding of how and why persons can come to agreement on issues.

Information and persuasion, and all the tools that fall under both approaches, will be used during the decision-making, or discussion, process. Communication will have moved toward the level where the intent is to formulate a mood or message that is agreeable to the participating parties. You could, in fact, consider all the previously discussed communication approaches as a part of an evolutionary scale. Such a scale would place the formulation of an idea by the self as the first step in the processes of evaluation. The last step would be that point at which decision-making is located in the communicative process. Consider the various parts of this text:

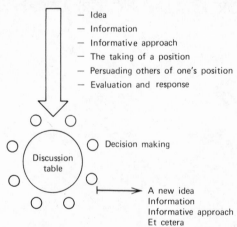

Each idea proceeds through the various levels of communication to the point where a decision is necessary—perhaps in the form of legislation. Decisions then generate new ideas that, when explored, again go through the various levels of communication.

This decision-making process is, therefore, a safety valve of democracy. Some persons hold strong and opposing viewpoints, but our culture has conditioned us to say that *sooner or later* those views will converge to produce a synthesis of all points of view. The steps by which this process occurs provide the subject matter of the following pages.

Discussion: The Tool of Decision-Making

Broadly defined, discussion is the interaction of ideas between two or more persons. In the context of this chapter, however, we will consider discussion as having specific characteristics and goals. The words that characterize the goals of good discussion are:

Agreement
Cooperative deliberation
Understanding
Satisfactory solutions
Exploration
Organization

It is these elements that make for the most productive discussion process. None of these terms, however, implies that free and open expression of positive and negative viewpoints is to be discouraged. Cooperation is an *ultimate goal.* It is the responsibility of each participant to seek out eventually, in spite of his opinions, levels of agreement.

The Purposes of Discussion

The purposes of two or more people gathering to discuss an idea can be for any one of three reasons.

There may be an *interactional reason* for the discussion. In other words, the people may be gathering simply to communicate with one another—to find out about one another's ideas, attitudes, and information. A conference may be held to reveal something about the people involved—to promote a better understanding of one another. This process is a first step in establishing a mood for later discussion on an issue. Conferences at the dinner table between diplomats serve an interactional function. The purpose is to "feel each other out" before harder, more substantive issues are discussed. Interactional

"*We deal with it by talking about it.*"

• • •

Drawing by Koren; Copyright © 1975 The New Yorker Magazine, Inc. Reprinted by permission of The New Yorker.

features of discussion, however, are not separate from a second purpose: the topical reasons.

There may be *topical reasons* for the discussion. The primary purpose is to explore the topic—to find out something about it. The discussion may begin and end with the sole function of bringing out into the open as much information about the topic as possible. Such discussions are generally held as a preliminary stage to another discussion at another time, or to present information so that the participants may draw their own conclusions and decisions from it. For example, the many facets of the energy problem and the methods of conserving energy could be initially explored with the intent that every member of the group should eventually contribute his own ideas at a later session. The intent may not be to come up with the ultimate solution but simply to generate thinking about the problem.

There may be *decisional reasons* for the discussion. In this case the ultimate objective is to come to some agreement concerning a policy or course of action. This solution may be put in writing, or it may be established merely as a common verbal agreement among the participants. Interactional and topical elements will, of course, be present in such discussions, but it is possible that the major considerations of interaction and topic will have been established before a particular communicative setting. The dominant thrust of the discussion will, therefore, be to work out the solution.

Approaching the Discussion Process

As you and other participants *enter* the discussion process, some awareness of attitudes *about* the discussion process should be reached. Certain predispositions about the function and purpose of the group can work positively or negatively to influence the proceedings and results of the interaction.

You should, for example, attempt to understand the point at which ideas are acceptable or not acceptable to either yourself or others. Where opinions are widely diverse, there will be greater need for time, exploration, interaction, and discussion. Discussion of deep-rooted values is likely to take place. There is likely to be considerable conflict between persons holding divergent views. Consider the following two scales pertinent to personality types and their attitudes on a topic:

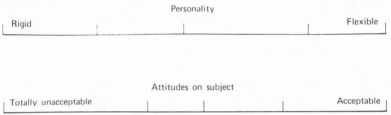

Depending on the results of your survey of yourself and the other participants, some preliminary exploration may be necessary—perhaps in the form of an interactional discussion on items not directly related to the topic.

You should also attempt to seek out the *levels of preparedness*. In Chapter 5 we discussed the importance of knowing the information. Persons often expect that in discussions ideas and information will flow freely without their having obtained background information. Unfortunately, lack of background information is an indicator of the fact that conflict will take place about unfamiliar facts. Solutions will be impossible because there will be little understanding of the actual ramifications of the problem. Consider the following four levels of preparedness and proceed to approach the discussion accordingly:

1. You are prepared, but the other participants are not.
2. You are not prepared, but the other participants are.
3. You are not prepared, nor are the other participants.
4. You are prepared, and the other participants are prepared.

The most productive discussion will take place among those in group 4; the least productive discussion will be among those in group 3.

Another consideration is the *level of commitment.* Many persons approach discussions thinking that they are fully prepared to discuss, agree, and act on the conclusions of the group, but the level of commitment is, in reality, quite low. Their good intentions may end prior to the policy-setting or action stage. For fruitful discussion to take place, it must be agreed that each participant is bringing into the discussion a healthy sense of commitment. Questions of commitment may be asked about group behavior as well. For example, how committed are the participants to cooperating with one another? How committed are they to allowing others to establish their positions with a full hearing?

Consider also the *levels of motives.* Each person has different reasons for belonging to, or joining a group. Some do so for acceptance only, with no real concern for the subject. There are those who join charity organizations, for example, only to associate with others—not to solve the problems of the charity. Others join groups to establish a power base. They think that the group will give them greater strength in dealing with others. Some persons bring the motive of manipulation into the group discussion. For the sake of personal profit or some other motive, they assume that they can bring a group—through various communicative devices—to their point of view. Their attitudes are characterized by manipulation rather than moderation and cooperation. In any of these instances—and there are many more—motives can play a large part in the direction that a discussion takes. Some understanding of these motives will establish clearer directions.

Finally, consider the *levels of structure.* Preconceived ideas about the actual structure and purposes of the group will influence people's attitudes about what is to transpire. The union negotiator, for example, will know that the bargaining table will be a battleground for victories or losses. His psychological approach, his levels of preparation, and many other variables will be affected by the setting and structure in which the discussion will take place. Three such structural considerations are:

1. Is the discussion to be formal or informal? Will participants be given certain time limits? Will they have to employ certain courtesies to get attention? Will they have to behave according to the dictates of the leader? Or will they be allowed to interact freely?

2. Is the discussion to be informational or controversial? Naturally, if the purpose of the discussion is to explore information, it is less likely to involve persuasion.

3. Is the setting likely to be confrontational or problem solving? Confrontational blocks are set up by persons thinking that one group belongs to a certain faction and the other belongs

to a different one. This subverts the problem-solving purposes of the discussion.

Format of the Discussion Process

The physical setting, including the arrangement of chairs either in relationship to the audience or the group itself, can influence the style of the discussion itself. Certain formats serve certain functions, and there are probably as many different formats as there are groups. Basically, there are a few illustration that indicate how a group can be set up.

The Informal Discussion Group

The informal discussion group, small in size, usually sits at one table. It is free to interact, or it may have a leader who structures the progress of the group. Three types are:

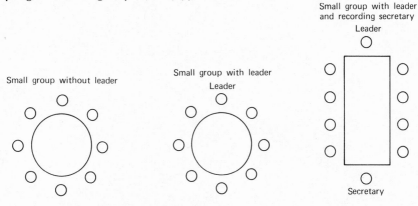

The Lecture Discussion Group

The lecture-discussion format usually has one main speaker and an audience. The format allows for discussion after the lecture and sometimes during it.

The Panel Symposium Group

The panel, or symposium, type discussion format occurs when a group of discussers sit before an audience. Each may be prepared with a certain side, or aspect, of the topic and be allowed to speak for a certain length of time. There is a moderator, and the audience is allowed to discuss or ask questions of the participants. Some varieties of this format are as follows:

Moderator

Audience

Moderator

Audience

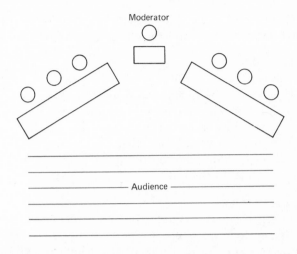

PROBLEM-SOLVING: THE FUNCTION OF RATIONAL DECISION-MAKING

Controversy may be a major or minor element of any group process. In either case it is a factor that, if not dealt with, will obstruct the decision-making process.

The elements of a pattern that may be used in part or *in toto* constitute what is called the *reflective thinking process*. Its essentials, developed by the American philosopher and educator, John Dewey, provide a method by which discussers can organize thoughts and opinions into a productive system for arriving at a decision. The system of reflective thinking presumes that the discussers, although they may hold differing views, will aim toward the selection of the most preferable option available to all representative viewpoints. The steps by which problems may be solved through *reflective thinking* are:

1. Recognizing the problem.
2. Describing the problem.
3. Considering the various solutions to the problem.
4. Selecting the best solution to the problem.
5. Acting on the solution.

Step One: Recognizing the Problem

The first step is to recognize the problem, to understand its implications and *initial* ramifications. The problem should be verbalized by the group in a form agreeable to each member. The territory of the topic has to be staked out. This process requires a few basic steps.

State the Problem

If the subject involves, for example, the problems of emergency medical care, it should be phrased in a question that sets the direction of the discussion and aims toward finding a solution. You might state: "What steps can be taken to improve the nation's system of emergency medical care?" Notice that the subject is phrased as a question so as to encourage open discussion rather than to establish positions for and against the topic.

Define the Problem

Certain terms can be vague. The result can be confused discussion of issues that were not properly defined. Avoid long and wordy discussions on the meaning of the topic by agreeing on its definition at the outset. In the topic above, you would have to define emergency care. Some questions of definition might involve:

Does emergency care include
ambulances?
out-patient departments?
Red Cross?
all safety agencies?
trauma research?
police departments?
fire departments?
all rescue organizations?
all emergency communication systems?
federal disaster area programs?

You can immediately see from the above questions that a seemingly limited topic can, without proper definition, expand into an extremely broad and potentially endless subject.

Limit the Problem

Closely connected with definition is limiting the problem. In effect, your definitions will limit your subject, but make certain that your topic does not allow for other topics to creep in. For example, it would be quite easy to enter into many other areas of medicine while discussing the subject of emergency medical care.

Thus, *step one* in the reflective thinking process is:

RECOGNIZING THE PROBLEM
State it.
Define it.
Limit it.

Step Two: Describing the Problem

The next step is to describe the problem by exploring it—putting all its aspects and implications on the table. This can be done in many ways, most of which we have discussed in previous chapters on evidence, the informative option, the persuasive option, and the logical option.

Some basic methods are:

Divide the problem into its major parts and discuss each part separately. Although you will ultimately interrelate all considerations of the topic in coming up with a solution, it is beneficial in terms of time and organization to deal with the problems associated with various sections of the topic. Consider how each participant could prepare a report on the following subdivisions of emergency medical care:

I.   Emergency vehicles—their problems
II. Emergency communications systems—their problems
III. Emergency agencies—their problems
IV. Emergency medicine—its problems

Second, examine all facts about each problem before coming to specific conclusions about each side. Ask the questions, "Have all the facts been explored?" "Do the facts describe the problem accurately." (Review the section on evidence.)

Third, examine the authoritative opinions on the problems. Explore how each authority came to his or her conclusions. Exclude biased viewpoints and those that are likely to add conjecture and guesswork to the discussion.

Fourth, explore the logical aspects of the problem. Look at the need areas, the advantages, and related problems. Does the evidence warrant the conclusions about the problem?

Fifth, consider the extent of the problem by looking at whom it affects, how much it costs, and the difficulties it presents to those who desire to do something about it and those who are already doing something about it.

Thus, *step two* in the reflective thinking process is:

DESCRIBING THE PROBLEM
    Divide it.
    Examine the facts.
    Look at the opinions.
    Explore the logic.
    Look at the extent of the problem.

Step Three: Considering the Various Solutions to the Problem

The next step is to consider what solutions, options, or combinations of solutions are available to solve the problem. Initially, it is best to explore the various solutions in the spirit of finding out how many possibilities there are. Consideration of various solutions may occur at several levels.

First, describe the solution. How does it work? Who can implement it? These are primary factors in describing what the actual solution does accomplish.

Second, discuss the advantages of each solution. Consider the full ramifications of how the solution will work to produce certain positive effects. Consider the following parallel solution to a problem:

Problem: Emergency Medical Care
Specific problem: The element of *time* in getting to the scene
                       of an accident.
Solution: Emergency helicopters will reduce the *time*.

Third, discuss the disadvantages of each solution. Examine the number of disadvantages and measure the extent and effect of each one. The above solution of helicopters, for example, might save on the time problem but create an additional safety hazard where air traffic is heavy in urban areas.

Fourth, discuss the cost of each solution. The cost of helicopters may be so exorbitant that monies will have to be taken from other social services. This may, in fact, reduce the quality of care in hospitals.

Fifth, discuss the practicality of each solution. An emergency helicopter system might possibly be too complicated, involving excessive administration for a problem that perhaps can be solved in other ways. It may be impractical at night when many serious accidents occur.

Thus, *step three* in the reflective thinking process is:

CONSIDERING THE VARIOUS SOLUTIONS TO THE
PROBLEM
    Describe the solution.
    Examine advantages.
    Examine disadvantages.
    Discuss the cost.
    Discuss the practicality.

Step Four: Selecting the Best Solution to the Problem

Finally, by the process of analysis and elimination, your group will seek out the best solution to the problem. This may be quite easy if the problem has been fully analyzed and each solution has been discussed at length. The result may be readily apparent. Some considerations are:

First, look at the solution that is comparatively better than all other solutions. Each solution may have its merits and demerits. It will be necessary to examine each comparatively—to see which is preferable, given all the considerations of each.

Second, consider which features of one solution may be combined with another to produce optimum results. Some solutions, however, are not easily combined, especially when their methods are totally different. If, for example, the problem involves the matter of facilitating transportation across a river in an urban area, the solutions might be: (1) a bridge or (2) a tunnel. A combination of the two would be incongruous and impractical.

Third, consider if there have been solutions to similar problems elsewhere and how they have worked. Remember that each solution you examine will be conjectural. That is, it will be based on the hypothetical assumption that it will work, given most circumstances. To choose which one is best, you can look at analogous solutions that have already been put into practice. Consider practicality, cost, and other aspects of that solution.

Thus, *step four* of the reflective thinking process is:

SELECTING THE BEST SOLUTION TO THE PROBLEM
Compare solutions with one another.
Consider combinations of solutions.
Look at similar solutions already in operation.

Step Five: Acting on the Solution

Having decided on the solution, you will next want to consider how this decision may be implemented. You may, first, want to put the decision through an experimental or trial run. However, in many cases this may not be possible.

Action will depend largely on the commitment of the group to implementing its decision. Whether or not persons outside the group will accept the decision is another consideration. This may have to be tested by the use of a poll. Another system may be to have the solution examined by outsiders, or authorities, to find out how well it will stand up to close scrutiny.

The most important feature of the action step is to make certain that your solution contains those practical and workable elements that your group will act on.

THE FUNCTION OF LEADERSHIP

Under most circumstances, some leadership is necessary to group decision making—even if it is only in the form of calling the group together. The purpose of leadership is to coordinate and guide rather than to dominate and direct. The ideal chairperson, or initiator, attempts to establish a harmony composed of democracy, productivity, and impartiality. The achievement of all three is believed often to be the product of "a born leader"—which is a questionable concept. Leadership can, in fact, be developed. The following options set forth methods by which you can lead in a group discussion. Or they can be used as principles by which you can make judgments about leadership qualities in others.

The traits and characteristics of leadership can cover a wide-ranging continuum from the extremely laissez faire and democratic leader to the outright dogmatic dictator.

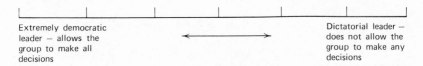

Extremely democratic leader — allows the group to make all decisions

Dictatorial leader — does not allow the group to make any decisions

By and large, our society is conditioned to seek out the person who is democratic—one who encourages all viewpoints but who also provides direction.

The measurement, or determination, of what style of leadership is most effective will depend on the circumstances of the discussion. You cannot formulate the ideal qualities of leadership in isolation from what the situation requires. During wartime, strong leadership is essential. In peace and during times of affluence, you have more time to reflect upon and discuss a wider range of options.

In an academic setting, where your discussions are likely to take place, two considerations have a great bearing on the type of leadership that is necessary: the subject and the participants.

Some subjects may need an instant solution. Or they may be so broad as to require much direction. In either case, leadership may have to be more direct and forceful than under other circumstances. Other subjects will be of such a nature as to divide opinions into very distinct and opposing camps. Under these circumstances, the leader will have to serve as a mediator—one who bridges the two camps by providing the way toward compromise and agreement. Finally, there will be those subjects that simply need to be explored—or aired out. The purpose will be to find out what people are thinking, or what it is about the subject that makes it important to the group. In this situation, a leader who questions and who takes a relatively passive role will usually be the most desirable person to have.

Participants will also determine the type of leadership that is essential. Some participants will be so boisterous or long-winded as to require considerable restraint. Others will have such deep-rooted biases as to call for a great deal of mediation explanation by the leader. Some members will not say much of anything. Leaders in this case will need to prod for responses, opinions, and interaction. Many groups will contain so many viewpoints and different types of personalities that a leader who is able to focus on the subject and direct attentions toward clear goals will be prized above others.

There will be many moments when the intangible qualities of tact and timing will determine the qualities of good leadership, but there are also obvious and acknowledged principles of effective leadership that can be set forth. Two categories of principles are presented below: (1) the topical elements of leadership, and (2) the interactional elements of leadership. The first applies to those things that must be done to explore fully the subject at hand. The second involves the dynamics of personalities as they function in the group setting.

The Topical Elements of Leadership

1. The leader should be prepared to start the discussion. By means of introductions, statement of goals, or giving some background about the topic, the leader can start the discussion by stating the actual topic. It may be the leader's function to define the topic and to introduce the participants to one another or to the audience, depending on what the situation requires.

2. The leader should be prepared to provide guidance with flexibility. An outline of the subtopics and various steps in the discussion will be useful. It may also be helpful for the leader to know the relative amount of time to be spent in each area. Urging the group members to stay within the boundaries of

the subtopics and the allocated time is usually essential to productive discussion.

3. The leader should know how to separate, balance, and develop fully each important aspect of the topic. Separation is essential so that subtopics can be seen clearly in their own context and with their own evidence. The quality of balance suggests that equal weight should be given to the main categories of the topic—especially if each is essential to the decision. Development of each area should be full; the leader must probe for information and opinions. Short discussion on major topics can produce shallow conclusions and decisions.

4. The leader should have a good understanding of the topic. To ask appropriate questions and to keep in check uninformed opinions, the leader will have to have knowledge of the topic. Facts, examples, and opinions will be helpful to the leader in setting the discussion on its right course.

5. The leader should be prepared to clarify and summarize the discussion. At various intervals, especially when the discussion has become cluttered with random statements, it will be essential for the leader to clarify the discussion by a summary and a restatement of goals. Through the use of a summary, the leader can synthesize the major areas of the subject matter and by doing so create a feeling of direction and accomplishment.

Interactional Elements of Leadership

Each discussion is dynamic, and its success will depend on how the leader adapts to the needs of the situation. The interaction of personalities and other factors will require the sensitive leader to step in at appropriate times to make the discussion an effective one. Some methods by which he can accomplish this are:

1. The effective leader should facilitate interaction. He or she must induce members to discuss their opinions with one another in a open and friendly atmosphere. By referring to "we" and not "I", the leader can promote an attitude of togetherness and group accomplishment.

2. The effective leader, although seeking out original and fresh viewpoints, must reinforce and emphasize those areas of agreement among the discussers. Areas of agreement are to be found in the intentions of participants although they may disagree on aspects of implementation.

3. Though disagreement is a part of any discussion process, it must be discouraged at the point where it begins to disrupt the flow of the reflective thinking process. Quibbles and especially conflicts among personalities can be reduced by shifts toward areas of agreement.

4. The effective leader must know how to stimulate perceptive and critical participation. Silent members should be encouraged to air their view. Talkative members should provide information, as well as opinions, to the discussion.

5. The effective leader should show patience with slow members of the group, allowing them to develop ideas.

6. Conversely, the effective leader should not allow dullness and boredom to set in. Questions that set the discussion moving in a more interesting direction might be necessary. Interruptions can be tactful if the question is drawn out of an area immediately relevant to the line of discussion.

7. The effective leader should be able to discourage apathy by relating the topic to the general interests of the group. Anecdotes, humor, illustrations, and stories may be used to set the group on an attentive and productive track.

8. The leader should know the balance between excessive formality and excessive informality. Of the two, informality is to be preferred, but if it results in interaction that is in no way germane to the intent of the discussion, it will be ultimately disruptive. Informal and friendly groups that have a sense of purpose are, generally, among the most productive.

PARTICIPATING AS A GROUP MEMBER

As a group member, you will be participating with the tools of communication thoroughly discussed in previous chapters. How you adhere to the topical purpose of the discussion and how you interact with other group members will depend largely on the attitudes that you bring into the group setting.

Perception of self plays an important part in how you relate to others in a group. Recall in Chapter 3 we talked about the various categories of self. Notice how each can have a bearing on your function in discussion:

Organizational self
Role-taking self
Information-filtering and information-processing self

Self-disclosing self
Linguistic self
Biased self
Attitudinal self
Social self
Script using self
Ritual self

Let us discuss each briefly *as it relates* directly to the group discussion process.

As an *organizational self,* you must facilitate the productivity of the group by keeping the goals clear and the discussion orderly. Aid the leader and other members in segmenting and developing important parts of the topics.

As a *role-taking self,* you must be aware of any roles that you assume that can either obstruct or be productive to the group process. You should not take an intellectual role in a nonintellectual setting (you would hardly want to use a polysyllabic and pompous vocabulary while discussing the subject of alcoholic refreshments at athletic events). Be perceptive of your roles—make sure they fit the situation. Are you being a sexist among women liberationists? If so, your discussion is not likely to be productive.

As an *information-filtering and information-processing self,* you must acknowledge your responsibility to the discussion process by having accurate, perceptive, and useful information. In short, you should be prepared. Whatever information you possess should be filtered for *pertinence* to the particular subject under discussion. Adapt what you know to the situation. Discard the irrelevant.

As a *self-disclosing self,* you should not be overly inhibited about telling the truth about yourself. Confidence and trust can be built up among other members of the group if you are willing to let facts be known about your experiences. Although certain groups are put together for therapeutic purposes, you need not approach each discussion as an opportunity for self-confession. Disclosure is useful in letting persons know about you because it may relate to the subject or group. Many members will not be interested in confessions about your past—especially if it is irrelevant to the topic.

As a *linguistic self,* you must be aware of the fact that you may use words that have different meanings to others. Make sure to qualify yourself—define when necessary—so that confusion may be held to a minimum. Keep in mind that others may also be using terminology that has different meaning in their own linguistic background.

As a *biased self,* you must be prepared to understand how your background and experiences will color your attitudes on given subjects. When bias is obstinate or takes on the characteristics of prejudice, then it is particularly destructive to the group process, and it can be subtly destructive if it alters any facts that may be pertinent to decision making.

As an *attitudinal self,* you should survey your feelings about related subjects prior to entering a discussion. If, for example, your attitudes about abortion are so strong that they are unmovable, you may wish to make this fact known prior to the discussion.

As a *social self,* you ought to be aware of the fact that by what you say you will manipulate the feelings of others, just as they will influence you. You are in a social setting and, therefore, you will have to realize that communication is two-way. You will need to listen and accept the opinions of others if you expect the reverse to occur.

As a *script-using self,* you must be aware of the fact that you may have already written an agenda in your own mind of what you expect to happen within the group. That is to say, your own attitudes toward the subject and the group may be preplanned in your own mind. Be prepared to allow for flexibility. The group itself may set forth a script, such as the reflective thinking process, which it will be useful in producing desired results.

As a *ritualistic self,* you must be aware that certain physical motions and social courtesies can signal ideas to others. Even pencil tapping can be a form of ritual; it may convey arrogance or pseudo-intellectualism. Politeness and respect are a form of ritual, and as such are quite useful in the discussion process. If, however, they are carried to the point of formalism, the atmosphere may become stiff. Members may become self-conscious as a result.

Thus we see that in addition to all the elements of message construction there are certain behavioral factors that will influence and determine the progress of the group. How you function will determine your effectiveness.

In an article entitled "A Survey of Small Group Activities Used in Beginning Speech Courses," Judith Runkle listed the following criteria for evaluating groups:[1]

CRITERIA FOR EVALUATING GROUPS

Quality of Contributions
Research
Accomplishing the Task
Organization, Structure of Presentation

Effectiveness of Presentation
Quantity of Presentation
Analysis, Reasoning
Knowledge and Involvement in Subject
Creativity
Group Effort
Listening
Preparation Participation
Knowledge of Group Processes
Communication Skills
Cooperation, Ethical Conduct
Leadership
Interaction
Group and Individual Presentation

SUMMARY

Discussion may have an interactional, topical, or decisional purpose. Preliminary analysis should consider levels of acceptability, preparedness, commitment, motives, and structure. The options for format include informal, lecture-discussion, panel, and symposium.

Problem solving can follow the steps of reflective thinking: recognize the problem, describe the problem, explore various solutions, select the best solution, act on the selected solution.

Your leadership style may range from the relaxed "let-things-be" approach to a dictatorial style. Know the hazards of both. Circumstances such as group size, time, and purpose will determine leadership style. Your tasks may include starting, guiding, developing, clarifying, and summarizing the meeting. The sensitive leader will be aware of the human relations needs of the members. He or she will balance discussion, giving opportunity to all. He or she will stimulate members, minimize disruptions, obtain accord from conflict, and promote thinking.

As a group member, you need to consider the attitudes that you bring to the discussion. Reconsider your various self roles so that they are productive and coordinated with the group effort.

Review and Exercises

1. List ten different groups with whom you have had contact. Describe their differences.

2. Attend a meeting of a group and report on its discussion patterns.
3. Compare an effective group with an ineffective one. Discuss why they appeared to be effective or ineffective.
4. Plan an agenda for a specific discussion topic, using the pattern of the reflective thinking process.
5. Evaluate your group role. Compare it with that of one other person.
6. Evaluate the leadership of a meeting that you have attended. Was the leadership effective or ineffective? Why?

Additional Readings

Bales, Robert, *Interaction Process Analysis,* Addison-Wesley, Reading, Mass., 1950.

Barker, Larry L., Cegala, Donald J., Kibler, Robert J., and Wahlers, Kathy J., *Small Group Communication,* Allyn and Bacon, Boston, 1974.

Maier, Norman R. F., *Problem Solving and Creativity in Individuals and in Groups,* Brooks/Cole, Belmont, Calif., 1970.

Patton, Bobby R., and Giffin, Kim, *Problem-Solving Group Interaction,* Harper and Row, New York, 1973.

Phillips, Gerald M., *Communication and the Small Group,* second edition, Bobbs-Merrill, Indianapolis, 1972.

Rosenfeld, Lawrence B., *Human Interaction in the Small Group Setting,* Charles E. Merrill, Columbus, Ohio, 1973.

Shaw, Marvin E., *Group Dynamics: The Psychology of Small Group Behavior,* McGraw-Hill, New York, 1971.

Footnotes

[1] Judith A. Runkle, "A Survey of Small Group Activities Used in Beginning Speech Courses," *Today's Speech,* **22,** No. 4 (Fall 1974), pp. 25–30.

CHAPTER 12 RATIONALITY THROUGH LANGUAGE

CHAPTER 12 RATIONALITY THROUGH LANGUAGE

We select words and phrases to explain and represent our ideas. The extent to which they accurately or inaccurately describe our thoughts determines our influence on others. Hastily chosen words will present vague, emotionally charged, confused, and weak concepts. Inaccurate impressions of what you are *really* thinking may result. That is why language choice is a most important element in creating the rational message.

You should consider the study of language as an on-going process. It can be improved by reading, by recognizing exciting expressions when you hear them, and by thinking of new ways of expressing yourself.

To suggest that rationality is obtained through language in *no way* implies that one type of language is rational and another is irrational. Words and meaning are determined by their context and their users. Even the most prejudicial expression can suggest rationality if used in an appropriate context. It is our contention, however, that the general principles of effective language usage can establish clear, rational, and convincing thoughts. The mere fact that you can choose to say "pigs" instead of "police" gives you an option. If you are cognizant of your choice, and if you find one expression preferable to the other, it is our suggestion that you have some control of your language. If your choice is "pigs," chances are that you will explain your meaning. In short, the application of the principles of language structure creates a rational mode of communication.

To obtain a perspective on the uses and meaning of language, we will discuss it from three perspectives:
  □ Language as a System
  □ The Function of Language
  □ The Effective Use of Language

LANGUAGE AS A SYSTEM

Language is extremely complex, and the factors that influence the meaning of words are incalculable. Nevertheless, if you understand that language is a dynamic entity—one that shifts with time and place—you can begin to understand how it functions and how it is used. You can begin to see how to use it rather than being a slave to it. Some definition of language should be attempted, and perhaps from this you can begin to understand its usage. The linguist, Archibald A. Hill, claims that language has five defining characteristics.[1] We have interpreted each characteristic as it may apply to the construction of a message for a communication setting. Some of the premises are debatable, but they do provide a perspective of language as a definable system.

The first characteristic is that language is a set of sounds. The extent to which you can manipulate sounds to create meanings will be the subject of another section. Keep in mind that the way in which you use sounds establishes your uniqueness as a communicator.

Second, the connection between sounds, or sequences of sounds, and objects in the outside world is arbitrary and unpredictable. In most cases the sound does not match the thing it represents. A building, for example, does not give off the sound "building." To be sure, there are words that sound like the thing they represent, but these words represent only a small percentage of our vocabulary. The "bow-wow" of a dog, for example, is expressed differently in other languages.

Third, language is systematic. In other words, there are certain patterns and designs in language. When a sentence is incomplete such as, "I went to the . . . ," we expect an explanation. Moreover, things are classified in our language according to tense, subject matter, and quantities. Manipulation of any of these systems by the communicator can greatly influence the meaning he or she wishes to present.

Fourth, language is a set of symbols. Language presents symbols to the sender and receiver, both of whom have their own interpretation of the symbol. The symbol has meaning in a special unique way to each person. The term "spaghetti" can have a visual and olfactory meaning to each person.

Fifth, language is complete. This does not mean that human beings have a word for everything but that they are capable of describing whatever phenomenon presents itself. Language is open-ended so that human beings can create new words to express new phenomena. This suggests to the communicator that he need not say, "I don't know how to describe it." You are in control of your language, and it is so designed that you may describe whatever it is that you wish.

Defined in this way, language can be seen as a product of civilizations that have created common symbols that allow their members to transact with one another. How languages have grown to be what they are is the subject matter of the fascinating study of linguistics. An in-depth study of linguistics here does not serve our immediate purpose, but it is an interesting area of exploration.

THE FUNCTION OF LANGUAGE

The purpose of language is to attach symbols to ideas, persons, places, and things. It is a method of restructuring reality, without actually *being* reality. According to S. I. Hayakawa, in his book *Language in Thought and Action,* it functions to: persuade and control behavior, transmit information, create and express social cohesion, and generate poetry and imagination.[2]

It is important to examine language from the stand-point of its being, as has been said, a set of *symbols.*

The Symbol is Not the Thing

Those who have studied the uses of language often refer to Alfred Korzybski's concept: The map is not the territory.[3] Essentially this means that a symbol is only a symbol and not the thing itself. Meanings are in people.

By assigning certain meanings to concepts we create our own verbal world. The use of the words "mama" or "daddy" will draw up particular feelings and emotions. In the process of making such designations, the child begins to realize that the term "mama" applies to most women with children. At this point, he or she begins to generalize. The learning process teaches the child how specific cases fit into larger groups and classes. He can then classify and differentiate ideas.

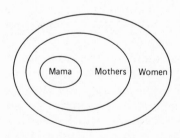

A process of abstraction is developing. As the class gets broader, the concept becomes more abstract. Ideas become fuzzier and more confusing. Notice how, in the following conversation, people can be victimized by the process of generalization and abstraction:

Daughter: Look at the birds.
Mother: Those are sea gulls.
Daughter: (somewhat puzzled) They look like birds.

Meaning and Attitude

The meanings of words are learned in context and from experiences. If you are always exposed to a specific symbol in a pleasant situation, you will remember it pleasantly. Cool swims in a lovely lake will produce nice connotations for the word "lake." But a brother who has pinched you, hit you, and abused you may very well produce an unpleasant reaction—in your nervous system—to the word "brother."

If you consider your own attitude toward certain events, for example, trips to dentist or visits to playgrounds, you will find that those experiences, pleasant or unpleasant, attached themselves to the label called "dentist" or "playground."

This pattern of attachment can be visualized in the famous Pavlovian studies. You can see a similar pattern built into your own neuroanatomy by the association of words with experiences.

```
Sound of Bell plus Food  = Salivating Dogs
    ''              ''    = ''          ''
    ''              ''    = ''          ''
Sound of Bell alone      = Salivating Dogs
```

Take this brief attitude test and see how this association pattern works for you:

Word	Pleasant	Neutral	Unpleasant
Establishment			
Security			
Freedom			
Hawaii			
School			

Several concepts can be drawn about symbols as they relate to meanings:

1. Meanings are the product of experiences.
2. Meanings change as the result of new experiences.
3. Meanings are different for different people.
4. Meanings are determined by attitudes.
5. Meanings are always changing.

Extensionality

Because meanings are a product of an ever-changing and dynamic world, the general semanticists as influenced by Korzybski, have created certain devices that are applicable to language as it changes. They are methods by which you may refine the use of your language and thereby contain it within identifiable areas. Because they both define and also adjust to the changing world of language, they are called "flexible extensional orientation" devices.[1]

Et Cetera

The concept of Et Cetera is a way of acknowledging that no statement can represent all the real world and that in spite of comprehensive knowledge about a subject, there will always be something else or something new to consider. It is a way of indicating to you that you should be flexible, be prepared to be flexible, and be prepared to adapt to things received by feedback or other unique features of a given communicative situation.

Dating

Dating is a way of acknowledging that because the real world changes with time so does language. Many communicators tend to ignore references to time changes and how, conceivably, it can change the nature of their ideas and referents. Lake Erie today is not the Lake Erie of 1900; pollution has changed both its image and physical composition. As you develop the rational idea, therefore, it is important to keep in mind the influences of time.

Hyphen

Your uses of language can suggest that things can be understood only in terms of specific categories. This may, however, limit your meanings. It is commonly called the fallacy of black and white—or seeing things only one way or another. The concept of the hyphen allows you the option of combining things to create new meanings and new identities. The use of the term "the military-industrial complex" is one example of how two concepts were merged to produce one. Similarly, expressions such as "liberal-Republican," "conservative-Democrat," and "socio-economic" are terms that imply more than if one or the other had been used.

Quotation Marks

You should remember that a particular idea or statement can be contained within quotation marks. This extensional device is a way of indicating that the statement is still questionable, or that it cannot be taken to be the absolute truth. Once the listener begins to work the words of the communicator into his own belief system, it is wise for him to keep in mind that certain ideas are "in quotes"—holding, therefore, that idea in limbo until it is further proven. The quotation marks concept is an excellent example of a rational extensional device—one that can keep things at a distance. Literary critic Susan Sontag defines things that are camp as those that we can put quotation marks around.[5] Lawrence Welk "music," for example, is that which we can consider "camp."

Indexing

The device of indexing recognizes the multiplicity and dissimilarity of things in the world. All snowflakes, blades of grass, and ants are different under amplification. Even standard models of automobiles take on their own distinct personalities according to bumps and nicks; some are "lemons," others are not. Indexing serves as a reminder that items, articles, people, ideas, and anything else are different and should be acknowledged as such. Basically, indexing encourages us to employ words which define the uniqueness of ideas and things. Apples are "red" or "green"—perhaps both. Some politicians are corrupt; others are not. Any tendency to index all things in one category as having identical characteristic creates problems in language. All modern art, for example, is not abstract.

THE EFFECTIVE USE OF LANGUAGE

Finally, there are qualities of language usage for which you should constantly be aiming. Some of them can be best understood by a comparison between speaking and writing.

Speaking versus Writing

Both speaking and writing are methods of presenting ideas and use the same language. However, there are some features you must consider when using one channel versus the other.

Consider, first, that one is oral and the other visual. Using written media means that the receiver can control the speed at which the material is presented. Second, he can control his length of attention. He can read for a while, stop, and pick it up again. Third, he can reread if he wishes. As he says to himself, "I don't understand that," he can go back over that section again or reread it at another time. The reader can take time out to check an unfamiliar word in a dictionary. He can generally pick out the surroundings for his reading task. He may be comfortable, alone, have soft music for a background, and so forth.

And finally, the reader has generally learned the features of written highlighting and punctuation systems. He recognizes a question by a question mark. He recognizes an exclamation by an exclamation mark. He recognizes emphasis by underlining or italics. The code system is fairly well understood by the reader. The communicator selecting the written format has time to select, to try out, to rewrite. He can put it away for a while, then reread it with a fresh viewpoint.

Consider now oral style. Here we find that the style *must be instantaneously clear.* This forces the effective speaker to unclutter and simplify his ideas. The speaker must preplan the response of his receivers and make adaptations in this dimension. In the written style the writer has no way of knowing just who his readers are. In the oral presentation the speaker may elect to use visual aids as a supplement to his oral style. Slides, blackboards, charts, models, and so on may be used to help the listener to understand and accept. The speaker may use both audio and visual channels.

Second, the oral style allows the transmitter to use both vocal and physical reinforcement systems. He can highlight ideas by vocal change or physical emphasis.

Third, the speaker can make maximum use of feedback. The listeners will send messages of acceptance or rejection, confusion, understanding, or approval. The effective transmitter will make adaptation to these messages from his receiver units. He may decide to define terms, to add additional examples, to rephrase or repeat.

Fourth, the speaker can give the listeners clues to the response he wants by his own transmission. He can give visible clues of acceptance by nodding his head in agreement as he asks, "Is this what we want?" and then answers "Yes, it is!" He can indicate rejection of ideas by physical reinforcement. He can communicate warmth by his tone of voice. He has a greater range of tools and more flexibility in their use than the writer.

Clarity

The theme that has been developed throughout this text is that there is no communicative virtue greater than clarity. Clear propositions, clear information, and clear logic all contribute to the construction of a rational message.

Also consider clarity from the point of view of language as well. The extent to which you accurately represent the content of your ideas will play a significant part in your effectiveness as a communicator. Four principles should serve as sufficient reminders of the main goals of clarity:

Be specific and concrete.
Avoid overly technical usage—strive for simplicity.
Understand your referents.
Define when necessary.

Be Specific and Concrete

The qualities of being specific and concrete are achieved by one simple principle: explain ideas with understandable information.

There are, as we have explained before, levels of abstraction. Concepts such as freedom and patriotism are among the most abstract. For your message to be specific, you need to explain abstract terms with real incidents.

Abstract	to	Specific
Freedom	to	smoke
Freedom	to	leave the country
Freedom	to	insult your boss
Freedom	to	march in a protest
Freedom	to	drive

Be as specific as possible! If you are talking about the "poor" quality of physical education in America (abstract), talk about it as it exists in the *specific* area of women's sports, for example.

Avoid Overly Technical Usage; Strive for Simplicity

The inclination to impress with the usage of big words is sometimes great. It may seem intellectual to dress up your message in impressive terms. The effect is usually the reverse: Either your audience will think of your language as artificial or they will simply not understand you. Consider how the following terms can be converted into simple ones:

Hagiolatry	the worship of saints
Paralogism	a fallacy
Poniard	a dagger
Somnambulism	sleepwalking
Escritoire	a desk

Understand Your Referents

By referents we mean the term that refers to certain things or concepts. A misunderstanding of the meaning that your referents can have to different persons can undermine the purposes and effects of your communication. A word symbol can change drastically in meaning. Consider the following:

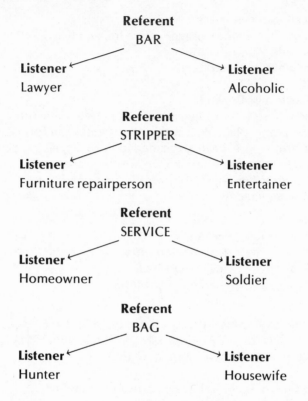

Referent
BAR

Listener
Lawyer

Listener
Alcoholic

Referent
STRIPPER

Listener
Furniture repairperson

Listener
Entertainer

Referent
SERVICE

Listener
Homeowner

Listener
Soldier

Referent
BAG

Listener
Hunter

Listener
Housewife

Define When Necessary

Some concepts even in their simplest terms may still be confusing. Use definitions to clarify the concept or thing that you wish to identify. Four techniques of definition are:

Negation. The process of saying what a thing *is not.*
EXAMPLE: By "military assistance" I do not mean the supplying of troops.

Illustration. The use of an example to clarify your meaning.
EXAMPLE: By "water pollution" I mean the dumping of refuse and garbage into the Platte River.

Synonym. The use of a similar word.
EXAMPLE: By "rising" I mean moving upward.

Analogy. The process of comparison.
EXAMPLE: The Gross National Product is an economic indi-

cator. Just as a light flashed when your generator is not working in your car, a falling GNP can indicate the lack of productivity in our economy.

Appropriateness

Of critical importance in language choice is the consideration of appropriateness. Trite expressions such as "early to bed, early to rise, make a man healthy, wealthy, and wise" are rarely appropriate. Be careful also of slang that is offensive or in poor taste.

The important question is "Does the language fit the listener, the situation, the message, and the speaker?" We have all seen mismatched styles and messages. Generally the effect is comical: The formally dressed minister who speaks with slang is one example.

Certain college classes establish a friendly and open atmosphere, whereas others are more formal. It is necessary to change your language accordingly. This is something that you can judge only with regard to the situation.

The Coloring of Language

Words frequently have positive or negative emotional connotations. For example, words used to describe the condition of a person who is overweight may be favorable or unfavorable. "Overweight" may be a neutral term used by the medical profession to describe a person who weighs more than he should according to ideal weight charts for his weight and body frame. If you want to attach negative connotations to that condition, you might use the words "fatty", "bloated" "huge", and so on. On the other hand, you might wish to describe the overweight condition with more favorable emotional connotations. Then you might describe or label the condition as "plump" and "huggable."

In the following list there are student choices for emotionally charged words. See if you agree with their choices. Certainly there is room for disagreement, for each of us has had somewhat different language experiences that have shaped our attitudes about words.

WORDS	NEGATIVE	POSITIVE
Coward	Yellow	Scared
Miser	Skinflint	Frugal
Vagabond	Tramp	Hobo
Dwelling	Shack	Palace

WORDS	NEGATIVE	POSITIVE
Automobile	Hot Rod	Car
Male	Peasant	Nobleman
Child	Brat	Angel
Liquor	Booze	Cocktail
Dress	Rag	Gown
Short	Dumpy	Small
Politician	Boss	Statesman
Religious	Fanatic	Pious
Upset	Irked	Concerned
Unkempt	Filthy	Neglected
Ambitious	Double Dealing	Hard Working
Look	Spy	Gaze
Nice	Pleasant	Delightful
Take	Grab	Clasp
Save	Stash	Treasure
Strange	Grotesque	Unusual
Eat	Gulp	Dine

Notice also how word choices create images. The meaning of the following information changes according to the alteration of the verb.

Charles University 29, Elwood College 6
Charles University defeats Elwood College 29–6
Charles University upsets Elwood College 29–6
Charles University smashes Elwood College 29–6
Charles University routs Elwood College 29–6
Charles University conquers Elwood College 29–6
Charles University whips Elwood College 29–6
Charles University victorious–29—Elwood College–6
Charles University overpowers Elwood College 29–6
Charles University drubs Elwood College 29–6

SUMMARY

Language is a symbolic system. It is the cohesive element in civilization because it enables people to communicate about reality and nonreality. To prevent potential communication breakdowns you must understand that language is a changing rather than a fixed system.

Words are only representative of things. The word is not the thing; the map is not the territory. Meanings are determined by experiences and attitudes. Because no two people have had identical experiences, each person's meaning is different from another's.

Oral communication must be instantaneously clear. We can provide different meanings and color to our language by understanding which option is most appropriate to the style of our message and the occasion in which it functions.

Review and Exercises

1. Select an article from a newspaper and condense it to half its normal length without losing the main point of the article.
2. Write out a list of words that represent a positive and negative aspect of the same concept. For example, an argument could be a *fight* (negative) or an *encounter* (positive).
3. List some words that may be used to describe different styles of walking (for example, ambling).
4. Write an introduction to a speech that is vague and pompous. Improve it with clarity and excitement.
5. Using the same topic and subject matter, write a speech in two different styles for two different audiences.

Additional Readings

Brown, Roger, *Words and Things: An Introduction to Language,* Free Press, New York, 1958.

Chomsky, Noam, *Language and Mind,* Harcourt Brace Jovanovich, New York, 1968.

Condon, John C., *Semantics and Communication,* Macmillan, New York, 1966.

Duncan, Hugh D., *Symbols in Society,* Oxford University Press, New York, 1968.

Miller, George A., editor, *Communication, Language, and Meaning,* Basic Books, New York, 1973.

Sapir, Edward, *Culture, Language and Personality,* University of California Press, Berkeley, 1961.

Wiseman, Gordon, and Barker, Larry, *Speech—Interpersonal Communication,* Chandler, San Francisco, 1967.

Footnotes

[1] Archibald A. Hill, *Introduction to Linguistic Structures* (New York: Harcourt, Brace and World, 1958), pp. 3–9.

[2] S. I. Hayakawa, *Language in Thought and Action,* second edition (New York: Harcourt, Brace and World, 1964), p. vii.

[3] Alfred Korzybski, *Science and Sanity,* fourth edition (Lakeville, Conn.: Institute of General Semantics, 1958).

[4] Korzybski, *Science and Sanity,* pp. 1–18.

[5] Susan Sontag, *Against Interpretation and Other Essays* (New York: Dell Publishing Co., Inc., 1969), pp. 277–293.

CHAPTER 13 IMPROVING THE COMMUNICATIVE ACT

243

CHAPTER 13 IMPROVING THE COMMUNICATIVE ACT

Every communicator is a performer. He or she is the focus of attention, the conveyer of information, and a source that is to be believed or not believed.

Considering that under many circumstances you will be at the center of the communicative act, it is necessary for you to pay some attention to those communication elements that establish a style of presentation uniquely your own. Each person draws on certain traits and personality characteristics in communicating with others. These factors establish your identity, as we have discussed in the section on self. However, in approaching the podium, many speakers allow other characteristics not typical of their everyday personality to dominate. Because the situation is different, their speech becomes different.

In the following section we suggest that you seek out your strengths. Learn to recognize and develop them. Likewise, seek out your weaknesses and discard them. This process is often merely one of identifying those characteristics that accompany your presentation of the message.

To establish you as a communicator who is unique and confident, we will examine the presentational options available to you: namely, the styles of presentation, your confidence and preparation, and the elements of communicative behavior.

STYLES OF PRESENTATION

In each communication situation, you will find certain styles of presentation best suited to you, the audience, and the topic. These styles may be imposed on you by the situation, or they may be ones that you have selected as best suiting your communication personality. Consider each style from either point of view, understanding fully its characteristics and usefulness.

Impromptu

Impromptu speaking occurs when you are placed in a situation that calls for a message that has not, necessarily, been structured for delivery at that moment. Conceivably, you will have the benefit of some background and information on the topic. If you do not, you may be presented with the opportunity to explore some of your initial attitudes and concepts on the subject.

One of the first considerations that should help you to improve and establish your mode as an impromptu speaker is, "Maintain a sense of control." Before commencing with your remarks, take a second or two to decide how to establish a communicative pattern. A quick start may get you going in rhetorical circles without a point of focus. The result may be the characteristics of a bumbling, fumbling, inept, and rambling speaker. If possible, think of what your *conclusion* will be—everything else should work in that direction.

You can train yourself to use that split-second time frame before you begin to select some options. You can decide, for example, whether your speech will take an informative or persuasive turn. If your option is informative, you can then decide whether your information will be positive or negative. You can then follow with explanation, illustration, comparisons, and hypothetical examples. Draw on those personal examples that are most familiar; by doing so, you will establish confidence. Similarly, if your stand is persuasive, then you need to establish a positive or negative stand. Your systems of development and support will be similar.

Consider how this approach might work in a message that involves the presentation of a single point. Consider the possibility of being confronted with a topic involving the conservation of gasoline. Allow your concept to work itself out according to the options established above, keeping in mind an opening appropriate to your point of view. Consider the following pattern:

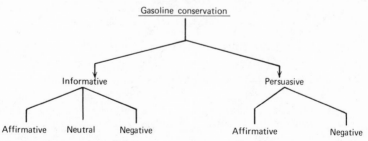

Possible opening statements:

Informative-affirmative: The development of the electric car offers some interesting possibilities.

Informative-neutral: There is uncertain information and research on both sides.

Informative-negative: The electric car will not be available for many years.

Persuasive-affirmative: We should all take steps to conserve gasoline.

Persuasive-negative: There is no way to save gasoline with voluntary systems. The government is going to have to do something.

The selection of a clear point of view will establish the direction on which the remainder of your message can hinge. Be careful, however, of timing. Do not overexpand. If an impromptu message is not choppy or too short, it is often rambling and too long. Maintain your message within a foreseeable structure: Those organizational structures mentioned in previous chapters are useful.

Consider the following guide for constructing your impromptu message:

1. Consider your goal—your point of view.
2. Make an opening statement that sets the tone and stand for your message.
3. Amplify your speech with appropriate supporting materials. Allow personal memories and examples to establish your fluency for you.
4. Close with a restatement of your opening position.

One final guide:

> *K* eep
> *I* t
>   *S* hort and
>   *S* imple

Manuscript

A style quite opposed to the impromptu approach is one that involves the use of a manuscript. By means of the manuscript, you commit to paper your exact wording, position, organization, and supporting information. This format has the advantage of developing your contentions in precise language. Politicians, who are sensitive to public opinion and the possibilities of being misquoted, rely heavily on the manuscript. Your concern for accuracy and precision might force you to do the same. The possibility of mistakes is slight unless, of course, you are prone to digress from your manuscript.

Another advantage of the manuscript is your ability to work on exact timing. Certain situations call for strict time limits—especially public forums and debates. Radio and television place similar restrictions on the speaker. At one medical conference, a directive was sent to all participating speakers that said: "At the end of five minutes your microphone will be disconnected." Those who save their juiciest point for last may find directives such as these disheartening. A manuscript allows you to plan.

In preparing the manuscript, you should appreciate the fact that people will be *listening to,* not reading, the comments. Your presentation style, therefore, should be *oral.* Recall the differences listed in the section on speaking versus written style. Avoid long, complicated sentences. Use direct and personal references to the audience. Use repetition frequently yet with tact; don't be too simplistic and condescending. In general, you should work for a style that is full of life. Avoid the stiff essay style.

The usual approach to the reading of a manuscript is one of unconcern—they are often dull, mechanical, and uninteresting. This need not be *your* pattern, however. With some preparation and some rehearsal time, you can easily eliminate some of the weaknesses of manuscript delivery.

Proper manuscript preparation involves the use of a clean and easy-to-read script. It should be typed—preferably in capital letters—with triple spacing to improve its readability. Include directions to yourself, if necessary, to slow down at important points, along with other remainders. A script might appear as follows:

THE CRISES WE FACE TODAY IS GRAVE. OUR ECONOMY IS BEING CHALLENGED BY BOTH OUTSIDE AND INTERNAL SOURCES. DESPAIR APPEARS TO BE SETTLING INTO OUR SOCIAL STRUCTURE.

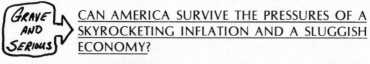

GRAVE AND SERIOUS → CAN AMERICA SURVIVE THE PRESSURES OF A SKYROCKETING INFLATION AND A SLUGGISH ECONOMY?

I SAY YES: ← EMPHASIS

IT MAY TAKE CREATIVITY, AND BELT-TIGHTENING, BUT IT CAN BE DONE. CONSIDER SEVERAL WAYS..........

It is generally preferable not to continue a sentence or paragraph onto a new page. Poor pausing can result.

In preparation, read the script aloud several times to gain confidence with the material. Check out your highlighting notations or whatever pauses you deem important. A tape recorder, or even a video recorder, can be helpful in eliminating ineffective mannerisms. Some freedom in reading the manuscript should be practiced. Several readings will allow you the confidence to make greater contact with the audience. This is especially important at the beginning, at important points, and at the end.

Memorization

Some speakers choose to memorize a speech rather than depending on a manuscript. This method presents both hazards and benefits. The pitfalls are many. First, there is always the fear of forgetting—a tension-producing element that can be extremely disconcerting. Memorization can also produce a recitative sing-song style that lends the impression of artificiality to your remarks. Additional communication barriers of this sort aren't helpful.

Some speakers will memorize parts of the speech—such as the introduction or conclusion. Quotations, or little asides, can when memorized add a dimension of professionalism to your speech.

It is not unusual for a speaker who has chosen to memorize his speech to bring the speech along as a security blanket. But if his memory fails him and he struggles to find his place, the effect can be disastrous. Some ability in impromptu speaking is therefore advantageous to the speaker who chooses to memorize his speech. When and if lapses do occur, you will have the option to expand and fill in with impromptu remarks.

Extemporaneous

The extemporaneous speech is one that is prepared but presented orally from either a memorized or notated outline. The speaker knows his categories of information including the position, the opening, the major topics, the sequence, and forms of support, but the speech is not intended to be memorized or read. Its style is that of the prepared impromptu—spontaneous in appearance but prepared in content.

A rehearsal is important for the extemporaneous message. Some experience in developing ideas without the benefit of notes is essential. If you do use notes, plan where and when their use is advantageous. Excessive reliance on notes can destroy the effect of the extemporaneous style. Abundant notes, as a matter of fact, will restrict your delivery, giving you none of the advantages of either the memorized, manuscript, or impromptu approaches.

Prepare your notes so they are uncluttered and easy to read. Quotations, statistics, and supporting materials from nonoriginal sources are materials suited for notes. Original ideas should be stated freely without any seeming constrictions of the notes. Maintain audience contact at all times. If possible, try also a rehearsal in the actual setting of the speech.

CONFIDENCE AND PREPARATION

Attitudes

We all enter the communicative act with attitudes. They may, in fact, be attitudes about the entire process of speechmaking. Conceivably, you may have the attitude that speaking is not important— it's what you do that is important, not what you say. If your attitude does reflect this point of view, chances are that you will not work very hard at being effective as a communicator.

Take a careful look at your attitudes and see if you have certain prejudices that are manifesting themselves in the way you prepare and present your message. Perhaps your negativism is a result of some feelings of inadequacy about speaking in public. It is necessary to attempt some modification of this attitude if it is, in fact, influencing your entire approach to communication.

Attitudes about yourself can interfere with your growth. An honest and accurate self-concept and self-confidence are two essential keys to establishing a pattern of development. An appraisal of what in your communicative skills needs improvement is essential. Accurate perceptions are likewise critical. Low self-esteem will make it difficult to consider any praise as valid.

You should establish, therefore, realistic attitudes about your potential for growth and what will be required of you. The feeling that your speech abilities are beyond repair can be extremely detrimental to growth. The mere attitude of being willing to try, along with a desire to speak whenever and wherever possible, will establish some very real paths for growth.

Ask yourself, "How do I react when suggestions are made concerning how I can improve?" Do you become aggressive, disinterested, sarcastic, emotional, critical, or antagonistic? Or do you listen and attempt to see areas for improvement?

Some motivation may be important for development in communication. If this is the case with you, study the value of communication. Look, if necessary, at its practical and economic value. How will it affect your chosen vocation? How will it affect your acceptance by certain persons or groups? How will it affect your own personal life? Your self-esteem? Your social and intellectual self?

Tension Reduction (Stage Fright)

Tension is created by all sorts of fears. If, for example, you fear that someone will stick you with a pin, you will have to prepare yourself for the event or choose to flee from the situation. Either choice of mental reaction will produce physiological reactions. Your heart may accelerate. Your mouth may become dry. Your respiration may pick up speed. You may perspire. Your muscles may begin to tighten. Many researchers in psychology call this the flight-or-fight reaction. Because your body is getting ready to respond, the system has become energized for action.

For many people, the prospect of facing an audience creates a similar reaction. Some prepare themselves to face the situation. Others become victim to what is called the "cycle effect," that is, they get tense about the situation; it produces more tension which, in turn, creates more tension about the tension. Magnified in this way, this build-up creates what is known as "stage fright."

This emotional stress can be an asset or liability. If you succumb to your tension about speaking, obviously it will be to your detriment. However, you also have the option of converting nervous energy into a state of readiness that can be used productively. There are, for example, outlets for tension in the speech situation. Energy can create an energetic speech style, if you can harness tension in some way. Some steps you can take are:

1. Accept the fact. Know and expect your problem. Convert it into constructive energy. Share your feelings with others: You will find that you are not unique.
2. Do not place excessive importance on the situation. Your audience is not there to judge your worth as a human being. In most cases, the audience will feel compassion for you if you are sincere.
3. Be active. Turn the energy into better vocal emphasis and physical movements.
4. Focus on the audience and the subject. The less concern for yourself and the more concern for the audience and subject will negate the cycle of tension.
5. Be prepared. You can approach the speech situation with

much more confidence if you are well prepared. A trial run with an audience of one can help to build your confidence. Knowledge of your subject will reduce tension considerably.

6. Accept your speech competency level. Know where you are. Do not compare your production with someone much more effective than you are. Set reasonable standards. Judge improvement as measured against your past performances.

IMPROVING COMMUNICATIVE BEHAVIOR

Vocal Presentation

Let us turn, specifically, to those aspects of oral delivery that can enhance your presentational style. An understanding of the elements of vocal presentation is essential.

Breath Control and Speech Production

Knowledge of your breathing and speaking apparatus can be important to knowing how to reduce tension by relaxation.

Human speech is produced by a compressed stream of air that is modified by the anatomical obstacles and chambers through which it must pass. The compressed air is produced by the expansion of the thoracic area. As the sides of the rib cage are raised and the bottom section (diaphragm) is lowered, the area expands and air is taken in through the mouth and nose.

The process is then reversed. The rib cage sides are lowered, the diaphragm is elevated, and the air is compressed. The compressed air stream goes from the lungs through the trachea, the larynx, the pharynx, and the oral and the nasal resonators. The sounds produced by the actions of the larynx are modified by narrow passages, the tongue, and the teeth.

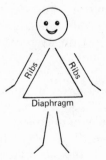

To use the speech apparatus effectively we must use the breathing mechanism efficiently. Research into operation of the compression system indicates that we (1) must have an adequate supply of air and (2) must use this supply efficiently.

The adequate supply of air for speech purposes will vary according to:

1. loudness of the production
2. length of phrases
3. breathing patterns.

If you find that you are not producing adequate loudness, running out of air, and breathing in the center of phrases, you should try to develop better breath supply and control.

One ineffective type of breathing is generally classified as clavicular. In this type, the rib cage is lifted by the upper chest muscles. This pattern produces shallow breathing and has a tendency to produce excessive tension in the neck regions.

In practicing to increase the efficiency of breath operation be careful that you are not merely increasing tempo or tension.

Phonation and Resonance

The phonation system produces the base from which we form the vowels and the other sounds. The process consists of closing the vocal folds, building up pressure, separating and closing rapidly enough to produce a basic tone.

The basic tone is varied by changes of the length, the thickness, and the tension of the vocal folds. We can produce lower basic tones by relaxing the tension in the system. Higher tones are more tense and produce more vibrations per unit of time than the lower base tones.

Clarity of Speech

As we have seen, speech is produced by the modification and manipulation of the breath stream by anatomical adjustments. Incorrect or imprecise movements or adjustments will produce speech that can be misunderstood. The differences between certain sounds are slight. The shift from one sound to another can be produced by a slight shift of tongue position, of lip position, of opening of the mouth, and so forth.

Practice in correct and precise movements and position will improve clarity of speech. If you are misunderstood or if people ask you to repeat what you said, you need to work on improvement.

One method of improving is to practice precision. Try reading aloud and focus on active and accurate articulation. Try pairs of sounds and ask a friend to identify the one that you produced. Some of the pairs that are confused are:

T–D   (for example bat and bad)
S–Z   (for example, his(z) and hiss)
F–V   (for example, half and have)
B–P   (for example, cab and cap)

Speech Emphasis

Just as the writer is able to highlight certain words, phrases or ideas by underlining, italicizing, or increasing size of print so may the speaker highlight by variety or change. Consider this statement: "John stole my best watch." Without emphasis the reader or listener is free to interpret this sentence in any way.

However, the phrase may have special meaning: "*John* stole my best watch." (Here it means that it could not have been anyone else.) "John *stole* my best watch." (He didn't borrow it.) "John stole *my* best watch." (not anyone else's.) "John stole my *best* watch." (not my old one.)

The speaker may also use change of pitch for highlighting or variety. Pitch is the quality of voice that gives it highs and lows. Generally upward pitches communicate questions and downward pitches communicate positiveness.

Yes? ↗   Yes ↘
Now? ↗   Now ↘

Tempo variety enables the oral communicator to produce greater excitement by picking a faster tempo, or greater involvement or emphasis by picking a slower tempo. We might consider trying these statements in a faster and slower tempo to see which seems more effective:

This is our last chance.
Come on in. The water's fine.
You must consider this alternative.

You might pick out certain words or phrases for tempo change as a means of highlighting the above phrases. The effective communicator has a wide variety of vocal tools at his command.

Extending the Meaning

Speech variations such as changes in pitch, tempo, and loudness may be used to add dimension to your communication. There are endless varieties of meanings that you can express with flexibility of speech. Developing more variation will develop a speech apparatus more responsive to meaning. Try to capture the meanings in the parentheses below by means of vocal variations. In other words, repeat "Come here" six times trying to capture the feeling and attitudes expressed in the parentheses.

Come here. (I'm glad to see you.)
Come here. (Or you'll be sorry.)
Come here. (You should see what I've found.)
Come here. (I can't believe it.)
Come here. (You are in danger.)
Come here. (If you want to.)

Nonverbal Behavior

Unless we are using a nonvisual communication channel such as the radio or telephone, we will be visible to our listeners. How we act, with our bodies, faces, and hands, is called visual behavior or, more commonly, *nonverbal behavior*. It is an area that has received considerable attention by researchers in communication, psychology, sociology, drama, and education—just to name a few. The effects of nonverbal behavior on the communicative act are considered to be extremely important. For our purposes, we will be concerned with several basic areas, each of which can be controlled and developed for a more effective pattern of speech delivery.

First, the body itself communicates. You communicate by the way you begin to speak. Your body may say that you are disinterested or tense. Your posture signals certain things. By leaning on the speaking stand, you may communicate a "I really don't care" attitude, or a mood of informality.

Second, your face is an important tool of communication. Many persons have a tendency to freeze their facial expression while speaking. Learn to use your face for expressing moods, feelings, and attitudes. If you say, as many speakers do, that you are happy to be here speaking tonight—and your face does not communicate that happiness—you are likely to create either confusion or doubt in the minds of your listeners.

Similarly, gestures—or movements of parts of the body—affect the meaning of what you say. A move of the head can reinforce a negative or positive message. Hands are likewise carriers of messages. They can be used to describe, suggest emotions, and add emphasis.

Control of distractions should be more of a concern than the planning of physical activity. If you are shifting your weight constantly, playing with your notes, or twisting your ring, you can distract an audience. Your objective should be to eliminate distraction while developing a natural, yet reinforcing, style of delivery. If you have difficulty in seeing, or understanding, what it is that you communicate with your physical activity, you ought to videotape a speech. A friend or trained communication instructor will also be able to provide some insights into areas for improvement.

Consider also that you communicate with your eyes. The use of eye contact is considered an important attribute in establishing contact with your listeners. Lack of eye contact can imply disinterest on your part.

Consider the following criteria for evaluating nonverbal behavior:

1. Does it contribute to an animated impression? Can listeners see and interpret your level of interest in the subject matter and themselves?
2. Does it have variety? A gesture that is repeated excessively will be distracting and perhaps boring.
3. Does it fit the content of what you are saying? Each subject carries with it certain moods. Nonverbal activity ought to fit accordingly. Solemn occasions do not call for hyperactive gestures.

Feedback

We have talked about feedback in previous chapters, but you should consider its special importance to the physical act of communication. Feedback works in such a way that communicators or transmitters influence receivers or listeners. And the same process occurs in reverse.

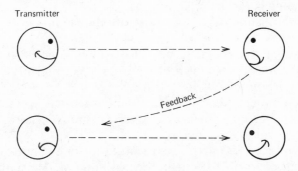

In the communicative act, the speaker may notice nods of approval, body activity that represents rejection, or puzzled expressions. Each of these clues is a transmission from the receiver. It is also called feedback, and it can be used to help guide you in adapting, simplifying, and clarifying your message.

Feedback is critical to the improvement of physical skills. Excessive movements, or too few movements, may elicit certain types of responses from your listeners, that is nervousness or laziness. Awareness of these responses can be a corrective device for modifying your own physical behavior.

SUMMARY

In the delivery of an oral presentation, you should be aware of where and how breakdowns can occur. Impressions are communicated by what the audience sees. Many cannot screen out distracting mannerisms.

Movement should be used purposefully, the voice should be used to emphasize, and gestures should be used to punctuate ideas. The key to all aspects of delivery is sincerity and moderation.

If you continue to have problems with stage fright, review the principles listed in the chapter remembering that with preparation comes confidence in your material and in yourself.

Review and Exercises

1. Evaluate your delivery as a communicator. Do so from a videotaped presentation if possible.
2. Using the same videotape, shut off the audio portion. Do an analysis of your nonverbal activity.
3. List the delivery characteristics of the most effective speaker you have seen recently. Which of his or her characteristics could you employ in your own style?
4. Select an article. Read it aloud attempting to get several different levels of meaning out of it: sadness, happiness, sarcasm, or humility. Try other emotions as well.
5. Speak impromptu into a tape recorder for one minute. Count the number of "ah's." Repeat the assignment. Have the "ah's" decreased?
6. Design the steps for self-improvement in your communication patterns.

Additional Readings

Birdwhistell, Ray L., *Kinesics and Context,* University of Pennsylvania Press, Philadelphia, 1970.

Bosmajian, Haig A., editor *Readings in Speech,* Harper and Row, New York, 1965.

Cathcart, Robert, *Post-Communication: Critical Analysis and Evaluation,* Bobbs-Merrill, Indianapolis, 1966.

Goffman, Erving, *The Presentation of Self in Everyday Life,* Doubleday and Company, Garden City, New York, 1959.

Hall, Edward T., *The Hidden Dimension,* Doubleday, Garden City, New York, 1966.

Harrison, Randall, *Beyond Words: An Introduction to Nonverbal Communication,* Prentice-Hall, Englewood Cliffs, New Jersey, 1974.

Knapp, Mark, *Nonverbal Communication in Human Interaction,* Holt, Rinehart and Winston, New York, 1972.

Mehrabian, Albert, *Silent Messages,* Wadsworth, Belmont, California, 1971.

Ogilvie, Mardel, and Rees, Norma A., *Communication Skills: Voice and Pronounciation* McGraw-Hill, New York, 1969.

Swets, John A., *Signal Detection and Recognition by Human Observers,* John Wiley and Sons, New York, 1964.

ABOUT THE AUTHORS

John C. Zacharis is professor and chairman of the Department of Speech and Communication Studies at Emerson College, Boston, Massachusetts.

He received a Ph.D. from Indiana University, and has served as a full-time or part-time faculty member at California Polytechnic State University, Lehigh University, Suffolk University, Indiana University, and Massachusetts Bay Community College. He has taught a broad variety of courses in speech and communication studies.

Dr. Zacharis has served as president of the Eastern Forensic Association, as a member of the National Council of the American Forensic Association, and as president of the New England Forensic Association. The Speech Communication Association and the International Communication Association are among the many organizations to which he belongs.

He has also written on the subject of women's rights and is author of the book *Your Future in the New World of Communication.* In addition, he has filled many speech-writing, teaching, and consultation assignments for Honeywell, the First National Bank of Boston, the United Steelworkers, the League of Women Voters, the federal government, and numerous other groups and individuals.

Dr. Zacharis has worked extensively in intercollegiate debate and forensics for the past fifteen years, and has coached students who have won over three hundred awards. He has a strong interest in the application of communication to careers.

Dr. Coleman C. Bender received his B.A. and M.A. from Penn State University and his Ph.D. from the University of Illinois. He is professor of Communication Studies and co-director of the Organizational Communication Division at Emerson College. He previously served as chairman of the Emerson College Speech Department for eighteen years. His other teaching assignments have included staff appointments at Penn State University, The University of Illinois, and the U.S. Air Force.

Other assignments include consultant appointments with the Harvard School of Public Health, the New Church Theological School, Massachusetts General Hospital, the American Institute of Banking, and the New England Law Enforcement Management Institute. Recently, he served as a special consultant in "Training The Trainers" for the State of Connecticut and for New England Correctional Trainers.

Dr. Bender has been a frequent guest lecturer for groups including the Naval War College, the New England Hospital Assembly, the Society for Technical Communication, the Boston Advertising Club, and the Administrative Management Society. He was honored with The Massachusetts Speaker of the Year Award in 1970.

One of his continuing interests is reflected in his co-directing of the Norfolk Prison Debaters. This outstanding group has been undefeated in nineteen of the past twenty-one years.

INDEX